LAURA CLAY AND THE
WOMAN'S RIGHTS MOVEMENT

LAURA CLAY
AND THE
WOMAN'S RIGHTS
MOVEMENT

Paul E. Fuller

With a Foreword by
A. Elizabeth Taylor

THE UNIVERSITY PRESS OF KENTUCKY

for Peg

Scholarly publisher for the Commonwealth,
serving Bellarmine College, Berea College, Centre
College of Kentucky, Eastern Kentucky University,
The Filson Club, Georgetown College, Kentucky
Historical Society, Kentucky State University,
Morehead State University, Murray State University,
Northern Kentucky University, Transylvania University,
University of Kentucky, University of Louisville,
and Western Kentucky University.

Editorial and Sales Offices: Lexington, Kentucky 40508–4008

Library of Congress Cataloging-in-Publication Data

Fuller, Paul E.
    Laura Clay and the woman's rights movement / Paul E. Fuller ; with
a foreword by A. Elizabeth Taylor.
        p.   cm.
    Includes bibliographical references (p.   ) and index.
    ISBN 0–8131–0808–X (acid-free)
    1. Clay, Laura, 1849–1941. 2. Suffragettes—United States—
Biography. 3. National American Woman Suffrage Association—
History. 4. Women—Suffrage—United States—History.
5. Women's rights—United States—History. I. Title.
JK1899.C55F84 1992
324.6'23'0973—dc20   92–14139

Contents

Acknowledgments

As is true with every scholarly work, this book represents a cooperative effort. Graduate school professors, friends, colleagues, librarians, foundations, and family have in varying degrees contributed to the publication of this study.

My greatest debt is owed to historians at the University of Kentucky who guided this work through the dissertation stage. Principal among these was Dr. James F. Hopkins, who has been generous with his time, wise in his counsel, and unfailingly patient as a critic. Professor Richard Lowitt skillfully pruned the manuscript, and Professor Mary Wilma Hargreaves made corrections and offered suggestions which have strengthened it greatly. Professor Enno E. Kraehe, now of the University of Virginia, immeasurably influenced my early graduate study, and his concepts of the teaching and the writing of history constitute the models for my own career.

Several librarians and archivists have given unselfishly of their time and efforts. I am indebted to Dr. Jacqueline Bull of the Special Collections Division of the University of Kentucky Library who believed that Laura Clay was worthy of study long before the current interest in woman's history, and to her colleague, Mr. Charles L. Atcher, whose friendship and aid consistently exceeded his official duties as University Archivist. Mr. James R. Bentley made research at the Filson Club of Louisville, Kentucky, a pleasure, and Miss Elizabeth A. Duvall, Bibliographer of the Sophia Smith Collection at Smith College, personally guided me through her archival material and took me on a memorable tour of the Connecticut River Valley. The writer also thanks Mrs. Marion Marx of the Schlesinger Library at Radcliffe College for much cheerful assistance.

Acknowledgments

The greatest joy of scholarly research is the sharing of information and ideas, sorrows and triumphs with one's friends and colleagues. I owe much to Dr. Jane W. Harbaugh, now Dean of the College of Liberal Arts at the University of Tennessee at Chattanooga, since without her advice and encouragement I would not have undertaken graduate study. My life has been enriched and my efforts supported through association with Joseph N. Binford, John H. DeBerry, Douglas W. Hatfield, Robert P. Hay, Frances and John D. Wright, and Edward T. Houlihan, all professional colleagues. During the course of my writing I met Professor A. Elizabeth Taylor of Texas Woman's College, who generously consented to criticize my manuscript and encouraged me to seek its publication. Professor L. Marcile Taylor, a colleague at Wesleyan College, was of particular help in the final stages of readying the book for publication.

Some personal debts are so great that only my family realizes their extent. My brother, Floyd L. Fuller, Jr., by inspiration and example, has influenced the direction of my life more than any other person. Peggy Kistler Fuller, my wife, has been of inestimable assistance. She has typed, corrected, prodded, attended to details so often and so well that in reality the book is as much hers as it is mine. To her and our children, Paul and Lisa Ann, for years of aid and understanding, I owe an infinite debt of gratitude.

Special acknowledgment is due the Eugenia Dorothy Blount Lamar Lecture Series fund of Wesleyan College, whose generosity has made possible the publication of this book. This fund was established by Mrs. Lamar to encourage research on some aspect of Southern literature, history, or culture. Two dissertation travel grants from the University of Kentucky greatly relieved the financial burden of my research trips.

Foreword

WHEN I BEGAN my research on the woman suffrage movement, I was only vaguely aware of Laura Clay. As I continued my research, however, I became increasingly aware of her woman suffrage activities in her native state of Kentucky, in other southern states, and throughout the nation. I recognized her as a person of superior ability and as a tireless worker for the cause. I learned also that there was a collection of her papers in the Margaret I. King Library at the University of Kentucky. The collection consisted of thousands of items relating to the status and rights of women. During the 1940s, however, the collection was not organized, and its importance was not as yet realized by professional historians.

During the early years of my research, I focused my attention on other states and had no special interest in Kentucky. I continued to find references to Laura Clay, however. She began to haunt me, and I realized that I would never be at peace until I had examined her papers. Finally, during the 1970s, I was able to spend several weeks in Lexington. By that time, the Laura Clay papers had been beautifully organized, and it was a pleasure to work with them. They were a storehouse of valuable information. Unlike many of her fellow crusaders, Laura Clay realized the long-term historical importance of the suffrage movement. Consequently she meticulously saved and preserved the records of her more than thirty years of active involvement.

Gradually but assuredly, the significance and scope of the Laura Clay papers entered the consciousness of the historical profession. They were consulted by Aileen S. Kraditor, Anne Firor Scott, and other historians of American women. The first person to use the collection extensively and in depth, however, was Paul E. Fuller. While a graduate student at the University of Kentucky, Fuller decided to write his doctoral dissertation on Laura Clay. He made this decision at a time when women's history was a developing field, and, in the opinion of some, not entirely respectable. His decision was a bold one, but time has shown that it was a far-sighted and wise one.

Laura Clay became active in the suffrage movement when she was in her early thirties. In 1881, she was elected president of the newly organized Kentucky Woman Suffrage Association. This Association had been formed for the purpose of conducting suffrage activities throughout Kentucky and was the first in the South to be organized as a state society.

Laura Clay filled this position until the Kentucky Woman Suffrage Association was supplanted by the Kentucky Equal Rights Association in 1888. She was elected president of the new organization and held that office until she was succeeded by Madeline McDowell Breckinridge in 1911. As the name implies, the Kentucky Equal Rights Association took a broader view of women's rights than mere enfranchisement. Its goal was equality for women.

The formation of the Kentucky Equal Rights Association gave immediate impetus to the woman's movement. In 1890, two years after its organization, the suffragists began lobbying the legislature, asking for property rights for married women and for the employment of women physicians in insane asylums. They secured ten thousand signatures on a petition in support of these demands. Laura Clay and her able coworker, Josephine K. Henry, presented this petition to the legislature and delivered addresses in its behalf in the House chamber during an evening session. The legislature ignored their demands but made a concession to women's rights when it enacted a law requiring employers to pay the wages of working women to the women themselves rather than to their husbands.

The 1890 session was a significant beginning. The suffragists lobbied during subsequent sessions, and their presence in Frankfort became a routine occurrence. They secured the passage of significant legislation for the benefit of women and children but were less successful in their demand for the vote. With the exception of school suffrage, they remained disfranchised until 1920.

When a convention assembled in September 1890 to write a

new constitution for Kentucky, the suffragists directed their lobbying efforts toward that body. They realized that they were unlikely to gain full suffrage but hoped for some concession. In an address before the convention, Laura Clay proposed that the new constitution authorize the legislature to enfranchise women by a simple act. If adopted, this proposal would eliminate the need for a constitutional amendment and would, thereby, make it less difficult for women to gain the vote. Unfortunately for the suffragists, the convention refused to adopt the proposal.

In 1895 South Carolina called a constitutional convention. Several weeks before it assembled, Laura Clay joined a group of women who traveled throughout the state speaking, organizing, and distributing literature in support of the cause. Their tour ended in mid-June.

When the convention met in September, Laura Clay returned to Columbia and remained for nine weeks. Together with several South Carolina women, she contacted delegates, distributed literature, attended hearings, and spoke whenever the opportunity permitted. On September 17th, she asked the convention to confer suffrage on women who could meet educational and property qualifications. Her proposal was discussed on the convention floor but was not adopted. Thus South Carolina women remained disfranchised.

Three years later, in 1898, Louisiana held a constitutional convention. At the request of the National American Woman Suffrage Association, Laura Clay went to New Orleans to lobby with Carrie Chapman Catt and Mary G. Hay of New York. On February 24, Catt delivered a major address in which she strongly advocated the enfranchisement of Louisiana women, and, during the week that followed, Clay, Catt, and Frances A. Griffin of Alabama conducted daily discussions of the issue. The convention did not enfranchise women, but it did grant a fragment of suffrage when it adopted a provision stating that women who paid taxes could vote on questions of taxation.

Laura Clay's willingness to leave her home in Kentucky and do suffrage work in other states continued after the turn of the century. In 1904, she spent several months in Warren, Ohio, with Harriet Taylor Upton, the treasurer of the National American Woman Suffrage Association. Upton's office was inadequately staffed, and Clay, who was knowledgeable about business matters, served as an able assistant.

In 1906, she did suffrage work in Oregon where the question of enfranchising women was to be voted on in May. In December 1906 she went to Oklahoma at the request of Anna Howard Shaw. There she joined forces with Ida Porter Boyer, a salaried worker of the National American Woman Suffrage Association. A constitutional convention was in session, and the two women lobbied for suffrage. In February 1907, Laura Clay addressed the convention in its behalf. When the convention voted on the issue, however, it was rejected.

In 1909, Laura Clay went to Arizona at the request of Anna Howard Shaw. She spent two months there organizing suffrage sentiment and lobbying the territorial legislature. The legislature refused to grant the vote to women, but her organizational and educational methods were to bear fruit a few years later.

One can but admire Laura Clay's willingness to travel far from her native state and to remain away from her home for weeks and months. Her absences often came at inconvenient times, such as during the planting season on her farm or when her house was undergoing repairs. Neither personal problems nor the hardships of travel deterred her.

Since 1895, Laura Clay had been a national officer in the National American Woman Suffrage Association. In 1911, however, she failed to be reelected. Nevertheless she continued to crusade for the rights of women. She did suffrage work in Ohio and Kansas in 1912, in Michigan and Wisconsin in 1913, in West Virginia in 1915, in Iowa in 1916, and in Rhode Island and New York in 1917. When crusading for suffrage, she was generous with both her time and her money. Her loyalty to the cause was beyond question.

In view of her strong dedication, one wonders why she opposed the federal amendment. Her opposition was in accord with her firm belief that suffrage was a state, and not a federal, matter. During most of her career as a suffragist, she did not consider the federal amendment a threat. She doubted that it would ever pass Congress and be ratified by a sufficient number of states. As the number of suffrage states increased, however, sentiment in favor of the federal amendment increased. Finally, in 1919, it passed

Congress and was submitted to the states for ratification. Laura Clay continued to oppose the federal amendment. In so doing, she was one of a small minority of suffragists. The vast majority favored it.

Kentucky ratified in January 1920. The thirty-sixth state, Tennessee, ratified in August 1920. The Susan B. Anthony Amendment thereby became part of the United States Constitution. Laura Clay's goal of votes-for-women was realized, but not in the way that she had expected or desired.

Few persons of her generation worked as long and as diligently for the advancement of women as did Laura Clay. She was active in the movement for more than three decades. She traveled widely in its behalf. She visited many states and did grass-roots work among the people there. She spoke, counseled, and organized in behalf of an improved status for women. She donated much of her time, her energy, and her personal fortune to the cause. Her dedication took precedence over personal pleasure and convenience.

Laura Clay was undoubtedly the South's leading suffragist. The papers that she left behind constitute one of the nation's most valuable collections relative to the movement for women's rights. Some fifty years after the ratification of the Nineteenth Amendment and some thirty years after her death, the University Press of Kentucky published *Laura Clay and the Woman's Rights Movement* by Paul Fuller. A long-time student of Laura Clay, Fuller examined her life and work thoroughly and in great detail, gaining valuable insight into her personality and character. He understood her role as a state's rights suffragist and its resulting conflict with the leaders in the national movement. His interpretations are thoughtful and well-reasoned. His style of writing is smooth and polished. His account of Laura Clay's role in the woman's movement is an excellent one. It might well be considered a landmark in the historiography of American women.

Fuller's *Laura Clay and the Woman's Rights Movement* is an outstanding book about an outstanding Kentucky woman. It is indeed gratifying that it is being republished during the celebration of Kentucky's two hundred years of statehood.

A. Elizabeth Taylor

I

THE EARLY YEARS

1849-1866

LAURA CLAY, who was to play an important and controversial role in the movement for woman's rights, was born less than a year after an event usually regarded as the beginning in the United States of the struggle for the emancipation of her sex. In July 1848 the Seneca Falls Convention, called by Elizabeth Cady Stanton, Lucretia Mott, Martha Wright, and other pioneers of the feminist movement, issued a Declaration of Principles modeled on the Declaration of Independence. Half a year later, on February 9, 1849, Laura Clay was born on her father's estate, White Hall, near Richmond, Kentucky. Born at the beginning of the struggle for woman's rights, she either witnessed or participated in the most important legal, educational, and political struggles for the rights won by her sex in the late nineteenth and early twentieth centuries. To know and to understand her life and motives are to comprehend much of the history of women's long campaign for equal rights.

The circumstances of Laura Clay's early life strongly influenced her career. Family connections and education prepared her for leadership; her devout Episcopalian faith and a native *noblesse oblige* demanded service to others; and her personal familial experiences made her painfully aware of the position of women and their legal disabilities.

Cassius Marcellus Clay, her father, was a wealthy landowner with a wide reputation as a bowie-knife duelist and as a fiery abolitionist. By 1849 he was a nationally known figure, mostly because of his antislavery efforts in a slave state but also because of his duels, political fights, and exploits in the Mexican War, which had attracted considerable attention in the press.[1]

Clay was often away from home. His volunteer service in the Mexican campaign, where he was captured and imprisoned, kept him away for eighteen months. Later, he was often absent while stumping for antislavery candidates or lecturing throughout the northern part of the country. During his long tenure of nearly nine years as United States Minister to Russia, his family was with him for only a few months. Little wonder that he should complain at one point that "his children did not really know him."[2]

Clay's frequent and long absences from home, the threats on his life and his wounds in political combat, and the strain of caring for a large household and a growing family were more than many women could have borne. Fortunately for the Clay family, its matron was an exceptional woman. Mary Jane Warfield had been one of Lexington's loveliest and most desirable belles when Cassius Clay married her in 1833. Her father, Elisha Warfield, was a doctor, horse breeder, and successful businessman; her mother, Marie Barr Warfield, was an able and strong-willed woman. The family was known for producing persons of strong intellect and vigorous physique who were "outspoken as to their political views."[3] During some forty-four years of turbulent married life, Mary Jane Clay needed all the strength and ability that good inheritance and upbringing afforded her.

Despite being born into what might be termed American aristocratic circumstances, Mary Jane Clay's life was anything but easy. She gave birth to ten children, six of whom lived into adulthood. During the first eighteen years of her marriage, nine of her children were born.[4] Many women cared for large families in nineteenth-century America, but Mary Jane's situation was complicated by almost constant worry for her husband's welfare and an unusual degree of responsibility in the management of family affairs.

During Clay's absence, his business affairs were nominally managed by his older brother Brutus, who lived in a nearby county. There is little doubt that the task was done primarily by Mary Jane. In this capacity she supervised everything from the production of butter to the vast renovation and enlargement of White Hall, which was undertaken and completed while Clay was serving as Minister to Russia.[5]

Mary Jane Clay's wide-ranging role in the management of her

husband's affairs was probably as much a matter of necessity as of choice. A banking company that Clay organized failed in 1855, and, during the following year, he had to admit a more general financial failure. He was unable to extricate himself from debt until the latter half of his ministry to Russia and then only with the skillful help of his wife. A daughter reported later that her mother had managed their 2,250-acre farm, "paid off a large debt on the property, built an elegant house costing $30,000, stocked the farm, and largely supported the family of six children, with money she made during the war."[6]

Mary Jane Clay supported her husband in his antislavery fight and was eulogized for it. Enmeshed in a great cause in an area where its advocacy courted danger as well as unpopularity, husband and wife were probably disposed to overlook their marital differences.[7] Later, when that cause was settled by the Civil War and most of the children were adults, Clay's infidelity, added to his long record of negligence and poor management in family affairs, brought the marriage to an end.

Laura was the eighth child of these two rather remarkable persons. Her birth came at a time when even the wellborn were not spared from typhoid fever, cholera, diphtheria, and respiratory diseases which caused so many deaths and struck particularly hard at the young, including three of her brothers and an infant sister. Nor were she and her brothers and sisters above the hard work that characterized rural life. The earliest record of Laura's activities depicts her as an eight-year-old, engaged in helping two slightly older brothers burn stumps at White Hall. "Ma gives us one-half cent for every stump we burn down to the ground," Cassius, Jr., explained to a cousin. "I do not like the business very much, but it is better to be doing that than nothing."[8] The combined family effort might have been partly a result of the severe financial reverses suffered by Clay in 1856, but, whatever else it indicates, it clearly shows that Mary Jane Clay was encouraging her children in hard work and providing them with a measure of incentive through a meager recompense.

Education was not forgotten in the Clay household despite the pressure for labor on a large farm. Since all the horses were needed for plowing, Laura, Brutus, and Cassius walked to the nearby

Foxtown Academy. Sitting under a master who required "all the scholars to write compositions or speak," the Clay youngsters all decided to become orators.[9]

Laura's narrow world, consisting of White Hall and Lexington, where her Warfield kin lived, was vastly expanded by a trip to Russia in 1861, when she was twelve years of age. The Republican victory resulting in the election of President Abraham Lincoln created jobs for the party faithful and her father was one of the recipients. Clay had aspired to a cabinet post, but finally settled for the ministry to Russia. He made it clear that money was a prime consideration, confessing to Lincoln that he sought public office as a means of extricating himself from debt.[10]

Although Clay had expressed concern about the expense of maintaining a family of seven and entertaining properly in Saint Petersburg, he nonetheless decided to attempt it, and the family departed from Boston on May 1, 1861. The voyage provided perplexities for the parents and excitement for the children. Laura and Brutus managed to become separated from their parents in the London train station, while Clay had difficulties in finding lodgings for his family in the English capital.[11]

After distressing United States Minister Charles Francis Adams by publicly damning the British for their neutral position in the Civil War, Clay and his entourage journeyed to Paris, where he again departed from diplomatic niceties in a speech warning the French against support of the Confederates. By June the Clays were at last in Russia, and there the new minister found sympathy for the Union cause. The Clays' background in the high society of the Bluegrass was a decided asset as they won new friends through a round of lavish entertainment. Indeed, both critics and friends of Clay's mission to Saint Petersburg found it "an indubitable success" in assuring Russian friendship for the Union cause.[12]

Soon, however, Clay was complaining to President Lincoln that his $12,000 salary was inadequate for maintaining his family and undertaking the social life necessary to his post. To cut expenses and, perhaps because the cold climate was disagreeable to his wife and at least one of the children, the minister allowed his family to return to the United States in February 1862 after only a few months in Russia.[13]

There is no available information on the long journey home which Mary Jane and the children had to make without Cassius's help. Upon returning to White Hall, the family found Kentucky caught in a struggle between Union and Confederate forces. It was an uneasy time for households that had their menfolk around and especially perilous for those, like the Clays', which did not. Full-scale military campaigns, raids by Confederate General John Hunt Morgan and other cavalry outfits, and guerrilla activity were all experienced in Kentucky. Both White Hall and Lexington, the Clays' second home, felt the ebb and flow of the conflict on more than one occasion.[14]

Mary Jane Clay was determined that her children should continue their education despite the dangers and disruptions of the war. Even amid the difficulties attending management of the farm and the vast enlargement of White Hall, she found time to send Laura and her brother Brutus to school and to encourage them in their education. Laura was enrolled in the Sayre Female Institute in Lexington in the fall of 1863. It advertised a curriculum embracing "all the branches of education usually taught in the best Female Seminaries." Specific courses included French, Latin, German language and literature, vocal and instrumental music, algebra, geometry, trigonometry, geology, chemistry, astronomy, history, English literature, and philosophy.[15]

It was an exciting time for a schoolgirl. Laura helped care for two wounded Union soldiers after the Battle of Richmond in the fall of 1862, and she and two friends at Sayre answered a "rebel fast day" with one of their own in April of 1864. Her sleep and the quiet of Lexington were broken at 5:00 A.M. on June 10, 1864, when General Morgan and his cavalry swept into Lexington for the second time. Although the feared raider held the town for only a few hours, the cause of education was undoubtedly lost for the day.[16]

When Laura was at home for holidays and summer vacations she found that White Hall was not escaping the effects of the war. The farm resembled an army camp as her mother secured horses and mules for sale to the Union army and contracted frequently to graze government livestock. "It looked like Camp Nelson had been removed here," she said, reporting that she had just grazed

1,000 mules and hoped to get another 1,000 within a month. With the mules came the troopers, of course, and they too occupied the scarce time of the mistress of White Hall: "I have had in the last month as many as fifty men here at once in some way or other to be attended to." She complained that she had "so much on my hands that I have not thought of others' concerns."[17]

Mary Jane's work for the Union army may explain why the Confederates raided White Hall in July 1864. Although it is not clear how much livestock was driven off, Laura witnessed the burning of a barn, two carriage houses, and three family carriages. Whether this was a part of General Morgan's last raid in Kentucky, which began in June 1864, or a segment of the widespread guerrilla warfare which characterized the fighting in Kentucky after the Battle of Perryville is not certain. On this occasion Mary Jane sent for her husband's brother, Brutus, of Bourbon County, to survey the damage and to give her counsel. There was undoubtedly some comfort in having a male member of the family available in emergencies, but, for the most part, both the worry of operating an estate and the burden of decision making were solely her own. Her only adult son, Green, had gone with his father to Russia and remained to prospect for oil. This meant that only Mary Jane, the four girls, and young Brutus were left at home.[18]

At this late date the abolitionist Clay family still had some slaves, who were entailed property belonging to the children and, therefore, under the law could not be set free. The Clays kept them and paid them wages, since to disavow authority over the slaves would have permitted the sheriff "to hire them singly to the highest bidder." Family letters show that these Negroes were both a comfort and a help in trying times.[19]

The experiences of this family are evidence that much of the usual nature of everyday life continued even in wartime. Laura's two years at the Sayre Institute found her doing and thinking about many of the things with which other girls of the time were concerned. In the spring of 1864 a circus came to Lexington and pitched its tents in the lot across the street from the house where Laura was boarding. Despite the nearness of the temptation, she hoped to resist its pleasures, keep her mind "on serious things," and give her allowance to the church. Like most other youngsters, then as now, she lost the battle, was lured across the street by the "delightful" music of the circus band, and soon parted with the fifty cents she had intended for the church.[20]

The diary that Laura Clay kept, off and on, for some sixteen years clearly indicates that she was conscientious, socially uncertain, and very religious in a traditional manner. She wanted to be well liked by others, yet believed herself "unfortunate in gaining people's friendship." "I would enjoy society very much," she wrote, "except I do not know exactly how to behave." Even in her own family, she believed the affection of others for herself to be less than she desired. She was elated when one of her sisters told her she would be missed when she returned to Sayre after Christmas vacation. "Oh! how glad I was," she exclaimed. "It always seems to me that they used to care so little for me, and not much now."[21]

Laura's feeling of insecurity can be explained in part by the fact that her sisters were either considerably older or younger than she. Separated by eight years from those closest to her in age, she was in one sense a middle child who at this time shared in neither the adult activities of her older sisters nor the attentions naturally given her baby sister. The young Laura Clay continued to be more socially reticent than her sisters and, while trying to overcome her shyness, confessed to one of them, "you know that naturally I am not sociable." Even in her relations with servants she did not feel as certain of herself as one would expect of a person born well. On one leave-taking from Lexington she was troubled because she had "but little money to give the servants as a parting present" and no knowledge on "how to give that with grace."[22]

Laura's education was not a great help in developing a sense of social assurance because it was more academic than was customary at most female schools in the South. Sayre Institute, where Robert Peter's lectures and demonstrations in chemistry were a featured offering, was a decided departure from the traditional female school where proficiency on the piano and guitar were at the core of a curriculum dedicated to teaching girls " 'the magic spell'— the ability to entice a man into marriage."[23] In short, while Laura's schooling gave her confidence in those areas where society expected men to excel it did very little to teach her the "magic spell" or to prepare her for the roles of wife and motherhood which she was expected to play. By developing an awareness of her own intellectual worth, Sayre seems to have bent her in directions which young ladies were not supposed to follow and, it may be suggested, was part of the reason she never experienced romantic attachments which might have chained her to a life of domesticity.

Laura did well in her studies, and her diary and letters show that she was continually pushing herself to even greater efforts. Frequently she resolved to study her lessons "diligently" and to quit reading novels and take up more serious works. The application of her talents gave her a degree of confidence about competition with males, an uncommon trait for a young woman of the time and one that was not likely to win her admirers among the opposite sex. While accepting the notion that men in general were intellectually superior to women, she avowed, "I am a woman, but I think I have a mind superior to that of many boys of my age, and equal to that of many more."[24]

Laura's strongest single characteristic as a young woman was her intensely religious nature. Her preoccupation with becoming a church member, discovering God's will, and faithfully fulfilling the duties of a Christian runs throughout her early years. She, as well as her sisters, accepted the Episcopal Church of their mother, but not without some mild objections from their father, who was not a regular churchgoer himself but leaned toward the evangelical sects. Her mother insisted that Laura receive Clay's assent from Russia before her baptism and confirmation because "he has shown a great deal of feeling upon the occasion of each member of his family joining the church." Although Cassius confessed that he usually had his "back up whenever a priest was in view," he gave his consent. Laura was baptized in June and confirmed in November 1864 at Christ Church in Lexington.[25]

Laura's membership began an association which lasted a lifetime, for, though she became less preoccupied with religion as she grew older, her loyalty to and support for her church never wavered. Her early religious impulses were mostly inner directed—a determination "to keep down many evil thoughts" and a concern about her ability to lead a Christian life. Yet she was honest enough with herself to confess that "the burden of my sin is not grievous to me." Evidences were also present that her religion was partly outer directed, mixing a concern for others with introspection. Reflecting upon a book on India, she wrote: "It makes me sad to feel that human beings are so low. I would like to be a missionary, and help to win them [the Indians] from their degraded state."[26]

The impulse to help others was thus part of her life from an early time, but the direction that impulse was to take became clear to her much later and then only after some painful personal experiences and long periods of soul searching. As a girl she was apparently unaware of any injustices to her sex and was certainly a great distance from her later commitment to the struggle for woman's rights.

In June 1865 she completed her work at Sayre Institute, one of six graduates among the 195 young women who were registered at the school. Her graduation caused some indecision about what she should do next. Most southern girls would have been presented to society and informally declared eligible for matrimony at this time or, at the latest, upon the completion of finishing school.[27] The Clay girls are a decided exception to this pattern, since there is no evidence of any parental pressure to rush into wedlock. By the standards of the time, they all married very late—Mary and Annie at twenty-seven and Sallie at twenty-eight. The disruptions of the war might have been partially responsible for the late betrothals of the two older girls, but whatever the cause it produced no comment and apparently no anxiety in the family. Mary Jane Clay's stout defense of the girls' continuing education and their late marriages suggests that she did not adhere to the traditional southern viewpoint on either of these matters.

Almost a year before Laura finished at Sayre, her mother was urging her to persuade "Papa to allow you to go to New York to school and devote your time to music and French." Clay, who had a traditional view on woman's education, had made his feelings on the subject quite clear some time earlier. In his opinion, "a few months of travel is the best of finishing for a young person when they [sic] have the entrée of good society." Both boarding schools and day schools, he concluded, were "not worth the expense."[28]

Whether the father, in Russia, finally agreed is uncertain, but

9

the children's education continued and Brutus and Laura felt a debt of gratitude to their mother for it. After both children had gone away to school, Brutus wrote Laura that "we can never repay Ma for the many kindnesses and hard work she has done for us, if it had not been for her we would not be where we are now gaining a [sic] education, but perhaps at work."[29]

Laura was sent to Mrs. Ogden Hoffman's Finishing School in New York City in the fall of 1865 and remained there for one academic year. The school, which enrolled about seventy girls, helped Laura improve her French to a good conversational level and provided work in voice and piano. Her ability in French impressed her father, whose efforts in that tongue abroad had resulted in some embarrassment to him. In one of his infrequent letters to her, he said he was proud that she was "speaking French habitually" and urged her to read, in addition to other works, the *Spectator* and Aesop's Fables, which are "full of wisdom for old and young." He also advised her on health matters, particularly warning her against the use of snuff on her teeth which was not as effective as "the brush and water."[30]

Clay had followed her activities through her letters home, which in turn had been forwarded to him. In the spring when he sent her a bracelet through the facilities of the American and European Telegraph Line, Laura was pleased that she could converse with that firm's agent entirely in French.[31]

The war's end did not reunite the Clay family. Cassius remained in Russia and Mary Jane was busier than ever with the management of the farm and the duties of chaperoning her two oldest daughters about Bluegrass society. As Laura prepared to leave the finishing school, the work on White Hall was at last nearing completion.[32] For almost three years Mary Jane had supervised the construction and her pride in the project was evident. Two Irishmen, she wrote to Laura in New York, were building a large terrace, set off with statues and vases. A circular flower bed, with a statue on a pedestal in the center, provided a perfect complement to the conservatory. "It is a grand house and so delightful . . . quite palatial," she concluded. "I hope I may be able to keep it in repair and keep up the grounds and fruit trees and garden."[33]

Her skillful management of the farm and Clay's ministerial income, plus profits from business deals made by him in Russia, were now providing the money needed to settle the family debts.[34] To meet them Cassius Clay remained in Russia almost three years longer, maintaining contact with his family only through the mails. His decision to remain through President Andrew Johnson's term of office left his wife with the full responsibility of a family which would soon be involved in the problems of courtship, marriage, and removal from the homestead.

While the year at Mrs. Hoffman's added to Laura's education, it did not perfect her social graces. Although she promised her sister Mary that she would try to improve her "social affections," she warned that it would be hard for her. She did make a close friend of Patti Field, a young woman who attended the school with her and later married Laura's brother Brutus.[35]

Laura returned to White Hall in the early summer of 1866. The war was over; the family debt had been almost liquidated; the palatial home had been completed. Laura had secured an education well beyond that of the average young lady of the day. Family portraits of the period show her to be an attractive young woman, with a lovely complexion and striking blue eyes that were emphasized by the arching, heavily marked eyebrows characteristic of the Clays.[36] One might have expected her, like her two older sisters, to marry into a good Bluegrass family and begin the management of her own household.

That she did not follow this course indicates that her life was beginning to turn in a new direction, a deviation from the norm, a course which demands attention and understanding. The why of the woman's rights movement is as important as the what, and, in most studies, the why has been neglected. As one author has put it, these accounts "tell little about why these women [the feminists] wanted the vote or why the movement arose where and when it did."[37]

Even in her early years, there are indications that Laura was not following the course prescribed for the typical young southern lady. Her education, her religiously inspired desire to do something for the oppressed, and her failure to develop those aspects of her personality believed to be most attractive to men inclined her away from the family context and toward service in a larger sphere.

Although one can discern in this early period inclinations toward the making of a feminist, concrete evidence of Laura's commitment to woman's rights does not begin until the 1870s, and it is not until the 1880s that she accepts the cause as her life's work. An examination of these twenty years gives additional answers to the questions posed above and provides greater insight into the making of an American suffragist, her motivation for entering the cause, the obstacles she had to overcome, and the program she pursued.

Had her home life been happier, one might speculate whether she would have ever entered the struggle for woman's rights. Certainly there is little evidence that she was resentful or willing to resist the inequality of the sexes until the longstanding friction between her mother and father led to their separation and eventual divorce. Although the end of this marriage was the trauma that awakened all the Clay women to the issue of woman's rights, it had the most enduring effect on Laura. During the years when the marriage was dissolving, Laura was closest to her mother's anguish and was probably her chief comfort. She was, after all, considerably the older of the two girls left at home; the other four children married and began families of their own early in this crisis period. Insofar as both age and marital status were concerned, Laura was more vulnerable to the effects of the family crisis than were her sisters and brothers. Of all the children, only Laura was caught between girlhood and adulthood by these events, as she struggled with the personal problems of choosing a career and finding a role in the woman's rights movement.

II

THE MAKING
OF A SUFFRAGIST
1866-1888

THE DISSOLUTION of the union between Cassius and Mary Jane Clay developed gradually over a period of several years. Their marriage had not been happy despite its long duration and the ten children which it produced. Years later Clay claimed that he had thrown away his wedding ring in 1845. Whatever the complete picture of their problems, financial difficulties were a recurring irritant. Mary Jane, the prudent and able manager, saw more than one of her husband's financial ventures fail as she labored through both the Mexican and Civil wars to attain solvency for the family. Although their marital situation was strained by Clay's long stay in Russia, Laura wondered if his anticipated return in 1867 was an event to be "more feared than hoped." [1]

Clay's absence left the mansion without a host and the girls without a father to give them away as brides. The eldest daughter, Mary Barr Clay, married Major J. Frank Herrick of Cleveland, Ohio, on October 2, 1866, and the second daughter, Sarah (Sallie) Lewis Clay married James Bennett of Richmond, Kentucky, on June 3, 1869. The entertainments associated with such events lacked the paternal presence and weighed heavily on Mary Jane Clay. [2]

For one who had grown up on the very edge of Lexington in an urban setting, Mary Jane found that rural White Hall, her husband's choice for a home, did not provide the social potential that she desired and she began to question, belatedly, the wisdom of putting so much time and money into its renovation. News of her low spirits prompted Clay to write, after nearly five years of continuous absence, that he had no idea "Ma's brain was suffering," and to claim that he would have returned home had he known.[3] And still he stayed in Russia for more than a year longer before relinquishing his office.

The extended absence, as well as the tiresome bout with debt, might have been forgiven and forgotten had not news of the Chautems affair reached the United States in the spring of 1867. This episode in the troubled ministry of Clay arose from charges by a Madame Chautems of Saint Petersburg that he had attempted to seduce both herself and her daughter. Clay admitted that he had befriended them by aiding the mother in setting up a boardinghouse, but he denied that he had made immoral approaches to the woman or her daughter. When a petition from the Chautemses to Congress was shifted from the House Committee on Foreign Affairs to the State Department and finally ignored, and when the Russian government refused to take action on the charges because of the minister's diplomatic immunity, Clay survived the incident at no more apparent cost than some public embarrassment generated by the newspapers; but his association with a woman who was a recognized courtesan was at best an act of incredibly poor judgment. The incident was one of several episodes which produced friction between Clay and William H. Seward, secretary of state. In December 1867 Seward asked him to resign, but Clay refused, pleading the protection of the Tenure of Office Act.[4]

The matter was not so easily resolved between White Hall and the American Minister in Saint Petersburg. While no correspondence between Clay and his wife is available for this period, he later claimed that she believed the worst in the affair and told him so in a letter. The Minister refused to answer her bitter charges and terminated their correspondence.[5]

The long stay in Russia ended on October 1, 1869, with the arrival in Saint Petersburg of the Grant administration appointee. Once back in the United States Clay renewed his political activities before even going to Kentucky to see his family. Joining some fellow Republicans in the cause of Cuban emancipation from Spain, he made a speech in New York attacking Grant's policy of neutrality. After laying the groundwork for what he hoped was a new political opportunity with the anti-Grant faction of the Republican party, he tardily made his way home, where he received a chilly reception. Years later, remembering this homecoming, he wrote that his wife treated him as a stranger and moved him into a separate room which had no fireplace and was so cold "that icicles froze on my beard." A short time after his return, during a conference on their financial situation, Mary Jane Clay charged her husband with breaches of their marriage contract, "enumerating many truths" against him both "at home and abroad, but also many calumnies." Clay claimed that he listened in silence as "the infuriated woman" poured "all the faults and escapades of a lifetime" upon his head "like a deluge," then, "with suave terms, bade her goodnight," returned to his room, and "locked the door . . . ever afterward" during her stay in his home. Within a few days after this stormy encounter, the mother, accompanied by Laura and Annie, the only children still at home, departed for Lexington where they took up temporary residence with Mary Jane's sister, Anne Ryland.[6]

The final blow to the marriage came in 1870 when a four-year-old Russian boy, whose paternity Clay did not deny, arrived at White Hall. The appearance of Launey, as the boy was called, put the marriage beyond repair. Clay legally adopted the child and attempted to introduce him into polite society, despite the expected gossip. The situation was extremely embarrassing for both Clay and his family. One callous newspaperman wrote that, in Richmond, "you see an early champion of freedom walking about boastfully with a bastard son, imported like an Arabian cross horse, and swearing at his family."[7] Such public indignities must have been hard for the children to bear; they were more than their mother could accept.

Clay claimed that his wife made an attempt at reconciliation, which he spurned before suing her for a divorce in 1878. Coming after nearly eight years of separation, the suit was based on the grounds of desertion. It charged that she had abandoned him for a period longer than the five years required by Kentucky law for divorce proceedings. Mary Jane did not contest the suit, which ended her forty-five year marriage on February 7, 1878.[8]

The dissolution of this marriage was a turning point in the lives of the Clay women. It brought them face to face with one of the greatest inequalities of American life: the vast difference between the legal and property rights of men and women. In some ways, Clay was more considerate of his wife than the law required. For example, his guardianship rights over the couple's only remaining minor child, Annie, were so absolute that he could legally have separated her from her mother. This right was not invoked and Annie lived with her mother and Laura into adulthood. Where property was concerned, Mary Jane did not fare so well. Clay wrote: "We . . . agreed that she should take every thing which she ever brought into my home, or bought with her own money and that she should relieve me of her right of dower." In short, Mary Jane was left without any stake in the fine home she had helped to build and the large farm she managed. Rather ironically Clay complained that he had not received "a single cent from her . . . for the rent of the place," which he alleged should have made her owe him about $80,000.[9]

In fairness to Clay, his claim that he sent more than enough money home for the work on White Hall and for the support of the family should be investigated, since he implies that his wife kept the difference. All the other members of the family are silent on this chapter of their history so the truth is difficult to know. Mary, who was Clay's favorite daughter, is the most impartial witness available. At the very time Clay in his *Memoirs* was praising Mary for her affection and loyalty while impugning her mother, Mary was giving her mother the credit for the very accomplishments he denied her. Mary's chapter in the *History of Woman Suffrage* relates that Mary Jane Clay built White Hall, stocked the farm, and largely supported six children "with money she made during the war."[10] It is difficult on the basis of this testimony to escape the conclusion that Mary Jane received neither compensation for her work nor interest in the estate she had been so instrumental in developing.

As one would expect, the sympathies of the girls were with their mother. Fortunately she had an inheritance in a trust fund from her parents and thus was able to live comfortably.[11] But what would have been her condition if she had not had it? The girls were confronted with the unequal status of their sex by the plight of their own mother, and all their interest and activity in the feminist movement postdates this crisis in their own personal lives.

In the case of Laura, the acceptance of woman's cause in these years is clearly evident. When she began to keep a diary again in 1874, she wrote that she hardly recognized the sixteen-year-old girl who had written in it nine years earlier. The principal change in her life had been brought about by "our own unhappy domestic life," leaving her "eyes unblinded to the unjust relations between men and women and the unworthy position of women." Still conscious that her first duty was to serve God, she believed that "the great cause of Woman's Rights" was "that sphere of activity in His service to which God has called me both through my feelings . . . and the education of life which has fixed the bent of my thoughts and opinions." She denied that her sentiments were prompted by jealousy of men and claimed that she desired only to see women awaken "to the higher life which God, through the advance of Christian civilization, has opened to them." Always an unusually fair person, she neither here nor elsewhere criticized her father. Rather she credited her antislavery parents with teaching her "to hate oppression and injustice" wherever she saw them.[12]

Laura had made a private commitment to the feminist movement, but it was to be some time before she embarked upon her public career. Two reasons apparently account for this delay. The first is that Laura had attained adulthood and was faced with the problem of making a living. Causing her further hesitation was the fact that she could not decide exactly what her role in the movement should be.

The problem of a livelihood was settled by her father's decision to divide part of his Madison County estate among his six children in 1873. The girls, Mary, Sallie, Laura, and Annie, as well as the boys, Green and Brutus each received a tract of land, ranging from 275 to 425 acres in size. The agreement drawn up between Clay and his children stipulated that each of them would pay him $360 per year until his death for the use of the land. Three years later, when Green sold his tract to his mother, the great bulk of the Clay estate was again in the hands of the females of the family.[13]

The generosity of Clay provided his daughters with a vocation and an income which Mary succinctly described: "Two of my sisters, Laura and Annie, and myself are practical farmers, each having under her immediate superintendence the workmen, both white and black, on 300 acres. We raise corn, wheat, oats, cattle and sheep, buying and selling our own stock and produce. We took possession of the land without stock or utensils, and by our observation and experience, prudence and industry, have greatly improved the lands and stock, and annually realize a handsome income therefrom." [14]

Like their mother, the girls were apparently good business-women, and none more so than Laura. She paid close attention to the smallest details of her estate, became a skilled and shrewd manager, and prided herself in the title "practical farmer," a designation she later used regularly when sending out autobiographical sketches for use in suffrage campaigns. She pleased her mother who relied on her increasingly as the years passed. "I am so fortunate," Mary Jane Clay wrote, ". . . in having you pass through my Farm to notify me of what is going on and to make suggestions." Still she kept a close check on her business. "Is the crib roof mended? Is the stone hauled and put on the dam?" she wrote from Lexington to Laura, who had remained on the farm to see that the final jobs were done before the onset of winter. Other tasks this self-reliant matron, now advanced in years, insisted upon oversee-ing herself: "I will go over [from Lexington to Richmond] when I think the sheep will need shearing as I wish to see it done." [15]

Laura's own work schedule settled into a routine which she seldom broke until the end of her life. Each year she would spend the planting and harvesting seasons and part of the summer on her farm, or in Richmond, which was about six miles away. Some of this time was spent with Sallie, whose home was located in Richmond, and during part of it she boarded with Mary, who had a house on her tract. When the harvest was in and tasks prepara-tory to winter were done, Laura would go to Lexington. She, her mother, and Annie made their home with Anne Ryland until 1873, when the mother bought a home on North Broadway in Lexington. When Anne Ryland died in 1892, she left her home, the famous residence of John Bradford at Second and Mill streets, to Laura, her niece.[16] Upon the death of Mary Jane Clay on April 29, 1900, Laura moved to her own home where she lived for the rest of her life, breaking her residence there only to oversee her farm or to work in a suffrage campaign.

Laura's preoccupation with learning the details of farm management was only part of the explanation for her failure to acknowledge publicly the advocacy of woman's rights she had already made in private. The other half of the explanation is that she simply did not know what course her dedication to the cause should follow. Strongly similar to her contemporary Jane Addams; she had great difficulty in deciding what role she should undertake for her Christian service. Unlike Addams, whose family desired for her marriage and the conventional woman's role, Laura Clay did not have to resist any family claims on her time or the direction of her life. Her mother and sisters committed themselves early to woman's rights and in the late 1870s and early 1880s were more active in the movement than Laura. Although her father was a bitter opponent of the movement, his influence on the direction of her life was minimal.[17]

In deciding upon her role in the woman's movement, Laura's range of choice was limited by the time she could spend away from her farm and her financial circumstances. She first hit upon the idea of going to college. Even then, however, she was not certain that higher education would answer her purposes. For what field should she prepare herself? "I know not. I only know that as I am, I am not fitted for any pursuit which will add to my happiness or that of my fellows." She considered a career in teaching and concluded, "I am competent, as a superabundance of others are also, not more."[18]

Since so many others were qualified in the field of teaching, it might do as much good to spend the time simply in improving her mind by going to college. She concluded that she would, but was perplexed by her belief that she owed more than an "ordinary service to myself and others." Told from her youth that she possessed more than ordinary mental abilities, her conscience would not let her off with ordinary service. But how much more? "I have no standard to go by," she complained. "O that my way was clear before God."[19] Implicit in her quandary was the recognition that her education, although superior to that of most women of the time, was inadequate for participation in the professional world, except for the field of public school teaching.

With the goal of a college education before her, Laura began to prepare herself for admission to the University of Michigan. Whether because she had been out of school for twelve years or because, as she understood, there was a difference between "the education thought necessary for young women and that which is necessary for a young man to enter college," she had to do a considerable amount of preparatory work. For three years she spent her spare time studying mathematics and other subjects while chastising herself for a laziness which kept her from progressing faster.[20]

In September 1879, her preparations over, Laura left Lexington for Ann Arbor. Her brother Brutus, a graduate of the University of Michigan, and one of his acquaintances there convinced her to enroll. Friends believed her decision rather sudden although it had actually been her "hope for years." On the other hand, they were not surprised at her desire to attend a "gentlemen's college," so it would seem that her belief in the equal ability of the sexes was well known.[21]

She spent one happy and profitable academic year at Ann Arbor. Despite misgivings over her failures "to go into society" frequently, she was acquiring warm friends and she gladly accepted them, whether from low or high stations. An aunt back in Lexington gently rebuked Laura for finding "a housekeeper . . . an agreeable and congenial companion" at her boardinghouse in Ann Arbor. Such distinctions apparently did not concern Laura, who continued to make friends from a wide range of acquaintances, both male and female.[22]

Her willingness to accept people of all social classes was prompted in part by the preaching of an evangelist, the Reverend George O. Barnes. Although a steadfast Episcopalian, Laura was a regular attendant at a six-weeks revival conducted by Barnes in Lexington early in 1879. Under the influence of his preaching, she began to worry less about her own salvation, accepting instead the comfort promised in God's love and seeking to become a means of transmitting that love to others through personal contacts with the poor and the outcasts of society. One aspect of this commitment was to visit the women in the Lexington jail two or three times a week from the time she heard Barnes until she returned to her farm.[23]

At the University of Michigan, in addition to working on the year of Latin which was required for full admission as a candidate for the bachelor of science, she took seventeen hours of course work. She continued this schedule for two semesters, attending classes in French, English, history, drawing, trigonometry, and geometry. At the beginning of the second semester, her sister Mary and her three sons came to Ann Arbor. Mary, who entered the premedical curriculum, and the boys were delightful company for Laura, and together they shared less expensive accommodations than Laura had been able to find earlier.[24]

Laura left Michigan after one year, thankful to God for the experience and for her happiness while there. She never returned to complete work on her degree. Her only other college experience was one semester at the Agricultural and Mechanical College of Kentucky (now the University of Kentucky) in 1886.[25] It is not clear why she failed to follow up her successful beginning in college. Perhaps the demands of farm management required her presence more than college work would permit; perhaps she decided that her desire to do something for womanhood would not be materially improved by higher education. Here again her indecision about how she could best advance the cause of her sex must have played a part in these beginnings and unexplained withdrawals.

Although her performance in college may have fallen short of her expectations, there seems to have been a general recognition of her ability to compete at that level. Diary entries indicate that she, her family, and her friends believed her talents to be well above the average. One correspondent urged her to become a lawyer, assuring her that she could complete the work for a law degree in less than two years. "When God has given a woman a talent," he wrote, "I am persuaded you know she ought to use it; and as regards the talent, we are all sure you have it."[26]

While Laura was still searching for a role in life outside the management of her farm, the other Clay women had become involved in organization and agitation for woman's rights. These sisters were not the first people to urge woman's rights in Kentucky, but they did establish the first lasting and effective suffrage organizations there. In 1853 Lucy Stone, a pioneer in the suffrage movement, "made speeches in Louisville and in other Kentucky towns on the Ohio river." Other notable public lecturers on woman's rights, including Anna Dickinson, soon followed Lucy Stone into Kentucky. The first suffrage organization in the state was founded at Glendale in Hardin County, where a society was established in October 1867. This group, however, did not have a continuous existence and Laura was unable to find any traces of it when she was seeking co-workers in 1888. Even the honor of being the first woman to address the Kentucky legislature in behalf of women did not go to natives of the state. In 1872 Margaret V. Langley of Ohio and Hannah Tracy Butler of Illinois visited the legislature and "received a respectful audience" when they asked for improved laws regulating married women's property rights. The chief significance of these early efforts, in Laura Clay's opinion, was that they showed Kentucky women that they would have to gain their rights themselves.[27]

One of the minor ironies of the Clay family's participation in the equal rights struggle is that Laura, who was to achieve such a wide reputation later, was easily eclipsed by her sisters in the early years of their activity. Mary B. Clay, now a divorced mother of three boys, initially involved herself, her sisters, and her mother in suffrage work. She attended the tenth anniversary meeting of the National Woman Suffrage Association at Saint Louis in May 1879. As a "self-appointed delegate" from Kentucky, she did not take part in the debates or program at the convention, but she and Susan B. Anthony did lay plans for the first significant effort to organize suffrage societies in Kentucky.[28]

During the autumn of 1879, while Laura was busy with her studies at the University of Michigan, Mary was making arrangements for Anthony's appearance in Richmond, taking care of advertising, accommodations, and itinerary. Anthony arrived in Richmond on the evening of October 25 for the first of three speeches. Her visit was a success, establishing a close contact with the Clay family which lasted until her death and marking the beginning of the Madison County Equal Rights Association, the first permanent woman's rights organization in the state. She spoke to "good crowds" at Green's Opera Hall and the courthouse, making a particular impression with her "Bread, Not the Ballot" speech which emphasized that the ballot was necessary for the economic protection that women needed.[29]

Anthony had a way of involving others in "the cause," as the women referred to their movement. Mary soon had "twelve or thirteen signees" to a petition to the state legislature and Congress urging legislative action in behalf of women. The other Clay girls joined her in asking newspaper editors across the state to publish woman's rights articles. By early 1884 Sallie Clay Bennett was writing a column on women's activities for the weekly *Richmond Register* and Annie Clay was handling a similar task for the *Kentucky Gazette* of Lexington.[30]

After the fall harvest in 1879, Mary Jane Clay returned to Lexington, where she made her home the center for suffrage agitation. The Clay women were knocking on doors to enlist supporters for a woman's rights organization and enjoying some success. "Mary has gotten 44 names of ladies," wrote Mary Jane, "and 102 of gentlemen." But the ladies' signatures had not come easily; most women required a lengthy discussion of the matter before agreeing to sign. A few held out even after the persuasion, "afraid of displeasing their husbands," according to Mary Jane. A short time later only six women attended the organizational meeting of the Fayette (County) Equal Suffrage Association. Obviously disappointed, Laura's mother commented, a little bitterly: "I expect we will find a good many masters standing in the way of the enlightenment of their slaves. Aren't you glad we have no masters?"[31]

But if the Clay women had no "masters," other women did, and the opposition of husbands continued to retard the movement in Kentucky. As late as 1884 Mary B. Clay reported that one husband had insisted that his wife return feminist literature because he did not want his "pleasant relations with his wife disturbed by her reading such books," and other men had forbidden their wives to go to suffrage lectures. Even the churches sometimes shut their doors to the women's meetings. In face of such opposition, concluded Mary B. Clay, many women lost heart at the very beginning and declined "to labor for what seems to them a far away and almost hopeless object."[32]

Despite these obstacles, the feminists were gaining some attention in Kentucky by the mid-1880s. "There has been some little agitation of the suffrage question throughout the State," wrote Mary Jane Clay, and lecturers had appeared in Louisville, Lexington, Frankfort, Paris, Henderson, Richmond, and "several other towns." The Frankfort meetings were held during the biennial sessions of the state legislature in 1882 and 1884. In the former year, Sallie Bennett, Mary B. Clay, and John H. Ward of Louisville were given a hearing by the Senate Judiciary Committee. They made a plea for the right to vote and for the improvement of laws governing married women's property and guardianship rights. In 1884 all four of the Clay sisters went to Frankfort, secured permission to use the legislative hall for their meetings, and were heard "by the best classes of the citizens . . . as well as the members of the legislature."[33]

Kentucky newspapers began to print news about the woman's movement and some provided column space on a regular basis. Perhaps the most hopeful sign was the growing strength in the state of the Woman's Christian Temperance Union (WCTU). Mary B. Clay believed that the temperance women would become suffragists as soon as they found out "how little influence in the country weighs without the ballot to back it."[34]

The first attempt to organize a statewide suffrage society came in 1881, when the American Woman Suffrage Association met in Louisville, the first such convention held south of the Ohio River. The meeting created considerable interest. One newspaper observed that, contrary to common reports, the convention was not solely a gathering of "strong-willed old maids" and noted that 90 percent of those in attendance were married, did not have short hair, nor dress in pantaloons.[35]

In an editorial on the meeting, Henry Watterson of the Louisville Courier-Journal opened an opposition to woman suffrage which lasted until he left the editor's chair in 1919. He admitted that it was a question that could not be scoffed away, but he doubted whether nine of ten women would know what to do with the ballot if they had it. Claiming that the franchise was a duty rather than a right, he questioned the wisdom of granting it to women and even suggested that they might be corrupted by the experience. Had not the extension of the ballot to the Negro—like women, an unprepared class—done more harm than good? Closing the editorial with one small gallant gesture, Watterson admitted that the woman's rights movement had done "tremendous good" in opening up some professions to women.[36]

Watterson's misgivings went unanswered and did nothing to dampen public interest in the convention. At its final session, "the Grand Opera House could not seat the great and sympathetic audience." Seeking to build on the enthusiasm aroused by the convention, a few suffragists founded the Kentucky Woman Suffrage Association, the first state society in the South.[37] The twenty-five members of the association elected Laura Clay its first president and Colonel John H. Ward of Louisville the vice president. Local societies in Louisville, Lexington, and Richmond affiliated with the state organization, but it was unable to create any new clubs.

Suffrage work in the state languished. Laura Clay attributed the association's failure to grow to its narrow purpose—the winning of the franchise, an objective that she believed was too abstract and far distant for the aspirations of Kentucky women at that time. In her opinion the organization should have started with a broad program directed toward improving woman's legal position and gradually worked up to a demand for the ballot.[38] Whatever the other reasons for the failure of the Kentucky Woman Suffrage Association, which maintained a paper existence down to 1888, one was the lack of leadership. Laura Clay never took the work in hand, and one familiar with her conscientious attention to duties in her later career is left to wonder why she accepted the presidency in the first place.

While the work was at a standstill on the local and state levels, two of the sisters were beginning to gain some national recognition. Mary and Sallie had gone to the National Woman Suffrage Association convention in Chicago in 1880, and the latter had addressed one of the evening sessions, which was attended by about 150 people. The next year Mary had been the family's most conspicuous representative at the national convention of the

American Woman Suffrage Association in Louisville. She was given a place on the credentials committee and made a speech in which she called for a revision of the Kentucky laws which would grant women equality with men, "nothing more, nothing less." [39]

The Clay women were members of two rival national suffrage associations—the National Woman Suffrage Association (NWSA) and the American Woman Suffrage Association (AWSA). These two organizations had resulted from a split among the feminists in 1869. The division was precipitated by personality clashes among the leaders and arguments over whether or not the suffragists should seek their own enfranchisement at the risk of imperiling the Negro's chances for the ballot. Both groups sought recruits for the cause, held national conventions, and attempted to establish auxiliary branches. Susan B. Anthony and Elizabeth Cady Stanton were the most prominent leaders of the NWSA, while Lucy Stone and Julia Ward Howe were the guiding spirits of the AWSA. The Clays maintained amiable relations with both factions, which were reunified in the National American Woman Suffrage Association (NAWSA) in 1890. [40]

Mary reached the height of her prestige in the suffrage ranks when she was elected president of the AWSA in 1883. She had the blessing of that organization's strongest leader, Lucy Stone, who wrote urging her to attend the convention in Brooklyn "because it is more than probable that you will be elected president for next year." She carried this newly won prestige to the halls of Congress in the following year when she spoke on woman suffrage at a hearing of the House Judiciary Committee. Her plea for the franchise was based on women's need for protection of their property, their children, and in their work. "Gentlemen, if your protectors were women," she argued, "and they took all your property and your children and paid you half as much for your work, . . . would you think much of the chivalry which allows you to sit in street cars and picks up your pocket handkerchief? . . . women need the ballot for self-protection." Not only would enfranchisement improve the lot of women, it would also cleanse the body politic: "you talk about the dirty pool of politics; if it is dirty, you alone are responsible . . . , because you have excluded the moral scrubbing brush of women. Let us in," she pleaded, "and we will soon change the face of things and bring politics to be the grandest theme of study for the human intellect."[41]

Later in 1884 when Mary gave her presidential address in Chicago to the AWSA, she "made a special plea for work in the South," a theme that was to remain especially dear to the Clay women. Noting that both Alabama and Mississippi had given married women equal property rights, she urged women to petition for similar legislation in other southern states. "For as long as women are dependent upon men for bread," she asserted, "their whole moral nature is necessarily warped." Such laws were important starting places in the struggle for full emancipation, "because pecuniary independence is one of the most potent weapons for freedom, and because that claim has less prejudice [than the ballot] to overcome." She recommended sending speakers and holding conventions as a means of awakening interest in the South where feminist feeling lagged behind the rest of the country.[42]

Laura, who was soon to be acknowledged as the leader of the Kentucky feminists, played only a minor role in the movement before 1888. Annie was recognized as the chief voice in the Lexington society, Sallie had the Richmond group in tow, and Mary spoke for Kentucky at the national level.[43]

Laura's talents had been recognized and solicited, but with little result. Susan B. Anthony asked Mary to remember her to Laura, "for whom I hope very much." Later she inquired, "Is your dear sister Laura going to devote herself to our cause by speaking and other ways? Or is she [going to be] a lawyer?" Lucy Stone, Anthony's rival for national leadership of the suffragists, also sought her services. "I wish your sister Laura could be induced to take Kentucky in hand," she wrote Mary, "hold meetings, organize societies, and push it to activity."[44]

Although Laura Clay dated her "systematic work" for equal rights from 1888, she was moving toward greater involvement in the cause at least two years earlier. In 1886 she was invited by the Association for the Advancement of Women to participate in a symposium on "Woman's Suffrage" at its national meeting in Louisville.[45] That her reputation at this point was strictly local is evidenced by the fact that her correspondent asked her whether she was for or against the subject of the symposium.

Laura prepared a paper entitled "A Practical View of Woman Suffrage," which she presented in Louisville on October 22. Her main point was that suffrage was a necessary component for woman's self-respect. Even in the all-important area of child raising, she maintained, women would "be held in contempt and disadvantaged" if the ballot was not won. Would sons follow their mother's lead on the questions of alcohol and tobacco if women were despised because of their powerlessness and abject meekness? No, "sons will imitate the vices of those they admire," she claimed, "sooner than the virtues of those they despise."[46] Since some 500 persons from many states attended the sessions, this speech may be regarded as Laura Clay's first national exposure.

Apparently her paper in Louisville impressed the association leadership, since she was asked to prepare another for the annual convention in New York the following year. Because she could not attend the meeting in person, her paper, "The Responsibility of Women to Society," was read by M. Louise Thomas, the president of Sorosis, the Women's Club of New York City. The paper hit at the disadvantages of "inferior education, dependence, poverty and political disability" under which so many women were laboring. In particular it urged that females be trained for a much wider range of jobs so they would not be forced into unwanted marriage by economic necessity. The responsibility of all women, Clay concluded, was to educate popular sentiments "to the belief that the true liberty of women consisted in her emancipation from dependence upon others for the means of subsistence."[47] Her conviction that "political disability" and economic dependence were closely intertwined was a theme that she returned to frequently during the years ahead.

How does one explain Laura Clay's quickening interest in feminist activities at the end of the 1880s? Here a definitive answer evades the researcher. The successful management of her farm had given her financial independence and perhaps made her more confident of her own abilities. She seems to have resolved in the negative her quandary about whether or not a college education was necessary to effective work in the cause of women. The two papers she wrote for the Association for the Advancement of Women were well received and could have convinced her that she was ready to participate publicly in the cause to which she had privately committed herself back in 1874.

Whatever her reasons for the decision, Laura Clay never faltered from her commitment to woman's rights in 1888. For the next thirty years, she was unquestionably the leader of her state's feminists, and neither the paucity of followers, the sting of repeated defeats, nor the indifference of the public ever caused her to waver from a staunch belief in the justice of female equality and its eventual triumph.

III

WINNING RIGHTS
FOR KENTUCKY WOMEN

1888-1895

ALTHOUGH LAURA CLAY had become a life member of the suffrage movement in 1881, she dated her active work from 1888. Marriage, family, and career had partially diverted her sisters from their work in the movement. Throughout the 1880s, Mary spent a considerable part of each year in Ann Arbor, continuing to work on her degree and keeping a boardinghouse, while raising her three boys. Sallie kept interest in the cause alive in Richmond, but could be counted on for little more because her five children, even with the help of her understanding husband, James Bennett, kept her occupied most of the time. Annie had married Spotswood Dabney Crenshaw on November 6, 1886, and moved to his home in Richmond, Virginia. With her removal from the state, Laura took up the column that Annie had been contributing to the *Kentucky Gazette*. The loss of workers to marriage and family responsibilities was a constant problem in the early history of the woman's rights movement. As Clement Eaton has pointed out, "There is probably a genuine correlation between the spread of the practice of birth control and the growth of woman's rights."[1]

So by default and by her own decision, Laura became the primary voice of Kentucky suffragists when she was almost forty years old. There is no evidence that she ever considered her rather late commitment an obstacle to good work and advancement in the cause, and compared to Susan B. Anthony, Lucy Stone, and Elizabeth Cady Stanton she was yet a young woman. Twenty-four years later when she decided to step aside as president of the state suffrage society, she did so not to decrease her activities, but rather to channel them in new directions.

It was largely owing to Laura Clay's active participation that the woman's rights movement took an upward turn in 1888. With the help of Henrietta B. Chenault, Laura reorganized the structure and redirected the efforts of the Lexington suffrage society. Like the Kentucky Woman Suffrage Association, the society's constitution "proposed work only for suffrage ... and this far distant object was too abstract for Kentucky women." Believing that opportunities for work in many areas should be open to women, Clay and Chenault issued a public call for a meeting in the old Lexington Library for the purpose of organizing a new society. The result was the birth of the Fayette County Equal Rights Association (ERA) in January of 1888.[2]

The objects of the new organization were "to advance the industrial, educational and legal rights of women, and to secure suffrage to them by appropriate State and National legislation." Laura hoped that this broadened scope of activities would make the organization palatable to a wider range of women while providing a Fabian approach to its ultimate goal, the ballot, which was still regarded as a radical notion by many persons of both sexes. These women were rightly called woman suffragists, said Laura Clay, but their wider claim was "absolute equality with men in the right to free enjoyment of every opportunity that ... civilization, the joint work of both sexes, offers for the development of individual capacity." To achieve this far-reaching goal, the women soon set up a number of committees, some of which— "Hygiene and Dress Reform," "Industrial Training for Women," "Bible Study," "Work among Young People"—were an attempt to reach every woman, regardless of her level of social, cultural, or political awareness.[3]

Laura Clay was elected president of the Fayette County ERA, which soon enrolled the members of the defunct woman suffrage association and sent a delegation to Frankfort to appeal for improved legislation for women. The work at Frankfort was directed by Laura and Mary B. Clay, who was at that time a vice president of both the NWSA and the AWSA.[4]

Following a speaking tour that carried her to Louisville, Lexing-

ton, ar... Mary Jane
Clay's ... paper at the
conver... 888 at Cin-
cinnat... vite all Ken-
tucky ... organizing a
new s...
De... wered Clay's
call a... sociation on
Nove... road program
of wo... m the Gospel
of Jo... he Truth and
the ... s were: presi-
den... rick and Mary
B. (... ner; recording
secretary, Anna M. Deane; and treasurer, ... I. Shepard.[6]

Speaking later of the new society, Laura Clay emphasized that it was attempting to win much more than the ballot, even though its members were commonly called suffragists. "The principle we are advocating," she said, "is more deep rooted and widespreading than the right of women, by the ballot, to have a voice in the making of the laws." Striking a strongly contemporary theme, she pointed out that women might have the franchise "and yet be so subjected by wrongful social customs, by deficient education, and by false religious views that the ballot in their hands would but weld and tighten the chains that bind them away from any true and noble liberty."[7]

The new society was then something of a paradox from the beginning. While its multipurposed program was designed to allay the fears of the timid and attract the widest possible range of members, it had nothing less than a societal revolution as its ultimate goal. By seeking absolute equality in every profession and every opportunity available to men, these women were seeking a goal that extended beyond the franchise and which had not been completely attained almost one hundred years later. They knew that the realization of this goal depended as much upon changing the people's attitude toward woman's place in society as upon changing the laws.

This women's quest had a somewhat inauspicious beginning.

The Kentucky ERA opened its campaign with only sixty-six members, failed to double that figure in its first year, and could muster only 400 members after seven years' activity.[8] Laura Clay, who was unquestionably the driving force of the movement, spent the first years of her active career primarily in three tasks: 1) building up the state membership and organizing new auxiliary chapters, 2) lobbying for feminist legislation whenever the state General Assembly was in session, and 3) encouraging women to enroll in the Agricultural and Mechanical College to which they had been admitted in 1880 and the Louisville School of Pharmacy which was opened to them in 1882.[9]

Laura began her efforts to build up Kentucky suffrage sentiment in the months just prior to the Cincinnati convention of the AWSA in 1888. She and Henrietta Chenault planned a speaking tour through the state for Zerelda G. Wallace, a noted WCTU lecturer, who was the superintendent of the Department of Franchise for that organization. The plan was for Wallace to include as much woman suffrage as possible in her popular temperance lecture, "The Home Versus the Saloon."[10]

All three women realized that there was much more sympathy in the country for prohibition than for woman suffrage. Wallace intended to bring woman suffrage in the back door of her lectures, believing she could better "reach . . . people and disabuse the public mind of prejudice" against the less popular movement in that manner.[11] This was a tactic which Laura Clay and many other suffragists were to use for years, and it was dictated as much by necessity as by choice. Most of the suffragists were believers in temperance, but like Laura they put the franchise first in their aspirations. Their problem was a simple one: they had to reach the people and that could often be done easier, especially in the rural areas, through a temperance lecture than through a straight suffrage talk. Perhaps Lucy Stone was correct when she attributed the greater popularity of the temperance movement to the fact that "it is so much easier to see a drunkard than it is to see a principle."[12]

The idea of mixing woman suffrage with temperance received a cool reception from women around the state. One correspondent wrote from Shawnee Springs that "it would not be expedient" to have Wallace give her temperance talk at that time. "We are fighting in the temperance cause and must let that be our first thought. Woman suffrage would do us harm now." [13]

Another correspondent was willing to have the lecturer come but warned that "Woman's suffrage finds few advocates here. My husband, my brother-in-law and myself," she wrote from Carrollton, "are all that I know of who are decided on that point." This was a discouraging note from a town of some 3,000 persons. A third correspondent replied from Paducah, a town of about 13,000 persons, "it is in my heart to say, 'send Mrs. Wallace to us,' but with the exception of myself, I know of no women in Paducah in favor of Woman Suffrage." Another woman complained that she could find "only two other ladies that endorse this movement" in Lebanon, which had a population over 3,000. "Being Southerners," she explained, "it is hard for us to advance out of the old routine," an excuse which Laura was to hear often as an explanation of southern conservatism. [14]

Despite the gloomy forebodings, Wallace toured the state and was optimistic about the results. "I was delighted with my trip in Kentucky," she reported to Laura Clay. "We have broken the ice and set the people to thinking upon the question of the woman's ballot from a new standpoint." [15] The new standpoint was the claim, common among temperance and suffrage lecturers, that the ballot in the hands of women was the surest way to prohibition and other social improvements.

In addition to planning tours for suffrage speakers, Laura Clay and other Kentucky suffragists began to give lectures themselves. Early in 1889 they announced the formation of the Kentucky Lecture Bureau, consisting of Mary C. Roark, Ellen B. Dietrick, Eugenia Farmer, Mary B. Clay, and Laura Clay. The bureau's purpose was to provide free speakers for any civic or woman's club anywhere in Kentucky. Laura was the most active of these speakers. At one of her earliest engagements, she spoke on "the rights, duties and responsibilities of women as citizens." Her lecture was an argument for exact equality before the law, including the right to suffrage of all citizens without regard to sex. Here, as in so many cases until after the turn of the century, Clay's audience was a District Convention of the WCTU. After hearing her speech, "nearly all the delegates . . . wore the yellow ribbon, the woman's rights color, with the white, the W.C.T.U. emblem. . . ."[16]

Like so many suffragists of her generation, Laura was a member of the WCTU. She differed from many of them in that she espoused suffrage first and sought to use her temperance affiliation to forward the rights of women. During the years she served as the superintendent of the Department of Franchise for the Kentucky WCTU, her first concern was the ballot for women, and that was her constant theme in letters and lectures.[17] Temperance societies seem to have been primarily a means to an end for her.

Although she later regretted the passage of the Eighteenth Amendment and claimed that her goal had been temperance, there is no evidence that Clay qualified her support of the WCTU program in the years of its greatest strength. While membership was largely a matter of expediency with her, she had no reservations about the foremost goal of the organization: national prohibition.[18]

The narrow line that Laura Clay had to tread when speaking for suffrage in temperance territory is indicated by a report of her appearance before another WCTU District Convention in Kirksville, Kentucky. Addressing herself to the subject "What Can Women Do for Temperance," she "held sway for an hour" in a crowded church. Her message was "deep, scriptural, and logical, touching lightly on woman suffrage, but . . . handled so skillfully that the men were almost persuaded to give justice to the plea that the salvation of fallen humanity from drink depended on the vote from the women."[19] It was a simplistic religious message on the evils of drink which was calculated to convince her rural audience that woman's suffrage was the shortest route to its eradication.

Laura took her dual message to the Eighth Assembly of the Kentucky Chautauqua at Lexington in July 1894. With "fervid eloquence," she declared that the temperance forces had discovered some time earlier that "moral suasion" was not enough. It had to be supplemented with legal authority in the form of local option or state prohibition. When these halfway measures failed to stop the liquor traffic completely, the temperance forces had begun to support national prohibition. While each step had done some good, she claimed that "each step had also shown the necessity of taking another."[20] She then suggested that it was time for women seeking to influence governmental decisions to take another step.

Instead of relying on "women's influence," which appeared "a little supercilious to their woman suffrage sisters," they must seek the legal authority necessary for a program of "direct action." The suffragists already knew that "women's influence" was not of "any great current value," and the temperance women were fast learning the same lesson. The ballot was the means to direct action and women could use it to "vote for prohibition and other righteous laws." Women had learned "that as human beings and citizens they are entitled to a ballot as well as to an influence." The local press reported that this speech of "the best known of the Woman's Rights lecturers of Kentucky" was followed by loud handclapping and cheers.[21]

Laura's speechmaking was not limited to appearances before women's clubs and WCTU meetings. The suffragists appreciated the advantage of securing endorsements from the political parties and usually petitioned them for recognition in their platforms. Success at the major parties' national conventions did not come until 1916 and their endorsement at the state level was out of the question during the 1890s in Kentucky. Because the People's party advocated a wide range of progressive and, for that day, radical measures, there was a greater likelihood that the women could win its approval.[22] This was Laura Clay's hope when she went to the People's party convention at Louisville in 1895.

Josephine K. Henry of Versailles accompanied her to the convention, and the two women anxiously listened from box seats as the platform was read without any mention of their cause. Finally a delegate near the women rose to offer a resolution that would make woman suffrage part of the platform and to request that the convention consent to hear Laura Clay in advocacy of his motion.

When the request was granted, Clay "roasted the People's representatives for overlooking the rights of one-half of the people —the women—who are the most miserable of all the prisoners of misery and toil and who have not the men's means to redress their wrongs." She pointed out that working women were even worse off than men of their class because they had "to suffer and bear their woes without having the power to defend by ballot the taking of bread from their mouths." She closed her "earnest and plaintive plea" with thanks to God that "she was a farmer and independent enough to say she desired to vote, something the school teachers and working women don't dare to demand for fear of losing their bread."[23]

Their consciences pricked, several of the delegates hastened to claim that they were "the friends of women," but unfortunately "the time was not yet ripe for the adoption of woman's rights." Clay refused to permit such fainthearted champions to carry the women's banner; she "dramatically came to the front" and denied that any men were their friends who did not "lift their voices for them and aid them with their votes."[24]

Her taunt reopened "the whole woman's rights question" in the convention and many speakers sought to gain the floor. One claimed that the adoption of woman's vote had hurt the People's party in Colorado, because women of "low character" were used to defeat its candidate. Another made the telling charge that not even a majority of Kentucky women favored suffrage, and a third feared that "too many isms would sink the platform." After some "noisy and prolonged" calls for the question, the resolution was voted down by a "tremendous majority."[25]

Although obviously disappointed by the rejection of their proposal, Clay and Henry lost none of their dignity in defeat. They walked out of the convention hall with their heads "defiantly tossed back in the air and without saying good-bye to anyone."[26]

Speaking wherever she could find an audience was only part of Laura Clay's suffrage work. Her steady correspondence with women throughout the Commonwealth, exhorting and encouraging them to renewed or greater efforts, was equally important to the growth of the movement. She made use of every contact available to her, those she met lecturing, and those who she had heard were suffragists, as well as the widespread network of WCTU chapters. All were urged to start an auxiliary to the Kentucky ERA and to circulate petitions seeking signatures in support of legislation at Frankfort. If time, money, or ability kept them from these tasks they were asked to send her the names of other women who might be interested in the work. It was often a discouraging task. Lida C. Obenchain (Lida Calvert Hall), who later achieved national attention for her novel *Aunt Jane of Kentucky,* turned down Laura's first entreaties to join the work. She wrote that two young babies would keep her from attending the meetings in Bowling Green, even if someone else could be found to organize an auxiliary. Laura refused to be put off permanently by such family responsibilities, and her persistence paid off when Obenchain accepted responsibility for press work shortly after the turn of the century. She was a valuable acquisition for the Kentucky ERA, bringing both her writing talent and her growing prestige to its service.[27]

The point of all this work—speaking, writing, organizing, and circulating petitions—was to mount a legislative campaign, both for the purpose of righting old laws unfavorable to women and of adding new ones. Clay realized that the proof of agitating and organizing lay in the women's success in Frankfort, and under her leadership the Kentucky feminists began their first successful lobbying.

Laura approached the task in her usual systematic and intelligent manner. Shortly before the Kentucky ERA was organized, she wrote Lucy Stone for advice on drawing up a married woman's property rights bill. Within a few days after the beginning of the new organization in Cincinnati in November 1888, she had secured a superintendent of Legislative and Petition work, who was to have charge of the work in Frankfort.[28] Josephine K. Henry was one of the ablest lieutenants Clay was to have in her long struggle for woman's rights.

Henry and Clay made an interesting and colorful team. Whereas Clay was called "a massive woman," "commanding in size and presence," Henry was "a small, slight woman," who wore glasses and was "so frail in her appearance that she would never be taken for the ardent . . . advocate of woman's rights" that she was.[29]

The talents of the one complemented those of the other. Clay was a good administrator and a fine tactician, less prone than Henry to alienate those they had to win to their cause with that abrasiveness and high indignation which characterized many suffragists. Henry, on the other hand, was a better writer than Clay and equally able as a speaker. By the early 1890s, they were the best known suffragists in Kentucky and were rising powers in the national organization.[30]

When Clay and Henry took their campaign to Frankfort in 1890, Kentucky laws dealing with the rights of women were among the most backward in the country, and those dealing with the property rights of married women were in a particularly "crude state." Kentucky law essentially followed the great English jurist William Blackstone, who wrote: "By marriage, the husband and wife are one person in law: that is, the very being or legal existence of the woman is suspended during the marriage, or at least is incorporated and consolidated into that of the husband."[31]

What this meant in practice was that a wife's property as well as the rents and profits that accrued from her real estate belonged to her husband. If she were a working woman, he had every legal right to her wages, with or without her consent. She could not sue without his accompaniment, nor could she make a will without his consent. In the case that death dissolved the marriage, the wife was entitled to a life's interest in only one-third of the husband's real estate, while upon her death he inherited all her personal belongings and a life interest in all her real estate. An extreme, but nonetheless possible, example of Kentucky justice was the following illustration used by Henry:

> A woman worth one hundred thousand dollars, that has not been settled upon her as her separate estate, marries a man not worth a penny, and it all becomes his in the instant he promises "With all my worldly goods, I thee endow." The woman comes from the marriage altar not even the legal possessor of the clothes she has on her back. She can not make a will, and, if the husband died one week after the marriage, fifty thousand dollars of the wife's money goes to his nearest male relative, unless he generously wills the defenseless wife her own estate.[32]

Insofar as suffrage was concerned, Kentucky women had been granted a minor voting right in 1838. A law of that year gave school suffrage to widows and spinsters in county districts who owned property subject to taxation for school purposes. It was the first instance of school suffrage on record, and no other state repeated it until Kansas gave its women the school vote in 1861. This limited suffrage extended only to such matters as school bonds and district school trustees. Most women were not, of course, covered by it at all, and since the right was not "generally known or understood, few women . . . ever availed themselves of the privilege." Aside from this legislation on school suffrage, Kentucky laws on the rights of women were among the most backward in the country, lagging behind the more progressive northern states and most of the southern states, which had incorporated advanced property and guardianship rights for women into their Reconstruction constitutions.[33]

Since the Kentucky legislature met biennially in the even-numbered years, there was one year between the founding of the Equal Rights Association in 1888 and the legislature's next meeting in 1890. Laura Clay used the interim period well, dividing her efforts between organizing new suffrage clubs and doing petition work. The latter effort was of particular importance because the small group of women who did the lobbying in Frankfort needed as many petitions as possible to support its pleas to the lawmakers. The petitions bearing 10,000 names which Clay and Henry carried with them to the capital in 1890 are indicative of the suffragists' work and their organization's successful beginning.[34]

The two women opened their campaign when the legislature met in January 1890. At the second annual convention of the Equal Rights Association in the previous November, they had resolved to seek laws protecting married women's property, appointing women physicians to mental institutions where women were confined, and enfranchising women in school and municipal elections. The House chamber was opened to the organization for an evening meeting, and Clay and Henry made addresses to "a good crowd," which included about fifty of the lawmakers, on January 10.[35]

Henry handled the appeal for new laws to protect women's property, while Clay explained why female physicians were needed in the mental institutions. Henry pointed out how paradoxical it was that Kentuckians, known "the world over for their chivalry, gallantry and exalted regard for women," should allow laws to remain on the statute books which almost make it "a crime to be a married woman." She cited examples showing that in Kentucky "the poor creatures seem to be worse off . . . than in any other State in the Union." "Her treatment of the subject showed much study," wrote one reporter, "and her presentation was very effective." He claimed that no one would have suspected a woman of such "small stature" to have possessed so much "intellectual force, but she proved a great surprise." Others who were prepared to scoff came away impressed: "Many of those who went were disappointed in hearing, instead of, as expected, a harangue from a misguided woman of her sex's right to vote, a clear, strong argument in behalf of the needed changes in the statute books, which now . . . smack strongly of barbarism and fossilized injustice that have been abolished in nearly every other State in the Union."[36]

Laura Clay followed Josephine Henry to the podium and made "a stirring appeal for the appointment of a woman assistant physician in every asylum in the State," pointing out "most forcibly how this would help female lunatics and imbeciles." She said that such provisions had already been made by the states of the North and West and that Kentucky should quickly follow their example. Noting her "distinguished appearance," one observer guessed her to be about fifty years of age and commented upon her "striking resemblance to her father." She was, he added, commanding "both in size and presence."[37]

While denying that the plight of women was as bad as they claimed, Henry Watterson of the *Louisville Courier-Journal* conceded that the laws demanded change. He warned that additional rights meant additional responsibilities for women and advised that whatever changes were made should be done cautiously. Bend as he did on the question of property rights, Watterson remained adamantly opposed to female suffrage. Only prohibition rivaled "the Silly-sallies and Crazy Janes" in the amount of "abusive," "exhortative," and "melancholy" comments received from his acid-dipped pen.[38]

The fruits of the women's first assault upon the legislature were meager. The sole victory was the passage of a bill that made it obligatory for employers to pay wages earned by married women to the women themselves. The purpose of this bill was to prevent "unworthy husbands" from gaining and wasting the earnings of their unwilling wives.[39] However small the victory it was a first step in a long campaign to equalize the rights of the sexes in marriage.

A more ambitious bill designed to protect a wife's personal and real estate from the control of her husband, was introduced by Judge William Lindsay, a member of the General Assembly from Harrodsburg. Laura Clay urged the readers of her weekly "Woman's Column" in the *Kentucky Gazette* to write their representatives in behalf of this bill. Although Lindsay's bill was passed by the Senate, it was defeated in the House, despite the efforts of Laura Clay, Josephine Henry, and Eugenia B. Farmer of Covington, who spent much of the legislative session in Frankfort.[40]

The constitutional convention that met in September 1890 provided a good opportunity for the feminists to further their goals. The primary purpose of the assembly was to bring the provisions of the constitution of 1849 into agreement with the important developments in the federal Constitution, principally the abolition of slavery. Since the state document had been built around the protection of slavery, extensive revision was long overdue and owed its postponement to partisan bickering between Democrats, Republicans, and various agrarian partisans.[41]

Laura Clay and her lieutenants hoped that this body would write a constitution which would protect married women in their property rights and would grant woman suffrage. If they did not secure these goals, the women would seek passage of a constitution that would be easily amendable in their favor in the future. Perhaps they hoped for too much from an undistinguished conclave. A chronicler of Kentucky history has written that this assembly "was composed of as motley a delegation of constitutionalists as had ever been seen in a convention hall. Kentucky would have been well served had at least fifty [of the 100] of these delegates remained at home."[42]

However undistinguished its personnel, the convention offered the women another chance to present their goals to the people. The deliberations were hardly under way before the Shelby County delegate complained that "the E.R.A. is now quartered here in Frankfort, making life a burden to the poor members." He attributed the "radical resolutions" on property rights and woman suffrage to the ERA and warned the delegates against "changes in the old constitution," especially in its Bill of Rights. Noting that the governor's wife, Mrs. Simon Buckner, had announced that she had more rights than she knew what to do with, he lamented, "if only other strong-minded women would take the cue."[43]

Despite such complaints, women used the convention's sessions, which lasted just over one year, as they had the last regular meeting of the legislature. They held evening meetings, buttonholed delegates, and even received a hearing before the convention. Laura Clay, Sallie Bennett, and Mrs. I. H. Shepard spoke to a "well-filled" State House during the early weeks of the convention. Clay, the principal speaker, asked for woman suffrage and changes in property rights. Suffrage was a matter of justice, she claimed, since women were taxed without representation, and a matter of necessity because the three million working women in the country needed the ballot to protect their interests. Displaying a knowledge of the impact of the industrial revolution, as well as a sympathy for working women, she reviewed the history of women as laborers and pointed out that their entire situation had been altered by the introduction of machinery into manufacturing. Forced out of the home and into the factory, women deserved the ballot for self-protection as well as for justice.[44]

Her speech received a mixed reaction. One delegate expressed the general opinion on suffrage when he claimed, "I love them too much to allow them to vote. If they were granted that right, the marriage tie would disappear inside of fifty years." Property rights, on the other hand, were an area in which the petitioners might expect some change.[45]

The highlight of the convention for the women came when Laura Clay was granted permission to address it. It was a hard-won right, and came after the women "had been lobbying many days." Even then it probably would not have been granted without the intervention of the permanent president of the convention, Cassius M. Clay of Bourbon County, Laura's cousin.[46]

In a "brief, well-worded and sensible" speech, Laura asked that the new constitution grant the General Assembly "the power . . . to extend suffrage to women on the same terms as it is now extended to men."[47] In short, she asked the delegates to empower the legislature under the new constitution with the authority to extend suffrage to women without going to the people for the customary approval of such constitutional amendments.

She complimented the "noble assembly" for the high ideas it had announced and added:

It has been my privilege and pleasure, in the last few days, to hear gentlemen recalling and emphasizing the great principles that lie at the basis of our government. I have heard the instruction with joy . . . as the gentlemen spoke of the sacred rights of humanity, in this Hall. It has been declared in the noble Bill of Rights framed by them, that they believe in equal rights to all, exclusive privileges for none. I have heard suffrage described as the crowning glory of the freeman. I have heard all these things, and seen with a joy which only a native born Kentucky woman can feel, that, amidst all the difficulties now surrounding us, there was an unfeigned and earnest spirit to preserve to our State the blessings which we have had of free government, and to secure good and free government to all.[48]

"Gentlemen," she went on, "I do not propose to argue woman suffrage. You have your own opinions; . . . I speak of justice, and justice only." Were not women to share in the equality and justice that the delegates had trumpeted through the halls for the past three months?

It occurred to me, could these men be speaking these lofty thoughts and not remember with any thrill of sympathetic pain, that there were others besides men as patriotic and intelligent, as law-abiding, as peace-loving—others who give as many hostages for the honor and safety of the States as they? Can they utter these noble sentiments, and yet exclude from any share in them the women of their homes? . . . Will the men forget that women also have rights, and that we have more right than simply to be governed for our good? That the highest right of a free woman, as well as of a free man, is self-government? . . . Women do not ever dream that they have more wisdom than man; but this we do say, that women have a different wisdom from men. Wisdom is not only manly but womanly; men are patriotic, women are patriotic. The laws touch women as they do men.[49]

Calling herself "as true a patriot as any man in this country," she asked for herself and her sisters the rights won by the revolutionary fathers. She reminded her auditors of words from the Virginia Bill of Rights which declared that "we cannot long preserve free government or the blessings of liberty to ourselves without a frequent recurrence to fundamental principles." The women of Kentucky, she asserted, believed it was time for a reaffirmation of honored principles and a significant step toward justice for women. Clay's speech stirred no comment in the convention. It barely paused long enough to allow Charles Bronston, a delegate from Fayette County, to gain permission to have the address published in the proceedings of the Convention.[50]

The press was more generous and somewhat disparaging of the delegates. One reporter was surprised that there was "no tremor" in Laura Clay's voice "which was the best the convention had listened to for many weeks." This was the first of four state constitutional conventions she addressed in her long career. She was to make similar appeals to equally deaf ears in South Carolina in 1895, Louisiana in 1898, and Oklahoma in 1906.[51]

Clay's eloquence and the goodwill of a few of the delegates were not enough to carry the ERA's program. The proposal to give the legislature the power to grant full suffrage to women was voted down, but the legislature was empowered to extend partial suffrage, that is, in school elections and in municipal and presidential elections. The effort to improve the property rights of married women fared even worse. After being favorably reported by the Woman's Rights Committee, the bill was tabled and never came to a vote.[52] Despite disappointments, the convention had not been a complete loss to the feminists. They had used the chance to put their question before the people and won converts and some concessions in the process.

The constitution, "with all its shortcomings," was adopted in 1891. One of its provisions, which was to prove especially troublesome to reformers, provided that only two amendments might be voted upon at a time. In effect, this meant that all amendments would have to vie for the two opportunities to change the constitution, and since the legislature met biennially, except for special called sessions, ordinarily only two amendments could be offered every two years. Furthermore, if an amendment were defeated by the people, it could not be put on the ballot again for five years.[53]

The General Assembly of 1892 had the task of bringing Kentucky laws into agreement with the new constitution. The work required a particularly long session of the legislature, occupying most of 1892 and stretching over into the next year. The ERA maintained its small Frankfort lobby throughout the session.[54]

A group of Louisville women led by Mrs. B. F. Avery joined Laura Clay and her lobby in the fight for a married woman's property bill. In an effort to secure executive aid, the women gained an interview with Governor John Young Brown, who reportedly "had been discreetly quiet since Mrs. Brown declared herself for the bill." The aid of such a highly placed friend notwithstanding, the women suffered another defeat when their bill failed to get out of committee.[55]

In 1893 the Kentucky ERA appointed a special committee, led by Mrs. Thomas L. Jones and Sarah G. Humphreys, to lobby for a revision of the age of consent law. After publicizing the issue in the press and gathering petitions supporting its position, the committee requested the lawmakers to raise the age of consent from twelve to eighteen years of age. One male supporter of the bill chastised the state for permitting "its children over twelve . . . to be called through the very gateways of hell by the demons who are ever ready at street corners to lure innocent girls into wine rooms, free shows, and dens of iniquity, because they have no fear of the law."[56] The bill was introduced and given a hearing in 1894, but the legislature adjourned without acting on it.

The work of organizing, petitioning, and agitating paid off for the ERA in 1894. For three years the organization had maintained an almost continuous lobby in Frankfort, urging its proposals on two legislatures and the constitutional convention. When success came, it arrived with a rush, giving married women equity in property rights and granting school suffrage to women of the three second-class cities, Lexington, Newport, and Covington.

Josephine Henry was the heroine of the passage of the married woman's property rights law. As superintendent of Legislative and Petition Work, "her efforts in writing and making speeches in its favor were of incalculable value," wrote Laura Clay.[57]

Clay recalled the events surrounding the bill's passage as "a romance in parliamentary practice." At a time when the bill seemed lost, since the House had rejected the amended version passed 21–10 by the Senate, Henry gave a speech on "American Citizenship" which many of the legislators heard. Speaking in Representatives' Hall on the evening of March 8, "she held a large audience in close attention for more than an hour while she applied the principles of American citizenship to the rights of women." "Her eloquence," wrote Laura Clay, "so moved our friends that they thought they would make another effort to pass the bill she had so much at heart."[58]

Judge William Beckner and Judge S. B. Vance, who had guided the bill through the House, went back to work. Beckner found a precedent by which the House could reconsider the bill. The House then brought up the Senate's amended version of the Beckner-Vance bill and passed it by a 76–14 vote. This meant success for the bill, "notwithstanding that the Senate had undergone a change of mind, and was quite furious that the bill had won at last." This greatest triumph of the feminists to date was signed into law by Governor Brown on March 15, 1894.[59]

The act, hailed by Josephine Henry as "a victory over fossilized ignorance, selfishness and tyranny," gave wives complete control of their own real estate and personal property, including its disposal through a will. It enabled them to carry on their own business independent of their husbands' interference and equalized curtesy and dower; that is, it gave the wife the same one-half life interest in her deceased husband's property (dower), as he had in her property under reverse circumstances (curtesy). Henry said it meant, in short, that Kentucky wives would no longer be "treated as outlaws and all their property confiscated at marriage."[60]

A second victory, accompanied by little of the fanfare of the Married Woman's Property Act, quickly followed the first. On March 19 the governor signed a law that permitted the women of second-class cities to vote on all school matters. Only three cities, Lexington, Covington, and Newport, were in this privileged class. The reasoning of the General Assembly was that only women of these cities petitioned the legislative committee which was preparing the city charters for the right; consequently, they received it, while the charters of the first-class, third-class, and fourth-class cities did not contain the enfranchising provision.[61]

While Josephine Henry was warning the public that these bills were only the first steps toward woman suffrage, Laura Clay's attitude was conciliatory and appreciative. She stated that Kentucky laws which had been among the most illiberal in the Union were now just and equitable. The results of the legislative session, she added, gave the suffragists cause for optimism and confidence. She concluded that "women will in the end win success for equal rights by unfaltering appeals to the love of equity which is deeply implanted in the hearts of men by the God of Justice."[62]

While pushing the work in Frankfort at every opportunity, the ERA undertook to advance women's rights in other areas. The introduction of coeducation at several of the state's colleges and universities was an early and unqualified success. Although the Kentucky Agricultural and Mechanical College had admitted women as early as the 1880–1881 session, the other colleges around the state had not followed its example. One of the first efforts of the Fayette ERA, following its organization in 1888, was to open Kentucky University (now Transylvania University) in Lexington to women.[63]

The association appointed a committee, led by Mary S. Hamilton, Anna M. Deane, and Laura Clay, to direct the campaign. The women interviewed a number of professors to secure their views and began collecting signatures on petitions requesting that the school admit women. In June 1888 the three ladies took "a bundle of petitions" to a meeting of the university's Board of Curators. Clay, the chairman of the women's committee, presented the petitions and made a brief address on the desirability of coeducation.[64]

The Board answered the women by appointing a committee, headed by the university's president, C. L. Loos, to investigate and make recommendations in the matter. Loos, who had been a warm friend of the project from the first, corresponded "with more than twenty principal colleges of the United States" and found unanimous support for coeducation.[65]

While the Board of Curators met in April of the following year, Loos and his committee recommended that women be admitted to the university. The board voted to admit women for the fall term of 1889 and made an appropriation to improve the buildings in anticipation of their arrival. Thus the oldest university west of the Allegheny Mountains, after 109 years of male isolation, opened its doors to women.[66]

Other schools around the state soon followed Transylvania's example. In 1892 Georgetown College, Wesleyan College at Winchester, and the Homeopathic Medical College in Louisville admitted female students. The Madison County ERA won a victory when Central University in Richmond agreed to its request for coeducation in 1893.[67]

The school suffrage victory of 1894 afforded the women of Lexington, Covington, and Newport an opportunity for civic activity and advancement of their cause. Laura Clay always maintained that women had a special interest in the schools; first, because a heavy percentage of their taxes went for school expenditures and, second, because women's special sphere was the health and education of children. Acting under these premises, the Fayette ERA petitioned the mayor of Lexington to appoint women to the city's School Board. Mayor Henry T. Duncan complied by naming Mrs. Wilbur R. Smith to the board in 1893. She was the first woman to hold such a position in Kentucky, and perhaps the first in the South.[68]

The women of Lexington used their newly won school suffrage to elect four women to the School Board in 1895. The WCTU, the Woman's Club of Central Kentucky, and the ERA joined forces at a mass meeting and planned their strategy for the campaign. Laura Clay presided and made the opening address. The nominations, made by a committee composed of representatives of the three organizations, were unanimously accepted. In the evening of the same day, the Citizens Association, with nearly 300 persons in attendance, endorsed the four women candidates.[69]

When neither the Democrats nor the Republicans would agree to form a coalition with the women, they added four men to their slate and called it the Independent Ticket. This ticket was elected in November, although the women did not turn out as heavily as was hoped from the number who had registered to vote.[70]

The election victory was an appropriate climax to the early years of the Kentucky ERA. Its vitality and efficacy had been proved and victories had been won. With the most important of its legal and educational goals achieved, the association was ready to turn its attention toward expanding woman's influence in the law-making process.[71]

In Laura Clay the cause of woman's rights in Kentucky had found able, devoted, and steady leadership, while she had found her cause in life. The early anxieties and doubts about her personal worthiness and the nature of her Christian service had vanished. She had found her niche. "I am in my element," she wrote.[72] "This work is God's cause, and He is the leader of all our campaigns."[73] Confident in the righteousness of her cause and growing in ability, she was prepared to play an important role in sectional and national suffrage affairs by the mid-1890s.

IV

SOUTHERN SUFFRAGISTS
FIND A CHAMPION

1892-1896

BY THE MIDDLE of the 1890s Laura Clay, the recognized leader of the woman's rights campaign in Kentucky, was prepared to play a broader role in the woman's rights movement. During this decade she became the champion of southern interests in the NAWSA, badgering it to expend more of its meager resources on the South, organizing suffrage affiliates in the section, and actively campaigning to get woman suffrage written into the new state constitutions which were replacing those of the Reconstruction period. She had become a familiar figure in suffrage circles, and the picture one can draw of her at this time does not change during the rest of her long public career.

Laura Clay was a commanding woman, large of frame and dignified in bearing. On one occasion she suffered silently during a discussion on woman suffrage while a popular newspaperman marshaled evidence against the reform before a convention of the Kentucky Federation of Women's Clubs. His clinching argument was that "women were not strong enough physically for the strain of politics; that they were indeed . . . clinging vines and men the sturdy oaks." Before he could reclaim his seat, Clay, who was to speak next, appeared beside him at the podium and, "towering above the speaker, replied laconically, 'O, I don't know.' " The "great laughter which swept the audience" proved that she had won her point.[1]

When a mature woman, Laura Clay was distinguished, rather than pretty, in appearance. She dressed simply, usually wearing a black dress with a white lace piece at the collar, a small brooch, and no hat. Her tastes definitely leaned toward the comfortable rather than the stylish, and she avoided fads, as, for example, the bloomer costume, realizing the adverse effects they could have on the woman's cause in the popular mind. Thick black hair, a short neck, a strong face containing large blue eyes and arching eyebrows caused Kentuckians to mark her striking resemblance to her father. "Her face is most winning," wrote one reporter who knew her well, "frankness and geniality beaming from her beautiful eyes."[2]

Laura Clay possessed a restraint and generosity which enabled her to put the shortcomings and offenses of lesser people in the best possible light, overlooking, rationalizing, and forgiving things that might have infuriated other persons. In a like fashion she refused to be pulled into the intraorganizational squabbling which too often characterized women's groups. A representative of aristocratic womanhood at its best, she believed that people might disagree on issues, but that they should never give in to petty backbiting and gossip. Alice Stone Blackwell, editor of the *Woman's Journal*, found her to be a person of "courage, highmindedness and absolute integrity." After praising Clay's business acumen, a newspaper added that among the suffrage leaders there was none "whose counsel is more judicious, whose estimate of persons and measures is more just or whose devotion to the cause of woman's enfranchisement is more marked."[3] Such was the woman who was to spend a large part of her public career trying to convince her fellow suffragists at the national level that the South was a ripe field for their work and her fellow southerners that woman suffrage was the answer to some of their most important problems.

In the area of woman's rights, as in so many others, the South was the most backward section of the country. In part, this situation was attributable to a carryover of conditions and prejudices from the antebellum South. For example, the early feminists, because of their close ties with the abolitionists, had earned the hearty dislike of the southerners. The views of the apostle Paul, which most churchmen believed put women in a subservient position to men, were widely accepted in southern churches and, consequently, were a deterrent to woman's rights. Furthermore, the romanticism of the section, which fancied man as a knight and woman on a pedestal, was incompatible with the notion of feminine equality. And, finally, the southern woman was generally ill-educated and overburdened with childbearing, making it difficult for her to comprehend, much less undertake, suffrage agitation.[4]

The backwardness of womanhood was compounded in the postwar South by the race question, which woman suffragists found at the very heart of the resistance to their goals. One southern woman described the situation succinctly just at the time the Clay sisters were entering the work: "The very existence of slavery put the South in a condition opposed to progress," she explained, "and the fact of negro women voting, if the ballot is given to women, will cause our men to fight every inch of the ground." In brief, the suffragists learned, as one historian has put it, that the bitter racial heritage of Reconstruction "becloud[ed] all issues" in the New South.[5]

At the time that Laura Clay was proposing a woman suffrage campaign in the South, the states of that section began a series of constitutional conventions, largely for the purpose of disfranchising the Negro. Mississippi led the way in 1890, followed by South Carolina in 1895 and Louisiana in 1898. Through either constitutional amendments and conventions or the poll tax and other such devices, North Carolina, Alabama, Virginia, Georgia, Oklahoma, Tennessee, Florida, Arkansas, and Texas also accomplished disfranchisement by 1910.[6] Because the conservative and the independent wings of the Democratic party had begun to compete for the freedman's vote, both began to look with favor toward his legal disfranchisement. Many Negroes had been kept from the polls by force, intimidation, and chicanery long before legal bars were erected. But so long as only "election methods and contrivances, . . . not sanctioned by law"[7] stood between the Negro and an effective voice in his government, there was a danger to white supremacy. Furthermore, since neither white faction was certain it could control the black vote as it wished, both became willing to entertain the thought of disfranchisement. Senator Henry Cabot Lodge's Force bill of 1890, which would provide for federal supervision of congressional elections, served to confirm the white belief that legal disfranchisement of the Negro must be undertaken.

Laura Clay's attitude toward the Negro vote was a mixture of the racial superiority common among her countrymen at the time and political expediency. Although strongly abolitionist, her parents were not believers in the equality of the races. Her mother sometimes complained of Negroes' lack of responsibility, and her father opposed integrated education at Berea College, which he had helped found. Laura later echoed the same thoughts in a letter to her mother shortly after the sudden and unexplained departure of their household help. "I am so sorry to hear you are still without servants," she wrote. "I do not understand why negroes should be so unreliable." She made her attitude more explicit in commenting on the difficulties an acquaintance was experiencing in raising an adopted Indian girl. "Whether the fact suits us or not, observation gives some of the best of reasons for believing that racial differences are not 'matters of complexion,' but run through the whole mental and physical constitution."[8] While obviously having reservations about the degree of societal development among Negroes, Laura insisted that they be treated fairly; she herself supported Negro causes in her church work.

Her earliest statement on the Negro and the woman suffrage question is a blend of political expediency and fairness toward the freedman. It came in 1890 in response to a newspaper article advocating the complete disfranchisement of the Negro. Noting the writer's claim that even northern Republicans would no longer condone black governments in the South, she refused to accept his conclusion that the country was ready to abandon the Negro entirely:

I believe Mr. Wilson is rash in thinking that the sense of justice in the people, either south or north, would permit a wholesale disfranchisement of a race. What the South has a right to complain of is not that negroes have a representation at the ballot box, but that they have a representation out of all proportion to the intelligence and virtue they bring to the support of Republican government, and the true problem set before the South is how she may restore a due supremacy of the more highly developed race without corrupting the ballot box, or repudiating the principles of true Democracy, which defends the right of every class to representation.[9]

Laura Clay then remarked that a new ingredient had been added to the longstanding debate on the race question. The new element was woman suffrage, a movement "rapidly growing in importance." She admitted that its progress in the South had been slower than in other sections of the country, "because to add an enormous number of ignorant negro women to the mass of ignorant negro men voters would be to invite an increase of the difficulties which are now scarcely manageable." [10]

Yet, she thought, woman suffrage could "neutralize all the alarming elements of the race question . . . without corrupting or intimidating the negroes, a present method that is fraught with reactionary danger to the integrity of our institutions." Her proposal was simple. The southern states should confer suffrage on literate women, "irrespective of the color line." Since the proportion of illiteracy was much greater among Negro women than among white, the effect would be to increase greatly the ratio of white over black voters. Suggesting that she was not opposed to an educational qualification for all voters, she foresaw that such legislation would involve practical difficulties. But there would be none at all in imposing literacy as a condition for women, "a newly admitted body of voters." [11]

Such a scheme of qualified suffrage, Laura Clay noted, would give literate voters a margin over illiterate ones, both white and black, "and leave a balance on the side of education." Even in South Carolina and Mississippi, where the blacks outnumbered the whites, the enfranchisement of educated women would give white voters a clear majority. To allay the suspicion of male chauvinists, she explained that they would still constitute a majority of the voters, thereby removing "an honest, though chimerical, fear" that the women might vote as a bloc and overwhelm them at the polls. [12]

The race question, she concluded, must ultimately be settled by the statesmen of the South, and "in a manner approved by the sense of justice of the whole nation." A "noble and honorable" settlement was at hand, the inauguration of "the next great triumph of Democratic principles for which the world watches and waits—woman suffrage." [13]

The position established at this time by Laura Clay is essentially the one she was following thirty years later. Whatever its faults by modern standards, it was an advance for the turn of the century, especially so for a southern woman of the upper classes. While obviously a believer in Anglo-Saxon superiority, she wanted to deal justly with the Negro by rewarding those who had overcome the disadvantages of their background and by encouraging others to improve their station through education.

Within a few months after Laura gave her initial public consideration to the race question, the Mississippi constitutional convention met in Jackson on August 12, 1890. Of the many plans proposed for disfranchising the Negro, two included woman suffrage. Delegate John W. Fewell proposed suffrage for "every woman who owned, or whose husband owned, real estate in the value of $300." S. S. Hudson, a delegate from Yazoo County, added an amendment to Fewell's bill which made education, as well as property, a requirement for female suffrage. It was reported that "the woman suffrage idea is growing in favor among the best minds of the convention, and unless safety from negro supremacy can be reached by other methods . . . will be adopted."[14]

The plan proposed by Laura Clay early in 1890 and similar ones prepared later in the same year at the Mississippi constitutional convention were enmeshed in the race question. Some white representatives from the black counties, where the whites were generally well-to-do, supported the plans because most of their womenfolk could meet educational and property requirements. But the small farmers of the predominately white counties were opposed because such plans, while barring many Negro women from the polls, would also keep a large part of their illiterate and propertyless white women from voting. Even worse in the minds of the poor whites, qualified woman suffrage would permit some Negro women to vote, a fact more galling to many whites than the loss of their own franchise suffrage. In short, qualified woman suffrage had much to recommend it to the black counties, but offered almost nothing to the white counties. Despite entanglements in the race problem, the woman suffrage proposal received the support of two-fifths of the convention.[15]

Although the attempts to incorporate a limited woman suffrage in the new Mississippi constitution were lost, the convention did radically limit male suffrage. In what came to be called the "Mississippi Plan," the legal disfranchisement of the Negro was accomplished by requiring literacy or an "understanding" of the state constitution and the payment of a poll tax.[16]

Laura Clay was a distant witness of these developments, and the fact that woman suffrage proposals had been brought to the floor of the Mississippi convention and given serious consideration with little or no organized female support did not escape her attention.[17] She began to undertake responsibilities for greater efforts in the South at the very time she and her fellow state suffragists were achieving their first important gains in Kentucky.

At Clay's urging, the NAWSA at its annual convention in January 1892 authorized the formation of a Southern Committee. She said that the past few years had convinced her that the South was the "most promising field" in the entire country for suffrage work. The convention gave her permission to organize the new committee whose primary tasks were to develop organizations in each of the southern states and distribute suffrage materials throughout the section.[18]

Laura undertook her task with zeal, writing prospective suffragists throughout the South for help and appealing for funds nationally through the pages of the Woman's Journal. Mrs. B. F. Avery of Louisville, a well-to-do suffragist, answered the appeal for funds with a check for twenty-five dollars, thus supplementing a small appropriation of fifty dollars which the NAWSA had given the committee. Most of the responses to the appeal for help were favorable, although the very reputations which brought these women to Clay's attention usually meant that they were already involved in some community work and could not promise full-time aid. Mrs. M. M. Snell, for example, wrote from Columbus, Mississippi: "I am crowded to overflowing with work. I have accepted work from the prohibitionists . . . to evangelize the state, to sow it with our doctrines . . . I have three children, . . . [do] Bible work in this city, . . . am also evangelist for the National W.C.T.U., [and] president for Mississippi on the Woman's Council."[19]

Some of the respondents were willing to accept part of the feminists' goals, but had reservations about others. "I am making first steps," claimed another Mississippi woman, "long having wished for a vote to suppress saloons, to vote women on school boards, to place them in police courts, to compel every female boarding school or college to employ a woman physician." On some of the other implications of full feminine equality, however, she held back: "But I cannot adjust jury and military service to my satisfaction. Personally I am retiring." A willing South Carolinian wanted Clay to understand that she was not recruiting a tower of strength. "Fancy to yourself a very small woman, barely over five feet," she wrote, "very timid, and quite wrapped up in home and husband, adventuring out on this stormy sea! That's my case!"[20]

The Southern Committee provided grounds for optimism as the first year's work ended. Laura Clay had been elected chairman and Clara A. McDiarmid of Little Rock, Arkansas, treasurer of the organization which counted representatives in Alabama, Tennessee, Louisiana, Georgia, Missouri, Texas, Maryland, Arkansas, and Kentucky. Despite illness and pressing business matters, which left her with only three months of concentrated effort, Laura managed to hold personal interviews with suffragists from Virginia, Texas, and Florida and to write, and receive answers to, more than fifty letters. In addition, she and her committee were able to establish new state suffrage organizations in Texas and South Carolina.[21]

At the NAWSA convention in 1893, the southerners were pleased with their progress and optimistic for the future. Virginia D. Young was reported as saying that if two hundred South Carolina women signed a petition, suffrage would be given to them "because," as she said, "we have nearly a pure Anglo-Saxon population, and . . . we recognize the truths that there must be no taxation without representation and that just governments derive their power from the consent of the governed." To illustrate the greater receptivity of the South to woman suffrage, she drew a parallel between a recent campaign in South Dakota and the constitutional convention in Mississippi. She related how the NAWSA had concentrated its efforts on the South Dakota campaign in 1890 and how some of the leaders "almost worked themselves to death" there in a losing battle. While at the same time in Mississippi, "not a finger was raised," except by the small state association, "and two-fifths of the constitutional convention declared in favor of woman suffrage." Why had the South not endorsed suffrage? The opposition was not the result of conviction, believed Laura Clay, "but only the conservatism of a people who have been too deeply engaged upon other pressing social problems to devote much thought to woman suffrage." If the race question, so obviously referred to here, were surmounted, reform politicians could be convinced that their parties would not suffer by adopting a woman suffrage plank.[22]

From her work with the Southern Committee, Laura Clay had learned a lesson, and the southern suffragists had found a champion. She resolved never to divert her attention "from the South until we are organized there so as to seize our opportunities." Indicting the NAWSA for being remiss in its southern effort, she concluded: "Since we claim to be national let us never forget that the South cannot be left out of our calculations. You have worked for forty years and you will work for forty years more and do nothing unless you bring in the South."[23]

The Southern Committee continued its work, while northern suffragists provided most of the funds for woman's newspapers and equal rights pamphlets which were mailed to potential members and state legislators throughout the section. By the end of the committee's second year, four additional southern states had organized and joined as auxiliaries to the NAWSA, leaving only North Carolina, Mississippi, and West Virginia without suffrage clubs. Some of these associations were largely paper organizations, a fact that explains why Mississippi, for example, was counted among the organized in 1890 and listed as unorganized in 1894. After a rudimentary society, often comprising no more than four or five willing women behind a dedicated leader, was set up in each state, Laura Clay planned to have NAWSA organizers come on the scene. Local women were essential for the purpose of arranging meetings, and it was hoped that the organizers could use the gatherings to arouse additional interest in the movement.[24]

By the end of 1894 the South was sufficiently organized to benefit from a suffrage tour led by the redoubtable Susan B. Anthony, aided by the NAWSA's most able speakers and organizers, Carrie Chapman Catt and Anna Howard Shaw. Anthony asked Laura Clay to plan the itinerary, writing that she hoped to hold two-day meetings in sixteen different cities. Her plan was to have Catt lead eight of the meetings and Shaw eight, while she herself shuttled back and forth across the South, making brief appearances in all the sixteen cities.[25] Arranging details of the tour occupied part of Clay's efforts during the summer and fall of 1894.

After some discussion among the leaders, they decided that the visitation should occur during the weeks just before the annual convention of the NAWSA in Atlanta, Georgia. This was the first time the convention was to be held outside Washington, D.C.; the touring leaders hoped they could create additional interest in it at the same time they were pumping new life into local associations. Laura Clay attended a meeting of the Executive Committee of the NAWSA, where the final plans for the southern tour were laid. A month later she was in Jackson, Mississippi, to make a speech at the State House and help the local suffragists revive the state association.[26]

Anthony and Catt made Lexington the starting place for the southern excursion. Following speeches there, they met engagements which Clay had made for them in Kentucky at Wilmore, Louisville, Owensboro, and Paducah. In Owensboro they made "an exceedingly favorable impression" and organized a local club for the Kentucky ERA. After their appearances in Kentucky, the two campaigners spoke in Memphis, New Orleans, Shreveport, and at cities in Alabama, South Carolina, Virginia, and Mississippi.[27]

The NAWSA meeting in Atlanta, from January 31 through February 5, was regarded by the southerners as the climax of their first concerted organizational drive. It was the first national suffrage convention in the former Confederate states, and it served to draw public attention to the activities of the southern feminists and to give many of them their first chance to meet the most important leaders in the movement. As one newspaper explained, the suffragists wanted to make clear to all that "they have decided to enter the southern field" and "educate the people."[28]

At the convention Laura Clay gave the report for the Southern Committee. Seven states in the South had been given financial assistance totaling $204.15. One of the year's signal victories for the committee was the establishment of the North Carolina Equal

Suffrage Association. Clay had sent the new society a supply of suffrage literature and advice on organizing additional local clubs. Only West Virginia, of the states assigned to the committee, was still unorganized. As chairman, Laura had "written numerous letters, distributed a great amount of literature, and sent out seven circular letters to other members of the committee." Susan Anthony commended the committee on its good showing and complimented Laura on her able chairmanship.[29]

One of the most important developments to come out of this convention was the creation of an Organization Committee. The moving force behind this step was Carrie Chapman Catt, who persuaded the convention that this committee should take charge of all the association's organizing efforts by putting speakers in the field, planning their itineraries, and directing special campaigns in those states where suffrage legislation was pending or constitutional conventions had been called. Catt, called "the general of the suffrage movement," planned to give suffrage activities the central direction and concerted impact which they had lacked in the past.[30]

Although Clay seems to have had an imperfect understanding of it at the time, the Organization Committee really supplanted the Southern Committee. The wings of her committee had been clipped at the previous convention, when it was decided that all funds should be placed in the hands of the national treasurer. This decision meant that the separate treasury of the Southern Committee was terminated, and that committee, accordingly, did not solicit the convention of 1895 for funds, as it had done for the past three years. A year later, Clay called for the dissolution of the Southern Committee, noting that the plan of the "Organization Committee . . . so nearly involves the plan of the Southern Committee that it has done little distinctive work during the past year."[31]

The end of the Southern Committee did not mark a slackening of her interest in the South, nor did it seem to cause any unpleasantness between her and Catt. Southern suffragists referred to her as "our great Laura Clay" and looked to her for "special protection" in the councils of the NAWSA and advice in their own state affairs.[32] Although she made important contributions to the national suffrage effort in a number of ways, Clay continued to regard herself as a special spokesman for the southern movement.

Catt, on the other hand, appreciated Laura's contributions to the cause of suffrage and credited her "eloquence" with convincing the NAWSA "that the South was ready to receive woman suffrage missionaries." Clay was named a member of the Organization Committee, and the South and the West were designated as the primary fields of labor.[33] She gave her time and money as generously to the new organization as she had to the Southern Committee and was its chief representative at the South Carolina constitutional convention in 1895.

The circumstances behind the calling of this convention were not unlike those which had produced the one in Mississippi in 1890. In both states the race question was at the core of the desire to write a new constitution. By the end of the 1880s Negroes had been all but eliminated from participation in politics, but this did not satisfy the followers of South Carolina's Benjamin R. Tillman, who sought to exclude them completely.[34]

In their imperfect understanding of the race question in the South, the suffragists, even those closest to the situation, as Laura Clay, failed to perceive the split within the ranks of the whites at the South Carolina Constitutional Convention. They understood that white supremacy was a principal goal of both the Tillmanite and conservative factions of the Democratic party, but they did not recognize that white supremacy was not enough for Tillman's followers. The Negrophobes of that faction demanded a solution that would not only overwhelm the Negro vote but actually eliminate it. The conservatives, while quite willing to disfranchise the illiterate Negro, saw no reason to make exceptions for the ignorant among the Tillmanites. The suffragists never grasped this fundamental difference between the two factions on the race issue. As a consequence, they continued to believe that any plan which would assure white supremacy would be acceptable to both groups. In point of fact, while woman suffrage with an educational qualification might expect to win some conservative support, it could not possibly serve the designs of the Tillmanites.

The strategy of seeking woman suffrage as a legal method of insuring white supremacy was not a purely southern proposal. At

the Atlanta Convention in early 1895, Carrie Chapman Catt recommended that the southern states should require an educational
qualification for their women voters, and the suggestion was warm-
ly received. Henry B. Blackwell, a former Boston abolitionist,
was the author of a pamphlet entitled "A Solution of the Southern
Problem." [35] It contained figures on the number of literate white
and Negro women in each of the southern states and pointed out
that all those states could insure white supremacy without resorting to fraud by granting woman suffrage with an educational
qualification. With both northern and southern suffragists agreeing, the NAWSA made this plan the heart of its plea for suffrage
in the South Carolina constitutional convention of 1895.

The women opened their effort in South Carolina in April 1895.
Virginia D. Young, president of the state society, and Viola Neblett, another South Carolinian, arranged a tour of suffrage speakers
designed to cover every county seat of the state. The meetings
began on April 29, with a two-day stop at Greenville, where Laura
Clay, Helen Morris Lewis of North Carolina, and Elizabeth U.
Yates of Maine joined the South Carolinians. The two-day meetings, featuring afternoon and evening programs, were continued
in Spartanburg, Columbia, and Charleston, which with Greenville
were South Carolina's four largest cities.[36]

After the Charleston meeting, the women split into two parties,
Clay and Young going on to hold meetings in one half of the state
and Lewis and Neblett covering the other half. Each pair of
speakers appeared in approximately eleven towns, organizing suffrage clubs if possible, encouraging people to join existing ones,
and trying to convince their audiences that the vote for women
would be an intelligent and progressive addition to the new constitution. The tour lasted from late April until the middle of
June.[37]

Female speakers were a novelty in South Carolina, and their
presence, more than their message, assured them of a good audience in most towns. People who had never heard a suffrage talk
came out to listen, if not to agree.[38] It was reported that at Charleston "the most distinguished audience which had gathered in that
city for years" turned out to hear the women. Every detail of the
speakers' styles was apparently of interest. A reporter made fun of

Young's nervous mannerisms as she spoke to a full house in Green-ville. The same reporter found Clay "an unusually attractive speaker" with "a full, clear voice" which varied "only a very few notes between her highest and lowest tones." In some ways he thought her a model for male speakers: "She talks with her hands at her sides, and is a living lesson to the very large number of men who seem to think that oratory is impossible without breeches pockets and coat lapels. By the way, at one time Miss Clay made a distinct motion to go into the pocket of her skirt and the audi-ence watched with breathless interest, but she found her handker-chief on the flower-covered table near her and went ahead."[39]

Although not a very demonstrative speaker, Laura Clay's facial expressions, he noted, ranged from "a peculiarly genial smile" to a countenance which could "in an instant become very grave and severe." She used hand gesticulations "gracefully and easily," and only "when she was very much in earnest . . . . Most of her points were emphasized by bending forward and she made a good many points."[40]

In her address, Clay used three arguments which she would revert to time and again in the South Carolina campaign. She opened her presentation by seeking to show that the Bible sup-ported feminine equality, a controversial claim in the South where religious orthodoxy was especially strong. According to a reporter, she "began at Adam and Eve and came down to the present time, without manuscript and without missing a word." Woman like man, she contended, was made in the image of God, and in the beginning was given a coequal status on earth. Because of the original sin in the Garden of Eden, she had lost her privileged place. It had been regained, however, under the new dispensation opened by Jesus Christ, who made no distinction in the worth of souls, whether male or female. She concluded that there was a direct correlation between the advance of Judaic-Christian civiliza-tion and respect for the rights of women.[41]

Turning to an economic argument, Clay asserted that the chang-ing role of women in a developing industrial society demanded new rights. She pointed out that fifty years earlier there were only seven occupations open to women. As she spoke, she said, there were three million working women "represented more or less in every trade, profession and pursuit except the army and navy." Their greatest misfortune, she insisted, was that they had no voice in making the laws which were their sole protection since they had been forced from their homes in search of a livelihood by "the great industrial changes of the last century and a half."[42]

The final and clinching point of Clay's talk was that woman suffrage with an educational qualification would insure white supremacy in the South. Speaking of South Carolina specifically, she noted that the census of 1880 showed that her reform would admit "75,000 white women and 18,000 colored women to the franchise, giving a white majority of 25,000 over the combined male and female vote of the Negroes."[43] She was proposing, in short, that the upcoming constitutional convention could achieve white supremacy without resorting to the fraud and violence that had characterized past elections.

The Greenville meeting was typical of the reception the suffragists received in South Carolina. They were greeted everywhere by large audiences that exhibited a noticeable reluctance to join the movement or to make contributions when the collection plate was passed. Writing from Marion, one reporter complained that interest in the "strange gods" of woman suffrage had caused most of the local women to forget their duty to the Confederate dead and fail to hold their usual Memorial Day services. The Charleston News and Courier was amazed at "the furor" created by "the suffrage demonstrations which begun [sic] here two days ago." It expressed the belief that the interest was "of a very ephemeral character, partaking of no sentiment more profound possibly than acute curiosity, but for the time the suffragists have the floor, so to speak, from one end of the city to the other."[44]

The general skepticism of the press rarely included any hostile criticism of the suffrage movement. A notable exception was printed in an up-country newspaper, the Laurensville Herald, which warned that the "packed and jammed audience," which heard Laura Clay, should not have been misled by her proposed solution to the race problem. It averred that an educational qualification would not have the desired effect because "nearly every Negro girl in her teens can read and write."[45]

The only other direct criticism of Laura Clay's position came

65

from the *Waynesboro* (Ga.) *True Citizen*. Observing that "the Constitution of the United States goes through some strange stretches of opinion these days," the editor feared that the Supreme Court might strike down the educational qualification. Since such a ruling would again give the Negroes a legitimate majority in some districts, he questioned the feasibility of woman suffrage. Aside from these two reservations, the press took no exceptions to the women's proposal.

Only the objection that the educational qualification would not act as a sufficient deterrent to the Negro women's vote had any effect on the suffragists' strategy. It caused Laura to consider the advisability of adding a property qualification to the educational requirement for the female franchise. While awaiting the opening of the convention, she wrote women and public officials in the various counties of South Carolina, inquiring as to the number of white and colored women who paid taxes on property valued at $300 or more. Of the counties responding, none had more than eight Negro women who would qualify under such a restriction, while from 300 to 400 white women would be enfranchised in each.[46] Hoping that this information could be used to placate the fear of the Negro vote, the suffragists decided to ask the convention for woman suffrage with a property qualification as well as a literacy test.

Clay and her co-workers concluded their preconvention campaign in the middle of June. The election of delegates on July 30 resulted in the victory of the Tillman forces, which were faced with the avowed tasks of eliminating the Negro voters, without the usual resort to fraud and intimidation, and, at the same time, protecting the franchise of numerous illiterate and landless whites.[47]

By the time the convention opened in September 1895, Clay and Neblett had arrived in Columbia. They established themselves in the Hotel Saint Jerome, where Young joined them, and began to lobby for woman suffrage. Clay remained in Columbia for nine weeks, helping supply the delegates with suffrage literature, appearing at committee hearings, and, finally, speaking to the entire convention and a large public gathering in the State House.[48]

There was some support for woman suffrage. George D. Till-man, Ben's estranged brother and a leader of the conservative delegates, noted that the women of the state were steadily sending in their petitions and that the movement had more advocates in the convention than "anyone dreamed of." Ben, the body's most powerful figure, had himself talked about "the elevation of the ballot" through literacy and property qualifications. General Robert R. Hemphill, a conservative delegate, was the women's staunchest defender in the convention and the founder of the suffrage movement in the state. His brother, James C. Hemphill, an unrelenting enemy of Ben Tillman, was the editor of the *Charleston News and Courier*, the organ of the conservative forces and the state's most powerful newspaper. Both the *News and Courier* and the *Daily Register*, ordinarily a Tillman organ, announced their support for woman suffrage during the course of the convention.[49]

The high point of the lobbying effort was the appearance of Laura Clay and two of her co-workers before the convention and the packed galleries of the State House.[50] The principal spokesman for the trio was Clay, who appealed to the delegates' state pride, reminding them of their forefathers' "bold adherence to noble political principles" and claiming that the nation was again looking for "something great" from South Carolina's "genius for statesmanship."[51]

She asserted that the nation, as well as the South, had a suffrage problem because of the "rash prodigality with which the franchise [had] been extended to all classes of men, regardless of their unfitness for such political trust by illiteracy, foreign birth, or other causes." This situation furnished South Carolina with an opportunity to set an example for the entire country. By extending the franchise to qualified women, the state could assure "the political supremacy of thrift and intelligence" and win the approval of the nation's conscience. Clay warned the convention that franchise restrictions of doubtful constitutionality would be struck down by the courts and urged it to accept a suffrage plan which was legal, fair, and far-sighted. In closing, she rose to the defense of working women and reminded the South Carolinians that many women were, of necessity, in the marketplace: "Men's tenderness for women has not enabled them to shelter the four million . . . working women and girls from the harshest contact with the world, contending for their daily bread. To exclude women from politics on any such ground is only to foster the luxurious delicacy of privileged women, already sufficiently protected by leaving the millions of their toiling sisters without the protection of woman's voice in the making of law, which men have found most useful to themselves and which is doubly needed by women."[52]

On the next day, Laura Clay and her associates were granted a hearing by the Suffrage Committee which was chaired by Ben Tillman, then a United States Senator. At the close of her presentation, Clay declared herself "willing and anxious" to answer questions. After she had successfully handled several of the delegates' queries, "Senator Tillman declared that Miss Clay was more than a match for any two men in the convention."[53]

However impressive the performances of Laura Clay and her cohorts, they were not enough to win the support of a majority of the delegates. When their proposal came to a vote, it was defeated by a 26–121 margin. The suffrage clause eventually accepted was much like the Mississippi Plan of 1890. Along with Neblett, Clay had remained at Columbia, pleading the woman's case with the delegates and hoping to the last moment that the convention would adopt qualified woman's suffrage as a legal and honest method of insuring white supremacy.[54]

Laura Clay was not badly disappointed by the outcome. She shared the view that the "understanding clause" of the new constitution, which permitted an illiterate to evade the literacy test if he could understand and explain any part of the document when read to him, would be overturned by the federal courts. The clause was designed to discriminate against the Negro by leaving to the discretion of the registration officers the determination of who could and could not understand the state constitution.[55] She applauded the statement of Robert Hemphill, who wrote:

> The suffrage plans presented to the convention are defective and unsatisfactory. They each have the quality of uncertainty, and of necessity can only be temporary. The most elaborate plan presented makes white supremacy depend upon the managers of elections and not upon an intelligent and open vote. Intelligent people know that such expedients will be in vain and of short

duration. No such uncertainty attaches to the plan of granting qualified suffrage to women. Their vote will secure the State from the debasing effects of fraud in elections and the control of ignorance. Woman suffrage is the only way out of the present difficulty.[56]

Just under this clipping, which she underlined, Laura wrote, "Glorious!" The federal action, which she expected to end such election frauds quickly, never came in her lifetime. In the meantime there was no need for her plan to secure white supremacy through partial woman suffrage and honest elections, because the country indifferently acquiesced in one of the great injustices of its history. As the *Plessy* vs. *Ferguson* case of the next year was to indicate, the Negro had been abandoned by the Supreme Court to the care of the several states. Indeed, as C. Vann Woodward has shown, "the Mississippi Plan had become the American Way."[57]

In addition to misreading the national temper on the race question, Laura Clay also failed to see that the power of her most probable allies in the South, the Bourbon conservatives, was almost a thing of the past. Her suffrage campaign in the South had begun at the time when political power was shifting from the patricians to the red-necks and Tillmanites.[58] The future of southern politics belonged to the Tillmans, Vardamans, and Heflins, not to the conservatives who were more inclined to listen to her proposal and certainly had more to gain from it. For after all, the conservative women would not be disqualified by an educational qualification, nor would they be outraged by the few Negro women who could qualify. The conservatives were also white supremacists, but, unlike the poor whites, they were not blinded by fear and hatred of the Negroes, and consequently were willing to permit "the better element" of the race to vote. The Tillmanites hated the Negro too much and had too many illiterates in their own ranks to consider rationally a plan that would offer the franchise to women of both races on an equal basis.

Such help as Clay found in South Carolina came almost entirely from the conservatives and their low-country stronghold; conversely, the available comment from the up-country Tillmanite area was adverse to woman suffrage. Thirteen of the sixteen towns that had ERA members were in the low-country section of the state. The Hemphill brothers, one of whom was editor of the *News and Courier*, were anti-Tillman leaders who favored woman suffrage. The first three resolutions seeking some form of suffrage for women were offered by delegates from Fairfax and Florence, both in low-country counties.[59]

Along with the *News and Courier*, the state's two other largest daily newspapers advocated woman suffrage. The action of one of them, the *Columbia State*, founded to oppose Tillman, supports the picture of conservative sympathy for and Tillmanite opposition to a qualified vote for women. Only the support of the state's third important daily, the *Columbia Daily Register*, breaks the pattern. This organ of the Tillman forces recommended woman suffrage and, afterward, lamented "that there was not enough statesmanship in the Constitution Convention for that body to recognize the wisdom, justice and expediency of woman suffrage." The *Daily Register* article carried a handsome portrait of Laura Clay and praised her for her intelligence, tact, and composure.[60]

The audience being reached by the suffragists were "of the highest social standing, educated and refined," not the rough-hewn farmers who had given Ben Tillman control of the state. "Judges, lawyers, doctors, ministers and Senators of social and political prominence" and their wives came out to greet the women and introduce them at suffrage meetings.[61] Unfortunately for the women's cause, the power that had belonged to these patricians from 1877 to 1890 had fallen into less refined hands.

Clay and the other suffragists, all women from the upper strata of society, did not understand that men of their own class were no longer in control of the South. If they had comprehended the shift in political power or understood the difference between Hampton and Tillman on the race question, they would have realized that qualified woman suffrage had little chance of enactment in the deep South after 1890. The goal of the politicians who were in power at the turn of the century was not to limit the Negro to an educated participation in government, but to eliminate his role entirely. On the other hand, the aim of the suffragists, like many of their patrician kinsmen, was to establish a government of the better people, meaning primarily the whites but not excluding qualified Negroes.

The basic misunderstanding of the changing political situation permitted Clay to carry her optimistic hopes for woman suffrage in the South to the NAWSA convention at Washington in January 1896. Carrie Chapman Catt, chairman of the Organization Committee, shared Clay's belief in the importance of continuing the drive in the South and asserted that a suffrage victory in the Democratic South would bring quick successes in the West.[62]

In her own remarks to the convention, Laura Clay asserted that the South "had less real prejudice against woman suffrage than any other section." Insisting that women of the South were "no less intelligent, progressive and open-minded than [those] of any other section," she denied that southern opposition was "wholly a matter of conservatism and ignorance." She attributed southern tardiness in espousing woman suffrage to the effects of the Civil War and Reconstruction. Preoccupied with the problems left in the wake of that conflict, especially the role of the Negro in postwar society, southern women had not had time to think much about the "new woman," Clay contended, but they had "been new women."[63]

Like Catt, Clay viewed the South as "the strategic point and . . . our most hopeful field after the West." Correctly seeing the country on the verge of a political coalition between the South and West, she believed that the West would not act on woman suffrage if it endangered relations with the South. "The West is ready to put woman suffrage into its program if it is not hindered by fear of the solid South," she said, "but no political party will antagonize the solid South for the sake of woman suffrage." If a southern state granted woman suffrage, the Democrats of the West would probably follow the example. Convinced of the movement's potential in the South, Clay wrote: "When we go through the South advocating woman suffrage, without attaching it to dress reform, or bicycling, or anything else, but asking the simple question why the principles of our forefathers should not be applied to women, we shall win. The South is ready for woman suffrage, but it must be woman suffrage and nothing else."[64]

In future years, Clay's belief was demonstrated by her continued efforts in the South and by her strenuous activities in campaigns in Oklahoma, Arizona, Oregon, and Kansas. Indeed, as a southern suffragist, she could find considerable grounds for optimism as a result of the convention of 1896. She believed that the defeat in South Carolina was only a temporary setback and that southern statesmen would be forced by the Constitution and the national conscience to turn to woman suffrage as a legitimate means of insuring white supremacy. Even the dissolution of the Southern Committee had not been a great loss since Catt had so heartily endorsed the need for a continuing effort in its field of responsibility.[65]

By electing Laura Clay first auditor of the NAWSA, the convention of 1896 gave southern suffragists additonal proof that their interests would receive consideration at the national level. This office gave Clay a place on the association's policy-making body, the Business Committee, and for the first time provided the southerners with a membership on the board of officers.[66] For the next fifteen years, she filled this position with distinction, bringing to it qualities of discretion, fairness, judgment, and unflagging service.

In part the office was a recognition of Laura Clay's distinguished role in the South Carolina campaign and of services that she had contributed without recompense.[67] It was also an acknowledgment that this Kentuckian, who viewed herself as the guardian of southern suffrage interests, had wielded an increasingly influential voice in national affairs since the early 1890s. Her election to the office of auditor was evidence that Laura Clay had transcended her state and sectional suffrage roles and had become a national leader.

V

STATE LEADERSHIP
AND GROWING NATIONAL
PROMINENCE

1894-1904

LAURA CLAY's election to the board of officers of the NAWSA could hardly have been a surprise to her or to other suffragists. It came after her contribution to the cause had won praise and her forthright stand on several controversial issues before the annual national conventions had gained public attention. Typical of the notice her work was receiving outside Kentucky was an article in the Springfield (Ill.) Daily Republican on January 19, 1892, which pointed to the growing influence of southerners in the NAWSA and acknowledged Laura Clay as one who "attracts attention by her fine appearance and her clear and impressive style of expression." Commenting on the discussions then under way at the NAWSA convention in Washington, the newspaper added, "If she were a man she would take a high place in the political arena on account of her good judgment, keen insight and logical reasoning. She has a well-trained mind, and with these qualities enthusiasm enough to make her a leader."[1]

At the national conventions, Laura's firm and reasoned stands often challenged the association's leadership, won admirers, and received public attention. One issue, which pitted her and other younger suffragists against Susan Anthony and a number of the older leaders, was the question of movable conventions. The annual meetings of the NWSA, and later the NAWSA, had always been held in Washington, D.C., in order to put pressure on Congress for a federal woman suffrage amendment. Clay believed that great benefits to the association could be gained by having these conventions in other cities, while continuing to come to Washington in alternate years. She tried vainly in 1892 to have the next year's convention scheduled in conjunction with the Columbian Exposition in Chicago, and in 1893, again on the attack, she cited the advantages won by Kentuckians when the AWSA had held conventions in Cincinnati in 1887 and 1888.[2]

Continuing the debate at the convention in 1894, Laura Clay argued that other people must be induced to join the ranks before success would be attainable at the national level. "How can the army march when there is no army," she asked. "Gather your forces and then march . . . . We must reach the people and then . . . we can come up [to Washington] and talk about influencing our Representatives." She and the younger suffragists won their point when the delegates voted, 37–28, for a movable convention, despite Anthony's strong objections. Although one historian has seen this vote as a victory for the states' rights faction in the NAWSA over supporters of the federal amendment, it was, in fact, no more than a tactical move which had support from northern and western, as well as southern, delegates. It could not have been carried without the support of Catt, who recognized that the effectiveness of a drive for federal action was ultimately dependent upon the strength of the movement in the various states.[3]

After the change was put into operation attendance at conventions in other cities was sometimes slightly below the Washington level, but new areas and new women were reached.[4] As Clay had stated during the debate, "Thousands of people have never heard of the National-American. The way to get them to know is by taking the convention where they will be compelled to hear us . . . . I maintain that we will have twenty states that have not been represented here before, that is the point."[5] Seventeen cities, from the east to the west coasts, received a firsthand acquaintance with the suffragists over the next twenty-five years.

Clay also played a prominent role in two other issues that were resolved at national conventions. Her view, in each case, brought her into disagreement with Elizabeth Cady Stanton, of New York, a pioneer suffragist and the first president of the NAWSA.

Because "the full development of women's potentialities," rather than woman suffrage, was her primary goal, Stanton devoted her abilities increasingly to other subjects in the last years of her long life.[6] Two of the causes that she supported, and Laura Clay opposed, were the opening of the Chicago World's Columbian Exposition on Sundays and the promotion of the *Woman's Bible*.

Resolutions advocating the Sunday opening of the fair had been introduced and discussed at the 1891 and 1892 NAWSA conventions, but had been withdrawn when opposition developed. Although thinly disguised, a third resolution, presented at the 1893 convention by Stanton, was designed to put the convention on record in favor of keeping the fair open on Sundays. Laura Clay realized at once the purpose of the proposal and moved to have it tabled. Anthony, who was in the chair, protested that a similar resolution the year before had been presented and tabled without discussion. Clay questioned the chairman's memory, claiming that the matter had been discussed for two hours before being withdrawn. After advisement the chair stood corrected, but the motion to table was defeated, 23–50.[7]

Failing to prevent consideration of the measure, Clay "scored the decisive point" during the debate on it. She "protested that the resolution, having nothing, directly or indirectly, to do with woman suffrage, was outside the province of the association." When Ellen Battelle Dietrick, one of Stanton's supporters, defended the proposal as "strictly proper" and "germane to the association," Clay called for the reading of article II of the constitution, which clearly stated that the association's aim was to secure woman suffrage through appropriate state and federal legislation. Having proved her point on constitutional grounds, Clay entreated the convention to "let each individual act as she chooses on the Sunday closing of the World's Fair, but let us not, as the Woman Suffrage Association, take any side on the matter." Her argument was decisive in the defeat of the resolution. In a later comment on the episode, Stanton remembered Laura Clay as the chief opponent of her proposal and claimed that its defeat was largely responsible for her decision to resign from the presidency of the NAWSA.[8]

In its impact on the suffrage movement, the Sunday closing

issue was similar to that, three years later, concerning Stanton's *Woman's Bible*. These two questions were also alike in that both pitted Laura Clay against Stanton. The *Woman's Bible* was not a new version of the Bible but rather a series of commentaries on woman's relation to God and man as depicted in the Bible. This difference seems to have been lost on the reading public of the day, which was led by the title to believe that a group of women had written a book intended to replace the Bible. The commentators in the *Woman's Bible* may be divided into two groups, one that viewed the Scriptures as a support for feminine equality and one that viewed the Bible as an obstacle to woman's progress. Stanton frankly admitted that she did not believe that the Scriptures or any religion were divinely inspired.[9]

Laura Clay considered the *Woman's Bible* blameworthy on two counts. In the first place, she believed that the degradation of women in the Old Testament version of original sin had been corrected by Jesus and the Apostles. She found the Bible a sufficient support for her woman's rights arguments and saw no need to attack some Scriptures and ignore others as the *Woman's Bible* did. In her opinion, the Scriptures were not detrimental to the woman's cause but a strong asset: "I believe that of all the means adapted to uplifting the prevailing ideas of what is just and true regarding the rights of women, the strongest and deepest teachings are the teachings drawn from the great source of moral light, the bible [sic]; and that a systematic study and proclaiming of the scriptural position of women will most completely and quickly convert people to the justice of our cause."[10] From Elizabeth Cady Stanton's viewpoint, the Bible was an obstacle to woman's advancement; for Laura Clay it was a document of freedom, in need only of proper elucidation.

An additional, more pragmatic, cause for opposition to the Stanton publication was that it appeared to jeopardize the suffragists' cause. During Clay's campaign in South Carolina in 1895, while the constitutional convention was in session, one of the state's leading newspapers devoted more than a column to a scathing review of the first volume of the *Woman's Bible*. At the same time, a prominent South Carolina suffragist wrote that the publication was doing great damage to the cause in the state. In some areas of the country, feelings were so intense against it that hecklers had attacked women speakers.[11] At the Washington convention in January 1896, other voices were raised against the *Woman's Bible*, and Carrie Chapman Catt, Anna Howard Shaw, Harriet Taylor Upton, Rachel Foster Avery, and Laura Clay were determined that the NAWSA should disassociate itself from the publication.

Susan Anthony and other friends of Stanton, who was not present, made a determined attempt to keep the convention from acting on the matter. They foiled Avery's effort to get it on the floor through her corresponding secretary's report and shelved the question in the association's executive committee. The opponents of the publication were undeterred, however, and succeeded in passing a resolution against it, "after an animated and at times rather personal" debate. The resolution, adopted by a 53–41 vote, declared: "this Association is nonsectarian, being composed of persons of all shades of religious opinion, and . . . it has no official connection with the so-called *Woman's Bible*, or any theological publication."[12]

Stanton was deeply resentful of the rebuke. She encouraged Anthony to resign from the NAWSA with her as a form of protest against the ungrateful organization. This the former refused to do, for she was openly resentful of the time Stanton had taken from suffrage work for a "futile, questionable digression" and advised her that both of them had a duty "to be at the next convention and try to reverse this miserable, narrow action."[13]

The dispute over the *Woman's Bible* was unfortunate for the feminist movement. Because the issues involved were irrelevant to most women of the time, an air of unreality pervaded the entire matter. In retrospect it appears to have been nothing more than a squabble among the movement's leadership, unrelated to women's problems, and detrimental to the cause of equal suffrage. It reveals, however, an important change in the suffrage movement by the mid-1890s. The defeat of the old guard on this issue was the signal that a new and more conservative generation of suffragists had gained control of the NAWSA. Highly practical, the new leadership wished to disassociate itself from radical causes and find a middle ground upon which a majority of American women

—and men, whose support was needed for success—could stand.[14]

Laura Clay was an influential member of this group. Her desire to conform to the sensibilities of her countrymen on most issues led her to write in 1896 a lecture entitled "The Bible for Equal Rights." It became a regular part of her repertoire and was given to church and rural gatherings throughout her suffrage career.[15] The argument over the *Woman's Bible* indicates that she wished to tamper with the status quo as little as possible. In matters relating to women and children, she was willing to take an advanced position, but, like most other Progressives, she sought changes within the traditional framework of American society.

Another event of the middle 1890s involving Clay was profitable to the women's cause because of the publicity it brought to their influence in politics, especially in Kentucky. This event was the widely reported breach of promise of marriage suit brought by Madeline Pollard against Colonel W. C. P. Breckinridge, after a liaison that had continued over nearly ten years and had been maintained in Lexington, Cincinnati, New York, and Washington. The trial conducted in Washington, D.C., occupied a considerable amount of the nation's attention for six weeks, from March to April 1894, and ended in a $15,000 judgment for Pollard.[16]

Had Breckinridge, a prominent Democratic congressman from Kentucky, a noted orator, and a former Confederate hero, decided to step out of public life at this point, he might have escaped the fury of aroused womanhood. This he declined to do, announcing on April 30, that he intended to seek the Democratic nomination for a sixth consecutive term in Congress. While the trial was under way, women around the country made it clear that they would not be passive spectators in any political activity Breckinridge undertook. At a meeting in New York City, the National Christian League for the Promotion of Social Purity decided to send a resolution to Congress "protesting against allowing Breckinridge to remain in his seat, and to send a communication to Mrs. Breckinridge . . . calling upon her in the name of womanhood to renounce her husband and to refuse to live with him longer." The League also asked the philanderer's church to expel him. The Woman's Rescue League, meeting in Boston, joined in the assault, condemning Breckinridge for the illicit affair and branding him "a menace to society and public morals." [17] Copies of the latter statement were sent to all Kentucky newspapers.

By the time Breckinridge arrived in Lexington on May 4 to open his campaign for renomination, local women were ready to do battle with him. The next day's *Louisville Courier-Journal* carried a first-page story entitled "Women of the District Protest Loudly Against His [Breckinridge's] Return to Congress." When some 2,500 supporters crowded the local Opera House to hear the Colonel's speech of "confession and defiance" not a woman was in the audience. [18]

As the congressman's campaign progressed, the women, who had at first contented themselves with long newspaper statements signed "Many Women," came more into open opposition. When the "best people of Fayette County" packed the Opera House for an anti-Breckinridge rally, a thousand women were among them. The house was full an hour before the meeting started and many people had to be turned away. The Breckinridge camp had expected the female community to be represented only by a few "women suffrage cranks" and was unprepared for the large feminine representation which frequently and loudly applauded the anti-Breckinridge speakers. [19]

Laura Clay began to receive recognition and thanks for the activities of the Kentucky ERA, which played a prominent role in the fight against Breckinridge. While declaring that there were few suffragists in Kentucky, the *Courier-Journal* admitted that women were the heart of the opposition to the congressman and asserted that, if he were defeated, "it will be their doing . . . . it is they who are fighting Mr. Breckinridge, and nothing like the interest taken by them in the race was ever before known in Kentucky." [20] By late summer, the anti-Breckinridge forces were rallying behind W. C. Owens of Georgetown, who had emerged as the incumbent's chief opposition for the nomination, and who was the ultimate victor in the election.

Women played a decisive role in ending Breckinridge's political career. According to Clay, their influence had gained the respect of politicians in Kentucky and had won for them the admiration of women across the country. The NAWSA convention, over four months later, adopted a resolution congratulating Kentucky on "the beneficial influence of women as shown in the campaign of last year."[21] Although Laura Clay was no more important than several other women in this campaign, she, as leader of Kentucky suffragists, derived from the victory an enhanced reputation in national suffrage circles. Election in 1896 to the position of auditor of the NAWSA was a reflection of the prestige she enjoyed.

Two things should be made clear about the office of auditor, which Laura Clay held for almost sixteen years. In the first place, an auditor had as much power in formulating policy as any other officer of the NAWSA. With the more prestigious officials, from treasurer to president, the two auditors served on the Business Committee, the body that decided the association's policy by a majority vote. Indeed, since the work of her post entailed only the annual auditing of the treasurer's books, Laura was left free of the daily tasks that burdened the association's two secretaries and treasurer. With time to devote to the overall direction of the organization, she soon became one of its most knowledgeable and powerful voices.

Second, Clay's long tenure as auditor was highly unusual. From the formation of the NAWSA to the turn of the century, it had been customary to change auditors frequently.[22] During this period, the office was often bestowed upon women who had arranged a convention or performed some other useful work in the preceding year. Clay raised the office to a level of prestige and power that it had not known before. In the thirty years from the organization of the NAWSA in 1890 to its transformation into the League of Women Voters in 1920, only Anna Howard Shaw, Harriet Taylor Upton, and Alice Stone Blackwell held office longer than Laura Clay.

Clay's first service to the NAWSA was as compromiser in a factional dispute. By 1899 Susan B. Anthony had become concerned about the wide powers being wielded by the Organization Committee, under the chairmanship of Carrie Chapman Catt. Catt and her close friend and assistant, Mary Garrett Hay, were able and energetic workers, but they had sometimes ignored the elected leaders of the NAWSA. Anthony believed that this committee had become so powerful that it was usurping the rights of the Business Committee. Her solution to the problem was to dissolve the Organization Committee and to hand its responsibilities over to the officers. After strenuous opposition from Hay, everyone concerned, including Catt, accepted this proposal.[23]

At the NAWSA convention in February 1900, two important developments occurred. First, in an emotion-filled transference of power, Anthony stepped out of the presidency in favor of her handpicked successor, Catt, who then received the overwhelming vote of the delegates. The second development broke the pleasantness of the convention for Anthony. Influenced by Hay, Catt persuaded Henry Blackwell to make a motion authorizing the continuance of the Organization Committee. Much to the consternation of Anthony the convention adopted the motion. Not to be outdone, Anthony carried the issue before the association's Executive Committee, composed of the NAWSA officers and leaders from the various states. After a lengthy debate, this body voted the Organization Committee out of existence. Hay thereupon resigned her post, and a breach was created between the old and new presidents, as well as among the officers who had taken sides in the matter.[24]

Clay was not involved in the dispute, for her attention was occupied by her mother's final illness, which began in the fall of 1899 and lasted until the following April. During this period Laura Clay's counsel and moderation were missed in suffrage circles. Anthony wrote to keep her abreast of developments, sometimes adding a note on the acrimony between herself and Catt, and making it clear that she wanted official restraints placed on the latter's independent activities. Anthony believed Clay's presence at Washington might have averted the trouble, since her "level judicial mind would have been a great help all around."[25]

Searching for a way to remove bitter feelings aroused by the Organization Committee struggle, Anthony decided to hold a Business Committee meeting and finally got the officers to agree to come to her home in Rochester in late August 1900. She wrote Clay that "less harm would come with all of us together at [a] later date, than to have even but one absent at an earlier time." She attached special significance to Laura Clay's participation: "I have told Mrs. Catt that I did not think our meetings could be effective without your presence. I felt last winter that we needed you very, very much. Indeed, we can't get along at all without you. Were it not for going further South and into a hotter atmosphere, I would even propose to go to your home to hold the meeting rather than have you absent." [26]

Clay was in a good position to act as a mediator. She had worked harmoniously with Catt, and each respected the other's ability and integrity. [27] Moreover, her mother's illness had kept her free of earlier involvement in the dispute.

On the other hand, Anthony's eagerness to have her present could have been for her vote, as well as her "level judicial mind." Of the seven active officers, Anthony could count on the support of Rachel Foster Avery, Anna Howard Shaw, and Harriet Taylor Upton. The new president had the vote of Alice Stone Blackwell, while Catherine Waugh McCulloch, a new officer, might align with either side. [28] If the latter sided with Catt, Laura Clay's vote would be needed to give Anthony's supporters a majority of the active officers.

The meeting was successful, and Clay was active in the discussions, although her exact contribution to the resolution of the difficulties cannot be established. The Business Committee was reaffirmed as the executive organ of the NAWSA, and the Organization Committee was thanked for its past services but left in the oblivion to which the recent convention had assigned it. Old misunderstandings were cleared up, unity was restored, programs were worked out, and the leaders of the association could now turn their energies again to the realization of their goals.

From a national viewpoint, Laura Clay's most important contribution in her early years as an officer was her chairmanship of the Increase of Membership Committee, established in 1902. This was an area of work which interested her greatly, and she initiated changes in the concept of membership which the association retained in its period of greatest popularity. When she had first entered suffrage work, a new member was expected to sign a card, pay one dollar annual dues, and attend all the society's meetings, usually held monthly except during the summer. The local societies sent thirty-five cents of each member's dues to the state organization, which, in turn, forwarded ten cents to the NAWSA treasurer, along with the names and addresses of every member of the state associations.[29]

Believing this procedure too cumbersome and time-consuming, Laura Clay urged a number of innovations. During the NAWSA convention of 1894, her motion that the membership lists be eliminated and only dues be sent to the treasurer was carried. The change saved bookwork on national and state levels and left to local societies the task of keeping membership lists.[30] In 1896 she moved that the constitution be amended in order to drop obligatory attendance at suffrage meetings and to open membership to any "citizen of the United States subscribing to the constitution, and paying not less than one dollar annually into the treasury of the Association." This proposal, which came to be called the Kentucky Plan, was based on the desire to retain the moral and numerical strength of people who supported the aims of the suffragists but were unable to attend regular meetings. Although the NAWSA declined to dictate what each state's membership requirements should be, it adopted, at the 1902 convention, a resolution urging its auxiliaries to adopt the Kentucky Plan. This convention also established a Committee on Increase of Membership and set it a goal of doubling the number of suffragists. Clay was appointed chairman of this committee, whose major task she described as winning the "argument of numbers."[31]

In the initial report of this committee to the NAWSA in 1903, she asserted that "the increase of membership should be the leading object of local Suffrage Associations." She noted that politicians who said that they were not opposed to woman suffrage claimed they were willing to concede the right as soon as a sufficient number of people indicated that it was a desirable reform, while antisuffragists contended that the small number of professed suffragists proved that women did not really desire to vote. Although unwilling to admit that these arguments should have any force in a government based on the principles of the Declaration of Independence, she recognized them as constituting a practical problem which had to be met.[32]

Laura Clay believed that the suffragists had to prove that public opinion was fast accepting their movement and that women were "able and willing to assume the rights and duties of full citizenship." Claiming that the difficulty lay not so much in creating suffrage sentiment as in enrolling that which already existed, she wrote, "if we could marshall all our sympathizers, we would present a force before which opposition would yield." Unfortunately, in her view, "only those who join our Association put themselves in a position to be counted on our side: and so far we have not enrolled more than one per cent of the number at which a conservative estimate places our sympathizers." [33]

The answer to the problem, she thought, lay in revising the techniques of organization "to focalize a vastly larger proportion of the sentiment which we know to be in our favor." She recommended further simplification of the requirements of membership. "Be careful," she advised, "to throw no duties upon the individual who does not care to assume them, except those which cannot be delegated." The duties for such members should include only subscribing to the principles of the association and paying annual dues. She also advocated writing off all back dues and reducing the required meetings to one per year for the purpose of electing local officers. State officers should encourage local clubs, through quarterly or monthly letters, to make full use of newspapers and to send organizers through their states as frequently as possible. Clay repeatedly urged suffrage leaders "to moderate their expectations" from newcomers and to remember that valuable work could be done by clubs "which could not exist if greater demands were made on them." [34]

The response to these ideas during 1903 was good. Laura Clay's committee published and mailed three leaflets, with a letter of encouragement, to all the state organizations. Replies from twenty-four states and the District of Columbia expressed interest in the committee's work and pledged to support it. The president of the Iowa Equal Suffrage Association promised cooperation and added: "What a busy woman you must be—looking after such a number of brain children." [35]

Clay's major suggestion to the convention in 1904 was the use of parlor meetings, small informal gatherings held in sympathizers' homes. Still seeking ways to bring the diffident into the suffrage ranks, she noted that such meetings could be attended "by friends too few or inexperienced to arrange successfully for public meetings." At the next annual convention, held in Portland, Oregon, in 1905, she was able to report an increase in membership of 20 percent. It was the largest gain ever achieved in a single year, raising the total to 17,000 persons. Again urging more states to adopt the Kentucky Plan, she assured the convention that many women would join under it "who now stood aloof because they will not perform club duties for which they feel themselves unfitted or for which they have no time or inclination." [36]

During the following year, Clay's ideas on membership reached final form. At the national convention at Chicago in February 1907, she argued that allegiance to the cause of equal suffrage rather than the payment of dues, should be the sole requirement for membership in the societies. The political parties, she believed, should be the models for the suffragists in canvassing and enrolling suffrage sentiment across the country, for, as she pointed out, the women had the same objective as the parties: "to rally every sympathizer, so as to bring his influence to bear for the success of his party. They work along the lines of the . . . political divisions of precinct, ward, city, county and state; and we should do likewise." Declaring, "We have been an overgrown women's club long enough," she added: "This system of gauging a person's devotion to the cause . . . by his or her attendance at meetings and pink teas isn't going to advance our cause much farther." She concluded trenchantly, "it is time we did something." [37]

Clay recognized that her plan would cost the suffragists part of their revenue, but she believed the loss could be more than made up by asking the members for donations. Money raised in this manner would enable the local chapters to pay assessments required for representation at the state and national conventions. The plan freed the officers from the onerous task of collecting dues, while accomplishing its major purpose of enrolling the timid and lukewarm friends of equal suffrage, as well as those who supported the movement but did not have time to attend meetings. [38]

Although Laura Clay resigned her chairmanship in 1907, she continued her interest in the membership committee and was frequently consulted about the Kentucky Plan. Since the NAWSA's decision was to leave decisions on qualifications for membership up to the various states, she did not miss opportunities to recommend her plan to other suffragists. Writing to the president of the Illinois Woman Suffrage Association, she reported that "we have a great increase in membership, and while the money has not increased in the same proportion, yet it has increased steadily as a result of the plan."[39]

Clay's leadership was reflected in the increased membership of the NAWSA, which, in the two years prior to the 1907 convention, almost tripled. This remarkable growth, from 17,000 to 45,501 persons, belies the contention that the years from 1896 to 1910 constituted "the doldrums" in the suffrage movement. While no new suffrage states were won, the period was important in creating enough suffrage sentiment to make the reform respectable, if not popular, by the latter half of the Progressive era. Laura Clay's innovations in recruitment of members came at a time when there was a growing participation of women in various phases of the Progressive movement and were instrumental in converting the suffragists into a political pressure group. Moreover, she advocated organizing from precinct level to congressional district before Carrie Chapman Catt introduced the idea in New York City in 1908.[40] Her proposal of non-dues paying membership had become accepted practice by 1915, when the suffragists numbered well over 100,000.

An increasing involvement in national suffrage affairs did not cause Clay to neglect work within her own state. Concessions for the improvement of the lot of women and children, whom the suffragists regarded as their special wards, were slowly coming from the state government. In 1896 the Kentucky General Assembly, responding to three years of joint effort by the WCTU and the Kentucky ERA, established two homes of reform for juveniles, one for girls and one for boys. Two years later the legislature enacted a measure, which Sallie Clay Bennett and Mary Clay had first advocated in Frankfort in 1884, requiring the presence of a woman physician in state mental institutions where women were patients. In 1906 the women secured the passage of a law, for which the Kentucky ERA had agitated since 1893, raising the age of consent from twelve to sixteen years of age. Laura Clay counted this act a triumph for the suffragists, although it fell short of the eighteen years of protection which they had been asking for.[41]

Taken together this legislation demonstrates the breadth of the woman's rights movement and indicates that Kentucky suffragists were in the mainstream of Progressivism. Laura Clay believed there was a direct correlation between the rights of women and the welfare of children, both of which were Progressive goals. Women are children's "natural protectors," she wrote, "and they will be protected very nearly in proportion to women's power to do so."[42]

Efforts to gain more equitable treatment for women at the Agricultural and Mechanical College were only partially successful. On at least one proposal—representation on the board of trustees—the women encountered a formidable opponent in James K. Patterson, president of the college, who reigned over the institution in the manner of a "benevolent despot" from 1878 until his retirement in 1911.[43]

The background of this confrontation had begun in 1895, according to Clay, when the Kentucky ERA resolved to petition the governor to appoint women to fill vacancies on the board of trustees. In compliance with this decision, Clay and Eugenia B. Farmer, the association's secretary, had notified Governor William O. Bradley that they believed "the interests of the young women students needed the supervision of some of their own sex on the Board" and had petitioned him to fill existing vacancies with women. Concluding that the law excluded women from service on the board, the governor had refused to accede to the request, whereupon the ERA, at Clay's instigation, had immediately set about the task of changing the law.[44]

When a bill embodying the desired change was introduced by Representative R. R. Morgan and sent to the House Committee on the Agricultural and Mechanical College, Patterson appeared in Frankfort to oppose it. In a long address he asserted that the education of 99 out of every 100 women had not prepared them for such a responsible position. When asked about the origin of the Morgan bill, Patterson, implying that Laura Clay brought it about, stated that the governor had told him there was a "Lexington lady who wanted to be a trustee of the college." Furthermore, upon learning that the law permitted only men to be appointed to the board, the lady was reported to have said that "she would have the law changed." Although some members of the committee favored the bill, the majority decided to report it unfavorably.[45]

Two days after Patterson's testimony, Laura Clay challenged his opinions. In a letter to the editor of the Lexington Daily Leader she undertook to clear up "the obscurity as to whence came the 'inspiration'" for the Morgan bill by recounting how the Kentucky ERA had resolved in 1894 to petition for female representation on the board of trustees and had instructed her and Eugenia Farmer to take the matter up with the governor. She disclaimed for both of them any desire to be on the board. In response to the statement that there was "not more than one woman in a hundred whose education fits her to fill such a position," she countered that the argument was "wholly irrelevant unless it could go so far as to prove that there are not a sufficient number of adequately educated women to afford an ample choice for the six or eight positions which are the most that is ever contemplated giving to women."[46]

Calling Patterson's appraisal "most mortifying to the self-respect of Kentucky women," she then questioned his administration of the State College. "If there is a shadow of justice in this opinion of President Patterson," she wrote, "it constitutes the most conclusive evidence possible that some change should be made in the supervision of the college." Noting that the institution had been open to women for sixteen years and that it claimed to give them the highest educational advantages, she expressed amazement that its president doubted that there were "enough highly educated women in the State to fill a poor half dozen positions on its board" and declared that there was no dearth of qualified women.[47]

A few days later, Senator C. J. Bronston, from Lexington, told a Joint Committee of the Senate and House on Municipalities that he thought the women's desire for school suffrage in all Kentucky cities was "orthodox . . . reasonable and just" and should be granted. Turning to the Morgan bill, Bronston saw the introduction of women into this place of power as a step in a general reorganization of the college which was long overdue. The institution, he said, had been running for fifteen years "in the same old rut," and "its standing was about that of a good common school." Blaming "old teachers and old presidents" for this state of affairs, he asked for an injection of new blood into every department, beginning with compliance to the women's request. His appeal made no headway.[48]

The disappointment suffered by the women in this instance was partially offset by other advances which they secured at the state university. As early as 1894, the WCTU and the Kentucky ERA had vainly sought a state appropriation for a women's dormitory. Women were not receiving equal advantages at the school and housing was one of the areas where there was a serious differential. At the urging of a committee from the WCTU in 1900, the legislature appropriated $30,000 for women's housing at the college. When the construction of the dormitory fell behind schedule, while a gymnasium which was appropriated at the same time neared completion, Laura Clay suggested that women on the board of trustees would see that as much attention was given to women's facilities as to men's. Women won a further concession in 1905 when the board of trustees, responding to the second of two annual appeals by some of the leading women of Lexington, whom Laura Clay served as spokesman, voted to establish a Department of Domestic Science.[49]

One of the most unusual reversals in suffrage annals occurred in 1902 when the Kentucky legislature repealed school suffrage for women in the second-class cities (Lexington, Newport, and Covington). This action resulted from a longstanding fear of black rule in Lexington, and illustrates the central role that race played in the history of the southern woman's rights movement.[50]

The precipitating event in the disfranchisement was the school board elections of 1901. In the voter registration for this election in Lexington, only 662 women registered as Democrats, while 1,997 joined the Republicans, and 139 considered themselves Independents. When male as well as female registrants were counted, Republicans outnumbered Democrats by 4,393 to 4,073. Nevertheless, the latter won the election by a 572-vote margin. The victory, as the Democratic *Lexington Herald* admitted, was far from an honest triumph. The polls where women were to vote did not open until eleven or twelve o'clock, meaning, of course, that a prime voting time for Negro domestics was eliminated. Every election officer was a Democrat. Taken together, the newspaper concluded, these conditions meant that the "ordinary Negro found it was almost impossible for him to vote at all."[51]

Apparently unwilling to trust to chicanery in the future, Lexington's Democratic delegation to the state legislature decided to take legal steps to prevent another Republican registration majority. Representative William A. Klair and Senator J. Embry Allen introduced bills in January 1902 to disfranchise women of the second-class cities. Noting that "1,900 colored women and only 700 white women registered and voted" in the Lexington school board election Klair suggested that the opponents of his bill should have been busying themselves in registering and getting white women out to vote. He contended that "colored women practically controlled . . . school elections" in Lexington, though he did not explain how the Democrats had managed to win despite being outnumbered.[52]

Laura Clay and other Lexington women, rallying against the Klair-Allen scheme, organized a Committee on Retention of School Suffrage for Women, comprised of representatives from the Fayette ERA, the Woman's Club of Central Kentucky, and the WCTU. The women circulated a petition and sent a memorial to the appropriate legislative committees, while Mrs. A. M. Harrison, a former member of the Lexington School Board, and Laura Clay went to Frankfort to lobby against the bill. From the beginning, their chances of victory were slight. The House committee reported the measure favorably, without even reading the women's memorial, and three days later, the House approved it without discussion, by a 67–20 vote. Only one Democrat joined the minority.[53]

Clay returned to Lexington for the weekend, disappointed and discouraged. Admitting that the defeat probably meant that the Kentucky ERA's bill to extend school suffrage to all women would also be lost, "she was," according to one report, "so disheartened that there were tears in her eyes." She was determined, nevertheless, "to pluckily stick it out to the last."[54]

Turning her attention to the Senate, she helped present an "appeal" which asserted that "more than 800 of the best class of white women," in addition to a number of Republican white women, had registered to vote, despite the fact that registration places had been placed in "negro cabins, barber shops and livery stables." The statement also charged that "local politicians" had worked to register and vote "an objectionable class of women in order to bring the school suffrage for women into disrepute."[55]

A large delegation of women, braving a snowstorm to go to Frankfort, was met at the station by Laura Clay and Mrs. J. H. Beauchamp, state president of WCTU, and attended a hearing on the bill before the Senate Committee on Education. There they heard Senator Allen "quite excited and reckless in his statements," claim that the group was "only a small coterie" which did not represent Lexington's womanhood. In a brief rejoinder, Laura Clay "showed cleverly and quickly the faults of his logic . . . and set all the spectators and even the Senators on the Committee to laughing."[56]

In late January, under pressure from Lexington women, Representative Klair offered to seek a substitute bill in the House which would exclude "the ignorant and illiterate class from the polls," while permitting the "intelligent women" to retain school suffrage. After brief consideration of Klair's proposal, obviously directed at disfranchising Republican Negro women voters, Allen rejected it, claiming that "over 90% of the intelligent women who patronize the public schools do not want the right of voting under any circumstances." The repealing bill passed the Senate, 23-12, and was signed into law by Governor J. C. W. Beckham.[57]

This loss of the limited right to vote in Kentucky provides insights into the complexities of the reform movement, especially in the southern states. This was the only instance in the history of the movement where the franchise, once won, was taken away by action of a legislature.[58] Repeal in Kentucky also raised the question whether school suffrage and other forms of partial enfranchisement were worth the work required to win them. Josephine K. Henry, a witness of the defeat in Frankfort, had been opposed to what she called "piecemeal suffrage," which, contrary to arguments of its advocates, had not made full suffrage easier to secure. To her mind limited franchise was a hindrance, since it gave "politicians a chance to find fault and bring charges which women in their hampered conditions cannot refute."[59] On the other hand, the great majority of suffragists, including Laura Clay, continued to agitate for partial suffrage, convinced that women would use it to prove the worth of their participation in politics and thereby induce the electorate to grant them a full vote.

Prior to 1902 Laura Clay had admitted candidly the "limited numbers" of the Kentucky ERA. After Klair and Allen had attacked the suffragists on this point and the friendly *Lexington Herald* had wondered if white women in Lexington truly wanted the ballot, the suffragists were forced to give greater attention to the argument of numbers. The operations of a small, elite group pushing for reform under the banner of all womanhood, were open to criticism in the name of democracy, which unfriendly politicians were quick to exploit. It is noteworthy that Clay's appointment to the chairmanship of the Increase of Membership Committee came at the NAWSA convention in February 1902, at the time the Klair-Allen bills were being debated.[60]

The direction and strategy of the national suffrage movement were influenced by the disfranchisement of Kentucky women. In a sense, this defeat, as well as general social conditions in the country at the turn of the century, tended to confirm suffragists, particularly in the South, in a racist mold. The original Kentucky law granting suffrage to women in 1894 had included no mention of educational qualifications. Following its repeal, the suffragists of Kentucky began to push for school suffrage for women who could read and write. Having been told that they lost the franchise because "too many illiterate negro women voted," the suffragists had to confront, not a theory on political equality, but an actual condition in the framework of American society. Denied the suffrage for all women, they reacted by trying to gain it for their own elite group. Nor were the northern suffragists innocent of this approach; Elizabeth Cady Stanton and Carrie Chapman Catt were willing to bar illiterate immigrant women from the polls if native females were given the vote.[61]

The southern suffragists' position on the race question was as much a matter of expediency as prejudice, and these women were scarcely more guilty in this regard than their northern sisters. Involved in the pursuit of a reform that they believed would bring additional good in its wake, they were willing to sacrifice egalitarian and democratic principles in order to win their prime objective. Progressive southern women, as the humane and widely admired Madeline McDowell Breckinridge, were determined that "the possible good of the present should not be sacrificed to the chimerical good of the future." [62]

The Klair-Allen legislation is a good example of the reactionary social and political attitudes that emerged in the wake of the assassination of Governor William Goebel in 1901. An authority on Kentucky history has written that the most important result of Goebel's death was that it forced the state into "a long period of partisan and factional war which prevented passage of much needed progressive legislation." [63] The wave of reaction also helped retract at least one progressive step, in the case of abolition of school suffrage for women. The woman's rights advocates now found themselves caught in a period of legislative inactivity, a situation that helps explain why the early successes of Laura Clay and her followers were not duplicated in the first years of the twentieth century. Not until 1912 did the Kentucky ERA again win the right for women to vote in school elections. This time the law applied only to women who could read and write, but it was statewide in coverage, unlike the 1894 law which applied only to the women of the second-class cities.

With progress of the suffragists in her own state caught in a web of partisan and racial friction and the NAWSA almost directionless following the resignation of Carrie Chapman Catt as president in 1904, Laura Clay gave the greater amount of her time and attention to suffrage affairs at the national level. It is somewhat ironic that her national prominence came only shortly after the painful and embarrassing defeat in her own state. For the next eight years of her career, she was at the zenith of her influence in the NAWSA, playing as important a role in its direction as any woman in the suffrage movement.

VI

CARRYING THE SUFFRAGE
BANNER OUTSIDE
KENTUCKY

1904-1910

LAURA CLAY attained the peak of her influence in national suffrage affairs during the period from 1904 to 1910, years in which the suffragists grew in numbers, though somewhat slowly, and won full suffrage for Washington in 1910. Although dwarfed by the rush of successes in the second decade of the century, the accomplishments of these women were important in laying the groundwork for future victories. By 1910 woman suffrage was a respectable, almost fashionable, cause, and such prominent and wealthy women as Mrs. O. H. P. Belmont and Mrs. Clarence Mackay of New York lent their names and some of their money to its goals.

Suffrage groups attained a sense of "self-consciousness" in this period. With associations larger and more conservative than the suffragists, such as the General Federation of Women's Clubs, adding their support to the suffragists' goals, the women were at last coming together to secure "a large part of that freedom of action which feminists had been demanding for so long."[1] As a leader in three state suffrage campaigns and as a central figure in the determination of NAWSA policies, Laura Clay played a role in this time of growing popularity and respectability as important as that of any woman in the movement.

Although she had been an officer of the NAWSA since 1896, her greater prominence did not begin until 1904. For two major

94

reasons, her second eight years on the Business Committee of the NAWSA were more prestigious and eventful than her first eight years as auditor. In the first place, Carrie Chapman Catt's retirement from the presidency of the association early in 1904 strengthened the role of subordinate officers. Catt, whose withdrawal was caused by illness and a need for a "rest from responsibilities" of office, was a splendid administrator and a good organizer, as well as an able public speaker.[2] During her presidency, however, she had turned infrequently to her fellow officers either for advice or for help in the operation of the headquarters. Her successor, Anna Howard Shaw, was an entirely different sort of leader.

Shaw, an ordained minister of the Methodist Protestant Church as well as a medical doctor, had already achieved prominence as a lecturer for the WCTU when Susan B. Anthony won her to the suffrage cause in the early 1890s. She is commonly regarded as the greatest orator produced by the suffrage movement. Unfortunately, her platform brilliance was not coupled with the tact, judgment, or administrative skills needed in the presidency of the association.[3]

During the early years of her tenure in office, Shaw was rarely present at headquarters and acted more as a representative-at-large of the association than as an executive. She relied heavily on the other officers in decision making and, with them, guided the organization by means of committee-type leadership, which helped propel Laura Clay into an increasingly important role. Not until 1909, when the headquarters was transferred from Warren, Ohio, to New York City, did Shaw abandon this method of administration, in a move that led to a series of disagreements among the officers and eventually to Clay's removal from office.

The second event that affected Laura Clay's role as a national leader was a bequest which she received in 1904 for use in suffrage work. The donor was Laura Bruce, a member of a prominent Lexington family who had studied art in Europe and had exhibited at the Paris Salon. Although it had taken the Clay women five years, from 1879 to 1884, to win her over to the cause of woman's rights, she became a valuable convert. By 1885 a warm friendship had developed between the two Lauras, and Bruce was soon an influential figure in the suffrage circle at Lexington. At her death in 1904, she left to Laura Clay real estate and stocks valued at $5,000. Because Bruce's mother and a sister contested the will, it was almost two years before Clay won an unfettered claim to the legacy, although she began at once to apply the income from it to the suffrage cause.[4]

Instead of converting the entire bequest into cash, Laura Clay retained a house at 718 North Broadway, which she rented out, and invested the remainder in stocks and loans. Returns from the rent, dividends, and interest were then expended in the suffrage movement. From 1905, when she paid the first increments to the NAWSA treasury, to 1925, Clay spent $8,881.99 of capital and earnings from the legacy for suffrage activities. Moreover, at the latter date she still held investments worth $1,980.75 which were turned over to the Christ Episcopal Church in Lexington to establish a Laura Sutton Bruce Memorial Fund for the purpose of paying the hospital expenses of indigent persons.[5]

The Bruce legacy was important in Laura Clay's growing influence in suffrage councils. It came before rich socialites began to take an interest in woman's suffrage and before Mrs. Frank Leslie made her huge gift of nearly $2 million, which she placed at Carrie Chapman Catt's disposal in 1914.[6] Since the Bruce money was used as Laura Clay saw fit, it gave her new weight in suffrage decisions.

The difference that Catt's retirement and the Bruce legacy made in Laura Clay's career was almost immediately apparent. In September 1904 she attended a Business Committee meeting in Warren, Ohio, recently selected as the site of the NAWSA headquarters, largely because it was the home of Harriet Taylor Upton, treasurer of the association. Working from two large rooms in an old vine-covered family residence, Upton, aided by Elizabeth Hauser, the headquarters secretary, and one or two other clerical assistants, carried on the day-to-day business of the association.[7] Anna Howard Shaw was rarely there, preferring to devote most of her time to speaking at state suffrage conventions, campaigning in states where amendments were being offered, or traveling on one of the Chautauqua circuits.[8]

Finding that the headquarters staff had more work than it could do, Clay remained in Warren after the conclusion of the business meeting and assumed part of the burden. Her stay, which lasted several months, established a firm bond among Upton, Hauser, and herself. Upton soon became the principal investor of money from the Bruce legacy, and Hauser was grateful for Clay's helpful presence at headquarters. For her part, Clay, who seemed to enjoy male company and discussion on political and agricultural questions, would recall years later her acquaintance with the father of her hostess, former United States Congressman Ezra Booth Taylor and "the pleasant days I spent in Headquarters."[9] Her work, which put her at the heart of suffrage communications, was one of the most memorable experiences of her career.

Two of the decisions made at Warren were to hold the next annual meeting of the association in conjunction with the Lewis and Clark Centennial at Portland, Oregon, in 1905 and to aid in the state's suffrage campaign. Since this would be their first convention in the West, the suffragists approached it with optimism. They had won their earliest victory in the West, when Wyoming Territory granted them the franchise in 1869, and because Oregon had adopted the initiative and referendum in 1902, they regarded that state as a particularly promising field. Mistakingly believing that the people were more likely to grant suffrage than their legislators, the suffragists resorted to the referendum procedure, determined to gather the necessary signatures in 1905 to put their question before the voters of Oregon in 1906.[10]

Laura Clay had hardly returned home from Warren and supervised the spring planting on her farm before it was time to make the trip to Oregon. Leaving explicit instructions for care of the farm with Howard Bush, an old Negro who had been in her employ for twenty years, she proceeded in mid-June 1905 to Chicago, where she met the other officers of the NAWSA for the trip to Portland and the opening of the convention on June 28. The long train ride was used for business meetings and for speeches from depot platforms.[11]

At the convention, in addition to hearing progress reports, electing officers, and holding public meetings, the delegates laid the final plans for NAWSA aid to the Oregon suffrage campaign. A salaried worker, Laura Gregg, was assigned to manage the effort and Clay agreed to remain in the state as a representative of the board of officers. The Kentuckian had not planned to stay because she feared that the work in her home state would lag in her absence, but her apprehension was overcome by the belief that a "victory in Oregon would be of more value in creating suffrage sentiment . . . than a ten thousand dollar educational campaign" back home. Placed in charge of securing signatures for a referendum, she directed the distribution of a ton and a half of petitions and accompanying leaflets, over 100,000 in number.[12]

As 1906 approached, she had some misgivings about the venture. Admitting to an old friend that "going among people in strange places" and trying to make "just the right impression" was an awesome burden, she added that she was "more than willing" to do the best she could. The experience, she thought, would be useful when she returned to Kentucky.[13]

Shortly after the campaign was launched, it came to a near disaster when Laura Gregg suffered what was termed an utter "collapse," which made her unable to inform officers back east of what had been done or what was being planned. Clay, who was personally fond of her, laid the blame for the problem on Gregg's failure to consult local workers for their ideas and opinions. To cite an example, she pointed out that Gregg added a young woman from Maine to the staff without conferring with the Oregonians. "That alone," Clay believed, "was enough to ruin us."[14]

With Gregg unable to continue as director of the campaign, Laura Clay took command and, in the words of Anna Howard Shaw, "proved a tower of strength." She and her co-workers gathered the signatures of the required number of voters and won a place on the ballot in 1906 for the woman suffrage question. Once the proposal was before the electorate, Clay began campaigning for its adoption. She made some fifty speeches, "ranging all the way from Portland to the extreme southern borders of the state."[15]

The suffragists encountered opposition, even among women, some of whom, commonly called "antis," opened a headquarters in Portland and caused one campaign worker to cry, "Why do they not stay at home where they say we should be!" When the NAWSA group did not find open opposition, they frequently had to combat apathy among members of their own sex. "I am glad that the women are not going to vote upon the question," one worker confided to Clay.[16]

When the proposition reached the voters in May 1906, it was defeated, 36,902–47,075. The suffragists sought consolation in the fact that a change in 5,122 votes from the negative to the affirmative would have given them a victory and, in explaining their defeat, named the liquor interests as the arch-villain. An Oklahoman claimed that breweries and liquor wholesalers had spent over $300,000 to defeat the measure. Clay also publicly indicted the "liquor trusts" and the keepers of saloons, gambling dens, and dance halls, with whose precinct workers she had exchanged cards at the polls in Salem. A share of blame for the defeat was placed on business corporations, which, Clay claimed, had "put out a letter saying woman suffrage would harm business interests." She had attempted to refute the charge by pointing out that neighboring states, more prosperous than Oregon, had granted woman suffrage. Alice Stone Blackwell and Harriet Taylor Upton also shared the belief that corporations had contributed to the outcome of the election.[17]

Writing candidly to members of the suffrage hierarchy, Laura Clay charged that "outrageous dissension" among the workers caused "injurious effects on the temper of the people" and contributed significantly to the defeat. Internal friction was a much greater problem than the suffragists admitted publicly or recorded in their publications and official histories. Disagreements between state and national suffrage workers, as well as jealousy between rival suffrage groups within some states, plagued the movement throughout its history.[18]

Laura Clay refused to let the outcome of the Oregon campaign discourage her. Writing to headquarters shortly after her return to Lexington, she claimed that suffrage work was a moral crusade: "I have learned to realize more that this work is God's cause, and He is the leader of all our campaigns." God, she concluded, would give the suffragists the victory in good time and "in the meanwhile for us to doubt would be disloyalty, to falter would be sin."[19]

Although she never returned to Oregon, Clay continued to be a strong advocate of aid to the state. When the Oregonians decided to launch another bid for the franchise in 1907, Abigail Scott Duniway, a leading Oregon suffragist, wrote NAWSA headquarters requesting financial aid and freedom for the state officers to run their own campaign. Her plea, supported only by Laura Clay and Alice Stone Blackwell, split the Business Committee. Clay urged that the money be sent, reasoning that $2,000 was "cheap to put the question to the voters," and that the "home people" should be allowed to run their own campaign. "If we have even a moderate confidence in the workers in Oregon," she argued, "we ought to be thankful that we can shift the burden of the campaign to their shoulders." Admitting that irascibility among suffragists was not confined to Oregon, she declared, "We must exercise some courage in working with disagreeable women, or we will be driven out of every state." By turning the money over to Oregon's board of officers, she pointed out, Duniway's direct control of it could be avoided.[20]

Despite Laura's pleas, the board of officers rejected the Oregon request by a 3–5 vote. One NAWSA officer wrote that nothing positive was possible in that state as long as the aged Abigail Scott Duniway lived. Clay expressed a contrary view: "Mrs. Duniway favored me with some pretty severe comments, I understand, but I never took them into consideration for a moment when I thought I had an opportunity to further the suffrage cause by overlooking them, or rather ignoring them." When Duniway sent a second request, this time for $500, only Clay and Blackwell supported it. "She is a terror," confessed Shaw, "my only fear is that Alice [Blackwell] and Miss Clay will send her some [money]. That would give her great encouragement in her abuse."[21]

Shaw's opposition did not deter Laura Clay from contributing to the campaign. As soon as the Oregonians had won a place on the ballot, she sent them $400, of which $300 was from the Bruce legacy. A short time later she made an additional donation of $100 from her own pocket. Her only stipulation on the use of the money was that it was to be placed in the charge of Mrs. Henry Waldo Coe, another Oregon suffragist, who was to spend it as the board of officers directed. Upton, who feared that Clay had denied herself to send her own personal funds, had no doubt that Duniway would spend the money on herself if she got the opportunity.[22]

These donations won the approval and lasting appreciation of the controversial Duniway, who sent hearty thanks and added: "I appreciate your cooperation all the more, dear Miss Clay, because you have been led for a time to believe me guilty of a breach of vulgar inhospitality toward you." She denied having spoken abusively of the Kentuckian. Four years later, she wrote that no other message commemorating her seventy-eighth birthday had given her as much pleasure as Laura Clay's, that Anna Howard Shaw must be replaced, and that Oregon wanted Laura Clay or Jane Addams for the NAWSA presidency. She closed her letter by urging Laura to attend the "jubilee" which Oregon was going to celebrate when woman suffrage was won in the approaching election.[23]

Clay's work and financial aid to Oregon were justified when the voters granted the franchise to women in November 1912. She must have felt that the victory was partly hers, for no other out-of-stater had worked so hard or contributed so much to building suffrage sentiment in Oregon. Laura Clay cherished the memory of her experience in Oregon, and her friends there sent her an Indian blanket as a token of their gratitude for her work and contributions toward winning their franchise.[24]

The only break in her constant support to the suffrage cause in Oregon had come late in 1908, when the Oregonians briefly sought the franchise with a tax-paying qualification. Laura Clay had informed them forthrightly that this proposal violated her principles, for it denied the ballot to many working women who needed its protection most. Her scruples against denying the vote to working women seem inconsistent with her willingness to deny school suffrage to women in her own state who could not pass an educational qualification. This inconsistency may be explained by citing her expectation that the majority of those excluded from the polls in Kentucky would be Negro women, while in Oregon, where almost 99 percent of the population was white, a tax-paying qualification would keep many native-born white women from voting. In short, Laura Clay, as most other suffragists, tended to think of reform as it affected native-born white people and saw no inconsistency of principle in excluding Negro and immigrant women from consideration. An educational qualification in Kentucky, therefore, was not regarded as a violation of her principles, while a tax-paying qualification in Oregon was.[25]

Late in 1906, only a few months after returning from Oregon,

Laura Clay, now something of a troubleshooter for the NAWSA, was asked by Shaw to go to Oklahoma to help in a suffrage campaign. Earlier in the year, President Theodore Roosevelt had signed an enabling act providing statehood for the Indian and Oklahoma territories and, since the convention that would be called would have the power to write woman suffrage into the constitution, this presented an opportunity to the suffragists.[26] Despite being in the midst of rebuilding her Lexington home, which had recently been badly damaged by fire, Laura Clay agreed to Shaw's request. She arrived in Guthrie, Oklahoma, on Christmas Eve 1906, there joining Ida Porter Boyer, a salaried NAWSA organizer, who had arrived with the purpose of establishing a headquarters.

The area was disliked by some suffrage campaigners, one of whom wrote that she "could hardly endure Oklahoma for the awful inconveniences and dirt and untidiness." She further reported that Boyer had not "had a decent or a clean meal for weeks, and a tub bath is unheard of," and she described the women of the Oklahoma City suffrage club as "unkempt and common" and usually dirty. By comparison she found her return to Denver, Colorado, like "coming back to civilization again."[27] Clay never complained nor let adverse conditions interfere with her work during the two months she was in Guthrie. Through January 1907, she and Boyer were busy interviewing delegates to the constitutional convention and getting the headquarters in working order.

The race question, a continual problem in southern suffrage discussions, was injected into the Oklahoma campaign. Clay referred to it in a letter to a local newspaper, in which she urged that all women in the South be given the vote provided they passed an educational test. Because of the far greater number of literate white women, she argued, the Negroes could not affect the outcome of elections. Her proposal would solve the race problem because it "would insure the most dignified position for the negro voters; [and] because it would be a guarantee that their votes would be as untrammelled as those of any other voters."[28] What here appears to a later generation to be blatant racism was a liberal position in the early part of the twentieth century.

During February Clay appeared before the convention's suffrage committee. Later, Robert Owen, one of Oklahoma's first United States senators, former Governor Alva Adams of Colorado, and she addressed the entire convention in a plea for woman suffrage. "She was the most effective of our speakers at the Constitutional Convention," Boyer reported. "She caught the Southerners. She's welcome to them! Alfalfa Bill and the whole bunch."[29]

Woman suffrage was the most debated topic in the convention and, for a time, appeared acceptable to the majority of delegates, notwithstanding the opposition of Charles W. Haskell, who was to become the first governor, and many of his Democratic supporters. Despite the solid help of organized labor and general support from the temperance societies, however, it was defeated, by a 37–50 vote. After the convention, Oklahoma suffragists continued to try to get their question before the voters and in 1909 appealed to the NAWSA for financial aid. Already short of money, the Business Committee was thrown into a quandary, as the officers split on the question of extending further help. Clay and Kate Gordon, the corresponding secretary, were strong advocates of doing all that was possible for the Oklahomans, while Shaw and Upton were opposed.[30]

Laura Clay's support for Oklahoma was part of her usual championing of southern suffrage causes. She was encouraged by the fact that suffragists there were united, and she believed that the temperance people, aroused by an attempt to repeal prohibition, could be counted on to aid in a referendum fight. An even greater influence in her thinking was the fact that in this campaign the suffragists had their only chance to create what she termed a "political situation." Led to this concept by Emmeline G. Pankhurst, an English suffragist, Clay believed that if Oklahoma, a Democratic state, granted suffrage, it would become politically expedient for Republican states to follow the example. Further, if one of the two major political parties made a move to enfranchise women, the other would follow suit rather than risk losing the support of these new voters. Her experiences in Oregon and Oklahoma had persuaded her, she wrote, "that this question of woman suffrage is going to be settled by politicians largely upon . . . grounds of party expediency, not on its ethical merits." For the first time, she was hearing the argument "that woman suffrage is bound to come soon—it cannot be staved off long."[31] Previously of the opinion that the suffragists would succeed because they were morally right, Clay's tactical thinking was becoming realistic by 1910.

In the end, the NAWSA decided to support the campaign in Oklahoma. Its chief contribution was the payment of Boyer's salary and the rental of a small headquarters, which was sometimes no more than a single room at her boarding place. Even this outlay cost $300 per month, and by early 1910 the treasurer was complaining that the NAWSA had expended $15,000 in the state since 1906. Upton contended that those officers who had voted to aid Oklahoma should carry the burden of raising the funds. In a characteristically diplomatic but firm reply, Clay stated that she did not believe her freedom to vote for what she judged to be the best interests of the association was limited by her fund-raising potential and that Upton and Shaw had as great an obligation to carry out the mandate of the board as those who had voted with the majority.[32]

Clay never slackened in her own support of the Oklahoma suffragists. During 1909 and 1910, while petitions were being gathered and the referendum campaign waged, she sent $1,267 into the state, only $300 of which was Bruce fund money. "Some way you seem to always come in the time when we are scared to death for fear we will be bankrupt," an appreciative Oklahoman wrote. Nevertheless, the hard work of the women who carried on the fight and the generosity of Laura Clay were not enough to win. In November 1910 the voters rejected woman suffrage by the margin of 88,808 to 128,928.[33]

Long before that defeat, Clay was already engaged in her third major campaign as a NAWSA officer. Early in 1909 Shaw asked her to go to Arizona, where the territorial legislature was scheduled to consider a woman suffrage bill.[34] As in the Oklahoma case, the Official Board (formerly the Business Committee) of the NAWSA hoped, by winning the vote from the territorial legislature, to avoid the more difficult task of amending the state constitution later.

On January 28, one day after the request reached her, Clay accepted it and notified Frances W. Munds, leader of the Arizona suffragists, that she would depart from Lexington immediately on the four-day trip by train to Prescott. For the next two months she conducted "a one-woman fight" to organize the women of the territory and to persuade the legislature to enfranchise them. She devoted most of her time at first to organizing suffrage clubs in accordance with her Kentucky Plan of membership without dues. Although the Arizona women gave her little assistance, she worked to create clubs at the local, county, and territorial levels, each with a chairman, who was elected if there was an active group at that level and appointed if there was not. Under Clay's direction, the suffragists held a convention and chose Munds their president.[35]

This campaign provides insights into the complexities of the suffrage movement and the widespread interest during the Progressive period in disqualifying some potential voters. Those to be disqualified were not, in every case, Negroes. Fearing the Mexican-American voters, nearly one half of the electorate in Arizona, Munds suggested that, when a constitutional convention was called, the suffragists should seek a franchise bill with an educational qualification in order to disqualify persons of foreign birth or of mixed parentage, who, she maintained, were always opposed to woman suffrage. Another worker presented the problem succinctly: "the Mexicans are opposed to woman suffrage because they are ignorant. The Americans are opposed because the Mexicans are ignorant—and there we are!" In short, suffragists often advocated a limited suffrage not only in the South, as is frequently noted, but also in the Northeast and West because they believed that the Mexican-American and the "new immigration" vote hurt them in two ways: first, it was not as enlightened as the native (Anglo-Saxon) vote and was thus cast against them; second, it kept the native voters from enfranchising them for fear of adding illiterate foreign-born women to the number of eligible voters.[36]

While in Arizona Laura Clay also found occasion to answer the contention that an election should be held to determine whether or not a majority of women wanted the franchise. Why should extraordinary tests be applied to find out the wishes of women, she asked, when such tests had never been required of the various classes of men admitted to the ballot? "Certainly women who want the ballot would never be any better satisfied, if the majority of women voted 'No,'" she explained, "to have their rights voted down by women any more than they are now satisfied to have them voted down by men." Unlike many of the suffragists of her generation, she did not expect the millennium to arrive with their enfranchisement, nor that women would vote in markedly greater numbers than men. "The indifference of many women to the right," she concluded, "seems to come from the immense difficulties in attaining it rather than to [any] indisposition to using it."[37]

Turning her attention to the territorial legislature, Laura Clay wrote each of its members, advising them that woman suffrage was fast winning the public's favor and that "its success in the near future can be as confidently predicted as anything else in human affairs." Since this was the case, it would be wise "for any party to meet the issue half way and by helping to gain suffrage for women to establish a claim to any party advantage which might come from the votes of the new electors." Though winning the appreciation and admiration of her new friends in Arizona, her efforts were not enough to sway the legislature. Her bill was defeated by two votes in the upper house and the lower chamber let it die in committee.[38]

By March 25 Laura Clay was back in Lexington. All the hard work, she assured Frances Munds, "will count in the long run." The Arizona campaign had convinced her of the need for male help, and she suggested employing a member of the American Federation of Labor to work with the labor unions. Whether the use of male speakers and organizers arose from her suggestion is not certain, but the NAWSA employed men in 1912 and the Kentucky ERA hired Urey L. Estes of Chicago as its field secretary in 1913.[39]

In examining their setback in Arizona the suffragists attached the greatest blame to the liquor interests and the corporations. Pauline O'Neill, wife of an Arizona politician, asserted that the votes which defeated their bill in the Senate were controlled by the corporations. The field reports of Laura Gregg, an NAWSA organizer, added credence to the charge. Claiming that the Southern Pacific and Santa Fe railroads and the Copper Queen and

United Verde mining companies were the chief enemies of woman suffrage in Arizona, Gregg reported that people in mining camps and railroad towns were in a position of "servile obedience to the corporations" and were unwilling to express an opinion on anything for fear of losing their jobs. Relating how a Copper Queen mining town had forced her to speak in the dark by turning off the lighting in the public square, she expressed apprehension that the corporations might have her jailed in order to stop her work.[40]

Another of Laura Clay's ventures as an NAWSA officer involved her in the race problem in Mississippi. The Negro population was still heavily concentrated in the former Confederate and three border states, and only in these states would the enfranchisement of women add a significant number of Negro voters to the lists. In 1910 the percentage of females of voting age in these thirteen states who were Negroes ranged from 59.2 in Mississippi to 12.7 in Kentucky. Oklahoma, where 8.5 percent of the women of voting age were Negro, ranked next, and Missouri followed with only 5.4 percent.[41] In the South as a whole, where Negroes comprised 25 percent or more of the persons of voting age, there was a response markedly different from that in other sections to the proposition of creating additional Negro voters.

In 1907 a plan to enfranchise the white women of Mississippi brought into bold relief the differences between northern and southern suffragists on the race problem. Kate Gordon of New Orleans, the corresponding secretary of the NAWSA, gave the issue focus by originating a scheme to grant the ballot in Mississippi to white women only. Always a strong critic of Negro pretensions to any sort of equality, she electrified the NAWSA convention at Chicago in February 1907 with a fiery excoriation of the Reconstruction policies which had enfranchised "cornfield darkies" and left "intelligent motherhood" on a meaningless pedestal. As she took her seat, "every woman in the hall clapped wildly, some waving their handkerchiefs and the applause continued for several minutes." Her ideas for getting the white women down from their pedestals took concrete form the following August, when she suggested to Laura Clay that southern feminists should push for state constitutional amendments which would give the vote to white women only. By linking the proposal with the suppression of miscegenation, she believed, the suffragists could win a large following.[42]

At first Clay refused on constitutional grounds to support the Gordon plan and maintained her usual advocacy of woman suffrage with an educational qualification, admitting that this would bar many Negro women from the polls while enfranchising most white females. During the next three months, however, she slowly underwent a change of mind. Her reasons are not entirely clear, but there is enough evidence to allow speculation. First, she was fond of Gordon and valued her aid when questions concerning the South came before the Official Board. Second, her own plan of appealing to southern legislators for woman suffrage based on an educational qualification had not been successful. Finally, she was influenced by the desire of Henry B. Blackwell, former abolitionist and longtime proponent of woman suffrage, to send Belle Kearney, president of the Mississippi Woman Suffrage Association, to the next session of the legislature at Jackson to lobby for the presidential ballot for women. Blackwell contended that the right to vote for presidential electors could be granted by state legislatures without popular approval, under Article II, section 2, of the federal Constitution, and hoped that this form of partial suffrage would be a major step toward full enfranchisement of women. While he objected to Gordon's plan, on constitutional rather than ethical grounds, he was willing to accept it if the southern suffragists insisted.[43]

As the time approached for the convening of the Mississippi legislature in January 1908, the only open opposition to the proposal for white woman suffrage came from Alice Stone Blackwell, recording secretary of the NAWSA and an editor of the *Woman's Journal*. The NAWSA officers had refused to give money to the campaign, although Shaw stated that she would have been willing to grant funds to Clay or Gordon, but not to Kearney. This was not really a matter of contention between supporters of the proposal and other national leaders, however, since even Clay was opposed to the NAWSA entering a white-women-only suffrage campaign.[44] Blackwell's objection, consequently, stands out as an exception to the general acceptance of the racist scheme, and it is important because it forced Clay to defend her own position.

At the bottom of her disagreement with Blackwell was Laura Clay's contention that "the condition of women requires the ballot in the hands of some women, at least, far more than the condition of negroes requires the extension of suffrage to negro women; or even that the negro men may vote."[45] Pointing to a number of states that yet had statutes discriminatory to women, she asserted that these laws would never be completely removed until "some women have the ballot." Even Negro women would benefit from enfranchisement of white females, because their votes would improve the laws that affected all womankind.

In extending the suffrage, Clay claimed, the electorate was motivated primarily by the question of how the newly enfranchised class would use the ballot, not by the abstract right of each individual to vote. She used the white voters' attitude toward the Negro in the South to illustrate her point: "The southern people have a horror of Negro suffrage from a painful experience, and from constant observation of what seems to them the incompetence of negroes for the government of a race different, if not superior, to themselves. It is scarcely probable that the southern states will easily consent to enlarging the negro vote, while they have no experience of the certainty of the white women's voting in numbers large enough to counteract the negro vote and have a surplus over."[46] In her opinion, the nagging fear that the eligible black women would vote while the white ones would not was the reason that the southern politicians had not accepted the argument that female suffrage with an educational qualification would enfranchise far more white than black women.

What she was asking for was an abstract policy for the NAWSA which would, at the same time, be expedient for the state associations. Such a policy would enable the national organization to continue to demand the ballot for all women, as a matter of principle, while leaving the state associations quite free to follow a course of opportunism. She agreed with Blackwell, for example, that no assistance should be sought from the NAWSA, thus permitting it "to remain the advocate of the abstract principle of the right of every fit person to have a voice in government." On the other hand, it should be "enough if the southern states are willing to admit the fitness of white women, without having to overcome the prevalent opinion that the enlargement of the negro vote would be disastrous to good government." In espousing the argument that the state associations could seek the ballot after their own fashion, Clay was conforming to her own states' rights beliefs and to the policy of the NAWSA, which since 1903 had recognized the doctrine of states' rights as governing the relation of local clubs to the national body.[47]

Southern politicians, experience had taught her, would discuss woman suffrage only if they were convinced that it would not "jeopardize the present white supremacy status." While believing that Negroes were "a childish and irresponsible race," she was not a Negrophobe, and she continued to advocate fair treatment and a dignified place in American life for them. She never succumbed to the abusive terms employed by Gordon in referring to Negroes, nor did she waver from her national position, as distinguished from her sectional stand, that every "fit person" should be endowed with the ballot, "as the rightful expression of the inalienable right of self-government." The deep South had a peculiar problem, and she believed that the states there had the legal power to handle the problem under their right to establish qualifications for the ballot. In her own state, she never entertained any idea of barring Negroes from the ballot box, except under the educational qualification, which would exclude white and black women alike. In Louisiana, where 43.1 percent of the population was Negro in 1910, Gordon was an extremist on the race question and sought white woman suffrage; in Kentucky, Clay was a moderate and refused to accept the right or desirability of racial restrictions on suffrage.[48]

The results of the plan to push for white woman suffrage in Mississippi were anticlimactic. With Clay, Gordon, and Blackwell prepared to finance Kearney's work with the state legislature in 1908, a conference was arranged with the Mississippi suffragists for early December 1907. Three Mississippi women, including Nellie Somerville, of later suffrage prominence, met with Clay, Gordon, and Kearney at Jackson. Five of this group then began a round of interviews with Governor James K. Vardaman, judges of the state's supreme court, and legislators to determine the feasibility of Gordon's plan. All but one of the persons consulted believed that white woman suffrage would be welcomed, but none thought it would stand the test of constitutionality.[49] Unfortunately for the progress of the plan, Gordon had not received a legal opinion from any of the lawyers to whom she had submitted her views.

The outcome of the conference was a decision to push for the Gordon plan, if reliable legal opinion sustained its constitutionality and "a selected number of political men, favorable to such a measure, advised that there was nothing in such an amendment to affect injuriously the present status of white supremacy." The latter condition, inserted at the insistence of the Mississippi women, is an indication of the difficulty in getting past the racial barrier. In case the required assurances were not forthcoming, the women decided to work for full suffrage "on the same terms men now exercise it," that is, with the restrictive clauses of the Mississippi Plan of 1890. In neither case would the Mississippi Woman Suffrage Association join Kearney in seeking Blackwell's presidential suffrage, for it agreed with Gordon that in a one-party state that sort of partial franchise would not be worth the effort required to win it.[50]

Laura Clay returned home in early December 1907, optimistic that Gordon's proposal offered much to both races. She confided to Blackwell:

> I am in great hopes that the words "white women" will prove constitutional; as it affords the best opening I have seen to interest men and politicians in our enfranchisement. When the [woman suffrage] movement extends to northern states, as I doubt not emulation will make it do, the fact that vast numbers of negro women will be enfranchised there ought to reconcile the friends of negro women suffrage to deferring their suffrage in the southern states; and the protection given both south and north to women's industrial and civic rights will rejoice us all, North and South.[51]

Early in the new year all hope for success in Mississippi was dashed. Gordon failed to obtain the needed legal opinions, and Kearney decided against making any suffrage proposals to the legislature.[52] Although disappointed, Laura Clay continued to believe that the South would eventually find a legal means of insuring white supremacy and that the Gordon plan, if it proved constitutional, might be the answer to the problem. It is ironic that both Clay and Gordon believed that the federal government would soon force the nation to abide by the Fifteenth Amendment and that the southern states would then have to turn from unconstitutional devices for maintaining white supremacy to legal methods, that is, to some form of woman suffrage.

Laura Clay's obtuseness in clinging to this notion is remarkable. Against mounting evidence that all branches of the United States Government had turned the Negro question over to the states, she continued to believe that the subterfuges written into southern state constitutions would be overturned by the Supreme Court. There is no evidence that she ever realized that the government's early program of protection for the Negro in his political and civil rights had been abandoned for a quiet national acceptance of the frauds which were being used to deny him his rights.[53] When a number of southern suffragists and legislators later supported the Nineteenth Amendment, it was not from a belief that all women, black and white, should be enfranchised, but rather from their conviction that the law would not be applied in the South. In the face of much evidence to the contrary, Clay continued to believe that the Constitution was the law of the land.

The years from 1904 through 1909 were happy ones for Laura Clay. Her close association with Harriet Taylor Upton and the headquarters' staff at Warren, her vote in all NAWSA policy decisions, and her participation in suffrage campaigns in Oregon, Oklahoma, and Arizona put her at the center of national suffrage developments. Although Washington was the only state to grant woman suffrage in this period, Clay and other suffrage leaders found grounds for optimism in their growing numbers.

During 1910 and 1911 organizational changes in the NAWSA produced dissension and recrimination among the suffrage leaders. The removal of headquarters to New York was a sign of growth in the association, but it raised administrative problems that had not arisen at Warren. In seeking a resolution to these difficulties, Laura Clay became involved in a partisan dispute which marred her last months on the Official Board and finally forced her out of national office.

VII

STRUGGLE FOR CONTROL
OF THE NATIONAL
SUFFRAGE MOVEMENT

1909-1911

THE INTERNAL DISSENSION that marred Laura Clay's last months
on the Official Board was similar, in some respects, to the bickering that both preceded and followed her sixteen years as an officer
of the NAWSA. Jealousies and rivalries were, perhaps, to be expected in an organization that included individuals with strong
personalities and firm opinions. The infrequent officers' meetings
contributed to failures in communication, and the lack of clearly
delineated areas of responsibility made clashes among some leaders
almost inevitable.

The dissension that existed from 1909 through 1911 differed
from that of other years. While earlier troubles were most frequently occasioned by personal antagonism, those of this particular period were caused in part by the growth of the suffrage
movement. By the end of 1909, the NAWSA had simply out-
grown the small headquarters at Warren, Ohio, and the administrative methods that had once been adequate. Warren was a poor
location for the advertising and selling of suffrage literature and
an impossible one for exploiting the publicity that large newspapers and the wire services could give the suffragists. From an
administrative viewpoint, greater centralization was badly needed
at national headquarters. Decision making by correspondence, a
method followed since 1890, except for a brief deviation during
the Catt presidency, was required for every transaction, from

buying a new typewriter to undertaking a state campaign. By 1909 this administrative system was too slow and cumbersome to allow an organization of some 75,000 members to function efficiently.

Both the personal differences among the officers and solutions to the organization's growing pains might have been worked out under a more able president. Anna Howard Shaw, who led the NAWSA from 1904 to 1915, was not equal to the task. Quick to take criticism personally and prone to alienate people with whom she worked, she had achieved the presidency largely through her powers as a public speaker and her devotion to the movement. Lacking in tact, judgment, and administrative ability, she compounded, rather than solved, the problems that confronted the NAWSA during her tenure in the office.

Shaw's deficiencies in leadership were not recognized at first because Upton was the actual executive of the association for the first five years of Shaw's term. While the president was on the lecture circuit or at her home in Pennsylvania, the nerve center of the suffrage movement was at Warren, where, from 1903 to 1909, the headquarters answered the association's correspondence, published *Progress*, the NAWSA's monthly paper, solicited funds, and advised and supervised suffrage activities around the nation.[1] The general tranquillity among the officers during these years was, no doubt, largely owing to the infrequency of Shaw's visits to Warren.

Even during these years, Shaw felt that she was being abused by Upton and resented her central role in the direction of operations. As early as 1906 Shaw wrote Lucy Anthony, her companion and confidante, that Upton "is ready to misjudge me on the smallest provocation." A little later she was complaining: "I must have my say about some things or let her [Upton] be president and run the whole shooting match." Shaw added that she was determined to become president in fact as well as in name by removing executive tasks from the treasurer's jurisdiction and turning them over to Anthony and Rachel Foster Avery, another close friend and vice president of the NAWSA. In 1908, after accusing Upton of usurping some of the president's responsibilities, Shaw instructed the other officers to adress all inquiries to her home in Moylan, Pennsylvania.[2] So long as the headquarters was in Warren, as Shaw must have realized, she was too far removed from the organization's administration to manage it as she desired.

Although usually getting along well with Shaw, Laura Clay did not entirely escape her wrath. The president was particularly displeased with Clay for persuading the NAWSA's Executive Committee to continue the Oklahoma campaign in 1908, an effort that Shaw wanted to abandon. Declaring that she would have her way more often and that the other officers could "like it or lump it," she asserted that she was "tired of being bossed and bullied by Miss Clay who does not digest a thing." In the following spring, word came to Laura Clay that there was a move to get her off the Official Board because she had offended Shaw in the Oklahoma matter.[3]

Money was the vital element in any consideration of the removal of headquarters from Warren, since the association could carry on its operations there with a modest budget. In the early months of 1909, however, a new development gave Shaw her long-sought opportunity to remove these operations from Upton's control. The growing interest of a number of wealthy society women in suffrage activities provided the president with a financial independence she had not enjoyed earlier and brought greater public attention to the cause of woman suffrage.

The most important of these socialites was Mrs. Oliver H. P. Belmont, a member of the New York "400" and owner of the Marble House mansion at Newport, Rhode Island. During her retirement from social life, following the death of her second husband, Belmont developed a commitment to the woman's movement which lasted until her death in 1933. She asked some of the suffrage leaders, including Shaw and Ida Husted Harper, "to come and help her understand the situation." In answer to her query about what the suffragists needed most, they replied, "Suitable headquarters in New York City, where the large newspapers, the press associations and many people of wealth and generosity are located."[4] Within a week Belmont made funds available for the establishment of the requested offices.

Belmont's generosity met with a mixed response. While Clay was not opposed to the removal of headquarters, she believed that Washington was preferable to New York, since the NAWSA usually carried on some lobbying activities when Congress was in session. Alice and Henry Blackwell agreed with her, for they feared that, if the NAWSA moved to New York, it would become involved in a rivalry between Belmont and Mrs. Clarence H. Mackay, another wealthy woman, who were competing for leadership of the suffragists there. The *Rochester Union and Advertiser* brought to public attention the Blackwells' fear when it claimed that the social rivalry of the two New York women had been extended "to the fight for women's rights." Newspapers tended to exaggerate the divisiveness in the suffrage ranks, but there was substance to the reports.[5]

The Executive Committee of the NAWSA, meeting on the eve of the convention in Seattle in July 1909, voted 27–3 to transfer the headquarters from Warren to New York. Only Clay and the two Blackwells voted against the action, which the convention soon ratified. The move necessitated changes in the board of officers and in the staff of workers. Gordon, who had served as corresponding secretary since 1901, resigned and was replaced by Mrs. Francis Squire Potter, who left her position as chairman of the English Department at the University of Minnesota to become a full-time suffrage worker. Mary Gray Peck, an assistant and friend of Potter at Minnesota, became the new headquarters' secretary, replacing Elizabeth J. Hauser, who temporarily resigned from suffrage work.[6]

Shortly after the headquarters was transferred to a spacious suite on Fifth Avenue in New York, Clay began to receive rumblings of trouble there. The problems revolved around two issues: the delineation of responsibilities among the officers, and the role of Lucy Anthony at headquarters. "I shall need your help more than I ever did before," Shaw had written Anthony, ". . . you are so useful that you will have to take a more prominent part in it [the work] hereafter." After the transfer to New York, Shaw gave Anthony a prominent role in the national office. According to Upton, Anthony began to receive dues, pay bills, and issue receipts, and, in general, play "the part of President and Treasurer." Since few members of the association shared Shaw's high opinion of Anthony's abilities, her new and unauthorized role caused a considerable amount of consternation, both at headquarters and among the other officers. Moreover, Potter and Peck had come to their jobs thinking that they were going to have the kind of freedom and authority that Upton had exercised before them. They found, instead, that Shaw, often acting through Anthony, intended to be in full authority and often unbalanced the association's bank account by confusing it with her own. Belmont, taking the side of Shaw in the ensuing dispute, reportedly said, "If the Pecks and Potters do not let Lucy stay, the National can get out."[7] The situation was all the more puzzling since Potter had been Shaw's personal choice for corresponding secretary.

Amid growing dissension in headquarters and "veiled protests from all parts of the country" that Belmont was about to take over the NAWSA, a meeting of the Official Board was called for December 21–23, 1909, in New York. In response to a suggestion that Potter be summarily dismissed, Clay insisted that she be given a hearing, both in fairness to her and as a protection against future accusations of injustice against Shaw.[8]

Clay was the chief compromiser at the meeting, which worked out a temporary solution to the strife. She stated her conviction that the difficulties had arisen because the association had never had such headquarters and, consequently, had neither rules nor precedents to guide the officers in their duties. Her reputation for fairness and impartiality was affirmed when the officers then unanimously elected her a committee of one to draw up a series of rules defining each officer's area of authority.[9]

On the final day of the conference, after all parties to the dispute had been heard, Laura Clay's statement on the rights and responsibilities of the officers was adopted. The settlement could be only temporary, as she realized, since there was no way the headquarters could be run efficiently as long as the president and the corresponding secretary were both present in the office and were at odds with one another. Clay's rules gave the president "the privilege of inspecting all the activities of headquarters at all times" and left day-to-day operations in the hands of the corresponding secretary. In case of disagreement between the two officers, a vote of the Official Board was to be decisive. This was a cumbersome solution but it was not likely that a better one could have been found on such short notice. It was hoped that a permanent resolution of difficulties could be postponed until the next convention in April 1910, when Potter and Peck were expected to resign. By implication Clay's settlement precluded Anthony, who had no official position at headquarters, from any role in its operations, a development greatly resented by Shaw.[10]

In fairness to Shaw, it should be pointed out that the concept her fellow officers had of the presidency made it an honorary rather than an executive position. Most of the officers had become accustomed to the old headquarters, in which Upton handled the administration, and were not prepared for the change that accompanied the move to New York. Upton certainly had the greatest adjustment to make. There was some justification for Shaw's assertion: "Harriet is at the bottom of this whole business. I wish Miss Gordon were on the Board. She [understood] Harriet and her attitude when she is in an injured mood."[11]

The new year made it clear that the December conference had not quieted the storm in New York. A flow of letters from Upton brought Clay news of the continuing strife and relayed gossip concerning the principal characters involved in it, including Belmont and Mrs. Mackay. The unhappiness with Shaw's administration was so great among suffragists that Upton, according to her own testimony, was subjected to immense pressure to stand for the presidency.[12]

As the NAWSA convention drew near, Shaw announced to state suffrage leaders that Potter and Florence Kelley, the second vice president, would not stand for reelection. The reason given for the latter's decision was that suffrage activities had left her too little time for her regular social work. "Health and family responsibilities" were cited in Potter's case.[13] These explanations provide a good example of the manner in which the national leadership tried to keep news of internal dissensions from the rank-and-file membership as well as from the newspapers.

The convention, which met in Washington, D.C., in mid-April 1910, was notable on several counts and especially because, for the first time, a president of the United States addressed a suffrage group. William Howard Taft was hissed when he suggested in his speech that woman suffrage had not yet proved to be a useful experiment in government. A newspaper reported that "hisses and catcalls" came from "all parts of the house," while suffragists contended that there were only a few and those from outsiders.[14]

The delegates used the occasion of the convention to present their Great Petition, which called upon Congress to initiate legislation for woman suffrage. Suffragists had originally sought one million names when the petition, a brainchild of Catt, was launched at the Buffalo convention in October 1908. Finally settling for 404,825 signatures, the suffragists formed a procession of seventy-six cars, with the officers in the lead, to carry their document to the Capitol. Laura Clay had worked hard, gathering signatures for the Great Petition in Kentucky, and had persuaded the NAWSA officers that a protest meeting should be held on the Capitol steps, if the appeal were not accepted by the House or Senate. Fortunately, Speaker Joseph G. Cannon accepted the petition, and the women found no reason to emulate their suffrage sisters in England, whose aggressive tactics under Emmeline Pankhurst's leadership were well known to the Americans.[15]

The convention also saw an intensification of friction among the organization's leaders. There was an ineffectual effort to unseat Shaw, when Upton ran a poor second to her in the balloting for president; but the election of officers in general was conducted without any bitter contests. Dissension among the officers burst into the open, however, when all of them, except Shaw, combined efforts in passing a resolution commending the work of Potter and Peck and expressing regret at their retirement. Shaw tried to keep all mention of the resolution out of the minutes of the convention and, failing in that effort, appended a dissenting statement to the commendation. In an attempt to keep the full extent of their differences out of the newspapers, the suffragists ordered all newsmen out of the meeting hall during the debate on the resolution. This unpleasantness among the officers was foreboding for the coming year, and the tension was compounded when Upton and Avery resigned their offices. Citing injustices to themselves which the convention had not corrected, the two women refused to serve another year under Shaw.[16]

With two positions on the Official Board vacated at the very end of the convention, it fell to the remaining officers to elect replacements. Clay's hope that the vacancies could be filled in "harmony and good feeling and without any more disturbances" was soon realized. Catherine Waugh McCulloch, who had been elected second vice president by the convention, was advanced to the first vice presidency; Kate Gordon was elected to the post of second vice president; and Jessie Ashley, a newcomer to suffrage leadership, replaced Upton as treasurer.[17]

Although there were now new faces and a better atmosphere at headquarters, some of the old animosities carried over into the new administration. While escaping Shaw's ire in the headquarters' matter, Laura Clay incurred it in discussions on the contract by which Alice Stone Blackwell's *Woman's Journal*, a weekly, was to absorb *Progress*, the association's monthly, and become the official organ of the NAWSA. Clay had supported the change because the association needed a weekly publication and the *Woman's Journal* was prestigious and enjoyed a wide circulation. Shaw, who had reservations about acquiring a larger and more expensive newspaper, wrote: "I voted against it and did my best to save us, now let those who voted for it see to getting the money." Clay's advocacy of the *Woman's Journal* and its editor, Alice Stone Blackwell, remained a point of friction between her and the three officers at headquarters for the rest of her tenure on the Official Board.[18]

In 1911 new problems developed between the three officers at headquarters and four of those not in residence there. Clay, Gordon, McCulloch, and Ella S. Stewart felt that they were being ignored by Shaw, Mary Ware Dennett, the corresponding secretary, and Ashley. A principal complaint stemmed from Ashley's failure to send out financial reports, a task Upton had always carefully performed. The trouble was, however, even broader, as Clay observed to Shaw: "I consider it a great mistake in the present management of business in Headquarters that the merest scraps of information come to the members who are not in New York; the principal source of their information being through the columns of the [*Woman's*] *Journal*. It seems to me that you are feeling so much what appears to you a lack of sympathetic effort on the part of some members of the Board simply because those members of the Board have very little touch with what is going on." Expressing her thoughts more succinctly, a little later, Clay questioned the treasurer's competency and complained, "I have never felt so entirely out of it as I do under this new Board." [19]

By April 1911, when a threat to stop voting on any matter, if treasurer's reports were not sent, had forced Ashley to send financial statements, another problem had arisen to widen the gulf between the factions. The new issue revolved around the pledge Belmont had made at the convention in April 1910 to continue financial support of the New York headquarters. Everyone outside of the New York office believed, as indeed the minutes of the meeting show, that her pledge of $600 per month was to be continued until the next convention. Great was the surprise and shock of the officers outside New York when Shaw informed them that Belmont had interlined the clause, "or until August 1, 1911," in the final contract between herself and the NAWSA and that she intended to implement it. [20] This meant that Belmont would withdraw her support August 1, over two months before the next convention was to meet in October 1911 at Louisville. Since the convention was the body that made decisions concerning the location of headquarters, the officers were faced with an embarrassing two-month interlude without money to pay the Fifth Avenue rent.

Belmont offered the officers an escape from the dilemma, but the stipulation she attached to her proposal only created another problem. She was willing to donate $1,000 to the NAWSA during the next year if the officers agreed to leave the headquarters in New York. [21] The condition brought protest from the four nonresident officers, who were soon referring to themselves as "the Insurgents" and were suspicious of any Belmont pledge, since they believed that the headquarters' staff had deliberately misled them as to the exact stipulations of the first pledge. They contended, furthermore, that the officers did not have the constitutional right to bind the next convention to a New York headquarters, as Belmont required in return for her $1,000. The Insurgents also claimed that the existing headquarters was too expensive anyway and that, if a move were necessary, it should be to either Chicago or Washington. In an attempt to work out a temporary arrangement, which would provide financial support for the New York office until the convention could decide the entire matter, Laura Clay offered to pay part of the rent herself. [22]

After much letter writing and manipulation of finances, Ashley wrote the other officers that Belmont had agreed to withdraw her condition and donate $500 for the six months following August 1. This settlement would permit the convention to remove the headquarters from New York after January 1912, if it so wished. Now, however, Ashley brought to light a second condition which Belmont had attached to her original offer, which made her contribution contingent on Shaw's election to the presidency for the coming year. Again the Insurgents protested that the Official Board could not guarantee the election of any person to office, since that right belonged to the convention and, consequently, could not enter into such an agreement with Belmont.[23]

Ashley assured those outside New York that Shaw had intended "from the first" to get Belmont to withdraw her condition about the presidency, but she admitted that it had not been done at the time the new contract was being drawn up. Claiming that "Mrs. Belmont has confidence in me and upon that confidence . . . has given every dollar she has contributed to the Association," Shaw promised the Insurgents that the objectionable condition would be withdrawn.[24]

Although Belmont's six-month offer without conditions was accepted, the damage was done to any possibility of harmony on the Official Board. The two factions continued to hammer away at each other. McCulloch expressed the sentiments of the Insurgents when she wrote: "This keeping some of the Board in ignorance of the exact facts and giving us erroneous conclusions from such facts does not seem to me ethical." Shaw gave vent to the feeling at headquarters when she openly asserted that the Insurgents' complaints were "unfair and unjust" and privately agreed that they were "acting like devils."[25]

While the argument over the location of headquarters was still under way, another dispute arose. Centering around proposals to amend the constitution of the NAWSA, it divided the suffragists along sectional lines: the eastern headquarters faction sponsoring the changes and the western and southern faction, led by the Insurgents, opposing them. Most important among the proposed revisions were those that called for admission to the NAWSA of any suffrage club with at least fifty members, and for the Official

Board to meet at least once a month, except during the months of July and August.[26]

While not opposed to easing the membership requirements for an auxiliary, Clay expressed the fear of the Insurgents when she wrote that admission of clubs of only fifty members would encourage the splintering of state associations. In many states this would divide the strength of suffragists and detract from their effectiveness.[27]

The second proposed amendment was even more objectionable. The requirement of monthly meetings, Laura Clay believed, would have "the effect of cutting off the election of any officers outside a restricted circle" extending from New York to Boston and Philadelphia.[28] Since the expense of bringing officers from New Orleans, Chicago, and elsewhere in the West and South to headquarters for monthly meetings would be prohibitive, candidates from the East would be the natural choices. Furthermore, since the amendment made five officers a quorum, the other two, even if elected from other sections, could miss the meetings and not affect the handling of business. They would, in effect, be "mere figureheads." The "main idea" of the changes, Clay asserted, was "to hand over the management of the National to a select few around New York; or at least in the East." "I have always stood for equal representation of all sections as far as practicable," she added, claiming that the new proposal would make the association a sectional rather than a national organization.[29]

Defenders of the proposal pointed out that the headquarters' officers needed more frequent and personal communication. The extended arguments carried on since the Washington convention had brought into question the adequacy of decision making via correspondence. Methods that had been satisfactory in the early days of the NAWSA were unsuitable as the organization's work became more sophisticated and its activities increased and broadened. The issues were being argued in the pages of the Woman's Journal as the two factions braced themselves for the expected confrontation at the Louisville convention.[30]

Attendance at the convention, including delegates and the general public, was so great that meetings had to be moved from DeMolay Hall to Macauley's Theater, the city's most spacious convention site. According to one newspaper, matters became heated as the convention began: "Lorgnettes were shaken as men would shake their fists, frigid stares were exchanged, velvet-toned but keenedged sarcasms danced about in the heated atmosphere as sun beams dance on water, opera glasses, looking like burlesques on double-barrelled shotguns, were leveled at the rostrum, and cheers rang out many times . . . . At twelve o'clock when wordy shot and shell were flying thickest . . . the reporter felt like a real war correspondent."[31]

Laura Clay quickly emerged as the floor leader of the southern and western faction, while M. Carey Thomas, president of Bryn Mawr College, assumed that role for the easterners. One clash occurred when Thomas secretly had a California delegate offer to establish a travel fund, provided by unnamed donors, for officers living outside New York, if the convention voted to accept the constitutional amendment calling for monthly officers' meetings. After a few questions were asked about the source of the travel fund, it was discovered that both the idea and the financial support for it came from Thomas, not the Californian. Clay secured the floor and denounced the offer as a thinly disguised attempt to bribe the convention into accepting the amendment. Hinting at similar conditional financial offers made earlier by Belmont, she concluded: "We would be unworthy suffragists to accept money with a string attached to it, and I wouldn't think so much of it, if it were the first time this kind of appropriation had been made to us." The encounter left Shaw "plainly rattled" and the usually suave Thomas "almost incapacitated from speaking by tears," while Clay appeared unruffled.[32]

Convention decisions are made by votes, not speeches, and the East plainly had a majority. The number of votes was based on state membership rolls rather than on the number of delegates present in the hall. New York was entitled to fifty-six votes and the College Suffrage League, which Thomas represented, qualified for twenty-six, making a total of eighty, although the two societies together had only twenty-one delegates present. Under this voting system, seven eastern states and the College League could decide any question which came before the convention.[33]

In light of these circumstances, the southern-western faction was probably fortunate in being able to water down the constitutional amendments. After an extended debate, the convention finally settled on bimonthly meetings, except July and August, rather than the number first proposed by headquarters. A compromise was also reached on the size of societies to be admitted to the association, when the convention agreed to a minimum of 300 members.[34]

In the election of officers, however, the southern-western faction was overwhelmed. The headquarters staff had begun, a month before the convention opened, to marshal forces to oppose any nominee offered by the Insurgents, while the latter group was handicapped by the unwillingness of prominent women from within its ranks to become candidates. Both McCulloch and Stewart, engrossed in work in Illinois and unhappy with the tension among members of the Official Board, had decided not to seek reelection. Gordon, about to embark on an extended vacation in Europe, was also unavailable. The only Insurgent willing to engage in unequal contest with the eastern group was Laura Clay, who was nominated for four different offices and decisively defeated in each instance.[35]

The method employed to administer the defeats was even more galling than the losses themselves. None of the four women chosen for office over Clay was present at the election, and among them only Harriet Burton Laidlaw, of New York, winner of the office of second auditor, knew that her name was going to be put in nomination. The other three were prominent people who were, without any knowledge of the plan to defeat the Insurgents, steamrollered through the convention by the powerful eastern faction.

While two of the new officers, Jane Addams and Sophonisba Breckinridge, were prominent in social work in Chicago, neither had sought NAWSA office, and both were surprised when informed of their election.[36] Upon learning that their names had been used to defeat Laura Clay, both offered to resign their posts if the Insurgents so desired.[37] Belle LaFollette of Wisconsin, who won over Clay in the balloting for the office of first auditor, had never done suffrage work, and there was some doubt whether she was a member of the association. At the insistence of a number of delegates, Shaw wired LaFollette to see if she would serve.[38]

The election of the three westerners was clever strategy on Thomas's part. It was difficult for the Insurgents' followers to criticize the selections, since the women were, after all, from the West and very prominent. If they should be unable to attend staff meetings or if they resigned, it would be to the advantage of the headquarters faction. Indeed, while the elections were under way, Anna E. Blount of Illinois had charged that the easterners were deliberately electing women who were so busy with other tasks that they would not be able to travel to New York regularly for officers' meetings. She pointed out that if the electees resigned, the Official Board, dominated by easterners, could elect more women from their section to fill the vacancies. LaFollette resigned her new office before the first of the year, and, as Blount predicted, the Official Board elected Susan W. Fitzgerald of Boston to fill the vacancy.[39] Even before Fitzgerald was added, the Shaw-Thomas forces had won a clear majority on the Official Board and could operate headquarters as they wished.

Since Clay and her sister Sallie Bennett had shared the expenses of the Official Board's lodging at the Hotel Seelbach in Louisville, the outcome of the convention could have been particularly irritating to them. If Laura Clay was displeased, she never let her feelings be known, and by her magnanimity and graciousness turned defeat into a personal triumph. In many ways, it was her finest hour as a suffragist, for never afterwards would so many people find so much to admire in her courage and character. McCulloch paid her an apt tribute: "The steam roller went over Laura Clay four times and she yet remains greater than the roller. Your magnanimity of spirit when you continued your constant helpfulness to Miss Shaw on convention business, your generous pledge, your alert attention to details no other board member remembers, all of this has won you friends among strangers and shamed many of the tools [of Shaw and Thomas]."[40]

Only a remarkable woman could have remained so charitable, dispassionate, and farsighted following humiliating defeats in her own home state. To her friends who criticized the convention, Laura Clay replied that it was "a magnificent success" because it had created so much suffrage interest in Kentucky. To those who talked of secession from the NAWSA, she wrote that a breach "between the East and the rest of the country" must be avoided. In regard to the candidates who had defeated her for office she wrote that the names of Addams, Breckinridge, and LaFollette "will confer great prestige on the Board and have a useful political effect in the states where constitutional amendments are pending." After learning of her own election, Breckinridge had wired McCulloch in anguish: "I don't see how it happened. I can't take Miss Clay's place. Help me do the right and loyal thing." Clay insisted that she would never suppose her to be "a party to anything which might be construed as a discourtesy or an unkindness." [41]

After more than fifteen years, Laura Clay's service as an officer had come to an end. Despite defeats in a number of state campaigns and unpleasant wrangles at headquarters, much good had been done during that period. The state of Washington had enfranchised its women in 1910, and the suffragists of both factions had been able to unite long enough at Louisville to applaud their recent victory in California. More important in the long run, suffrage sentiment was growing rapidly all across the country: newspapers were giving greater space than ever before to suffragists' rallies and conventions; socialites, as Belmont, Mackay, and Mrs. Quincy Shaw of Boston, were joining their names and fortunes to the cause; and it was becoming fashionable to be a suffragist. [42] The glamor of the movement was growing as parades, street-corner meetings and automobile tours became standard parts of the varied suffrage activities. Finally, the changing nature of American social and economic life was thrusting women into a wider range of responsibilities, which in turn led them to demand greater privileges. Suffrage was succeeding, often in the face of the indifference of a majority of women, and sometimes despite the errors, jealousies, and dissensions of the suffragists.

While dutifully accepting at Louisville the chairmanship of the NAWSA Membership Committee, Laura Clay did her principal work after 1911 at the state and sectional level. Turning, in her sixty-second year, to new tasks in her fight for woman's rights, she wrote encouragingly to an old comrade: "Because one clique has triumphed is no reason there is not plenty for all the others to do for the final great victory." [43]

VIII

PUTTING IN THE SICKLE

1912-1916

WHEN LAURA CLAY found time to take stock of the recent events at Louisville, she wrote a friend that she found "considerable consolation" in the convention's outcome. She admitted that her continued presence on the Official Board, following her recent clashes with Anna Howard Shaw, "would not have been without a nervous strain" and that her only suggestion for the association's financial problems would have been economy, "which there seemed to be no disposition to practice." So, she rationalized, perhaps her removal from authority was for the best, and others could take up the task of finding money to finance the policies that the board would determine. She also found comfort in the thought that the interests of southern suffragists, always one of her principal concerns, would now be looked after by Sophonisba Breckinridge, a native of Kentucky, who gave assurance of her willingness "to serve the cause in general and the South in particular" in whatever way Clay thought best. "Tell me," the new vice president wrote, "how Miss Addams and I can be of the most use." [1]

Clay was further reassured by a belief that "the disintegration of the N.A.W.S.A. would not seriously check the suffrage movement." The long years of work in the states had helped develop associations which, she believed, would see the suffragists through the final victory. So, while she counseled other suffrage leaders against "open contention and secession" from the NAWSA, she placed her hope in efforts within the individual states. [2]

At the same time, she was convinced that changes were needed in the leadership and methods of suffrage associations. "In these new and stirring days, the young people will think they must try their experiments," she wrote to another veteran of suffrage battles, "and I really suppose they are more in touch with some of the more recent aspects of the question." She believed that new leadership would move beyond the educational methods of older suffragists and prove to the country that woman suffrage was a question which could not be ignored. Older workers had placed the movement before the public; the younger ones could better convince politicians of the inevitability of woman suffrage and the expediency of action in its favor.[3]

In order to assure adoption of the changes she sought, Laura Clay prevailed on the 1911 convention of the Kentucky ERA, which immediately followed that of the NAWSA in Louisville, to amend its constitution. Thereafter, half of the officers, including the president, would not be eligible to succeed themselves in 1912, and all officers in the future would be limited to three consecutive terms. An officer could, however, switch to another post and thus serve beyond the three-year limit.[4]

With the constitution amended to her satisfaction, Clay's next task was to find a suitable replacement for herself as president. In Madeline McDowell (Mrs. Desha) Breckinridge, she found the ideal woman, who, however, was reluctant to take the job. Breckinridge, wife of the editor of the Lexington Herald, was the outstanding female civic leader in Lexington and in all respects one of the New South's best examples of progressivism.[5]

Breckinridge had made her mark in civic and philanthropic work before devoting her talents to the cause of woman's rights. In 1900 she had become a charter member of the Lexington Civic League, an organization dedicated to the general betterment of city life. She also was a founder and the first vice president of the Kentucky Association for the Prevention and Relief of Tuberculosis in 1909 and, with other members of her family, was instrumental in building the Blue Grass Sanatorium in Lexington. Because of frail health and her many activities, she was an uncertain choice as Laura Clay's successor in 1912, but in the end, she agreed to stand for the post. Like so many other women of her generation she had come to believe that the enfranchisement of members of her sex would make possible the improvements in education, public health, and child and woman labor that she so much desired.[6]

Breckinridge had not always been happy with the aid she had received from Clay and the ERA in civic improvement programs, and she had once voiced a strong complaint. "I have had the experience a number of times of being left virtually to hold the bag in cooperative work with her," she had written to Kate Gordon, "and as the Equal Rights Association is not going to help me hold the bag on any of the jobs I have already obligated myself for, I feel it is not only fair to myself but to them not to undertake more than it is possible for me to do in a new work." The charge was probably true. In her own reform work, Laura Clay subordinated all other activities to the full enfranchisement of women. As a consequence, she and other suffragists would often work for a reform only until they could get another woman's group to take up the effort; at which time, they would divert their energies to another feminist goal, while continuing their moral support of the first cause.[7]

A major difference in the careers of Clay and Breckinridge lay in the background of their commitment to woman suffrage. Clay had set out to right the legal and political wrongs of women, of which the denial of the ballot was the foremost. Once full suffrage was gained, she believed that other good would follow in due course. "Our cause does not touch the people's feeling," she noted, "because so few women realize the connection between the ballot and the rectifying of evils." Wary of distracting suffragists with resolutions on world peace, Sunday closing laws, or penal reform, she would sometimes vote against resolutions, not because she opposed their goals, but because she believed they would spread the suffragists too thin. "When the evil relates to women and children I am willing to incorporate it" into the suffragists' program, she asserted, but even then it must always be subordinate "to getting the ballot for women."[8]

Breckinridge, on the other hand, had grown up in an extremely close-knit family and in her early life was not impressed with the disadvantages of women. Although she was an avowed suffragist as early as 1904, she consented to take a leading part in the movement only after years of struggling, with partial success, to get politicians to vote the funds needed for her humanitarian projects. For her, woman suffrage was a necessary step in the eradication of social and economic evils, while for Clay the ballot was the most important goal in the winning of full equality for women. Other reforms would come as a natural consequence, but she was insistent that they wait their turn.

By the time Breckinridge was elected president of the ERA in November 1912, she had led Kentucky women to victory in their fight for school suffrage. The struggle to regain this right had gone on continually since 1902. In the sessions of 1908, 1910, and 1912, Breckinridge, as chairman of the legislative committee of the Kentucky Federation of Women's Clubs, had directed the effort in Frankfort. When the state Democratic party added a school suffrage plank to its platform in 1911, the desired measure was practically assured, since the Republicans had supported it in the 1910 session. Remembering the accusation that illiterate women had voted in greater numbers than literate ones in 1901, the women asked for and received school suffrage for only those of their sisters who could read and write.[9]

The only other victory won during the last part of Clay's tenure as ERA president had been the co-guardianship bill of 1910, which gave the mother and father of minor children coequal rights over them, leaving questions of their upbringing and disposition to the courts in case of separation or divorce. Prior to the passage of this law, drawn up by Judge A. R. Burnam and championed in the House by the suffragists' old enemy, William Klair, the father's legal claim to control of his children was undisputed in his lifetime and, through a will, could reach beyond the grave to designate a guardian for them after his death. Only the mothers of illegitimate children had unfettered legal claims to them. During the legislative session of 1910, Clay and Mary C. Cramer had made three trips to Frankfort to lobby for the guardianship law, which erased a longstanding blemish from Kentucky justice.[10]

Breckinridge's election to office began an exciting era in the history of the woman's rights movement in Kentucky. She was Kentucky's version of Carrie Chapman Catt: a good public speaker, an inspiring and innovative leader, and a skilled administrator. Clay was correct when she wrote, "now that our question has become political she can carry on the work better than I can, and success is what we are working for." Interest in suffrage grew rapidly. Mrs. S. M. Hubbard of Hickman, a suffragist of Laura Clay's generation, inaugurated the day of large ERA budgets in Kentucky by donating $1,000. "I scarcely know whether I am hovering near sixteen or sixty-five," she wrote, after the school suffrage victory.[11] With more money available and imaginative leadership to use it, several innovations were quickly made.

Early in 1913 the Kentucky ERA hired Urey L. Estes of Chicago as its first full-time field secretary and opened its first headquarters in Lexington. Most of Estes's time was spent in filling speaking engagements and organizing new suffrage clubs. The efficacy of the new program was quickly apparent in the growth of membership, which rose from 1,779 to 4,655 persons in Breckinridge's first year as president. At the end of the following year, the membership had climbed to 10,577, representing all but one of the state's 120 counties. Growth was particularly spectacular in Louisville where suffrage sentiment had never before been very great. Building on the interest created there by the NAWSA convention in 1911, Louisvillians were anticipating a membership of 5,000 by the end of 1913. In Lexington, where the suffragists had always been strong, a house-to-house canvass was conducted in the search for new members.[12]

Announcing that there was "no reason we should make a funeral of it," Breckinridge made suffrage campaigning interesting and entertaining. The suffragists of Louisville had done their part to get the movement out of parlor, courthouse, and church meeting places and into the public's eye by participating in a parade through the downtown in 1913. Coming only two years after the first suffrage parade in the country marched down Fifth Avenue in New York, it marked the first time southern suffragists had participated in such an event.[13]

Breckinridge was quick to try new methods. She encouraged hiking for suffrage as well as automobile trips with the suffragists' traditional "yellow banners flying." Urging her followers to "get all the fun out of the thing there is in it," she suggested that they hike along the Cincinnati-Southern Railroad from Covington to Lexington, stopping in small towns, where suffrage was seldom heard, long enough to make talks and hand out pamphlets. "The railroads," she explained, "could take tired ones home and bring fresh ones to take their places." She sent her compliments to a Covington suffragist who was speaking for the cause between vaudeville acts at the Colonial Theatre and who had arranged for the display of a parade of suffrage dolls in department stores there and in Cincinnati.[14]

After the new campaign techniques were employed in the summer of 1913, Laura Clay expressed reservations about them. "I want again to warn you," she wrote Breckinridge, "that in my going about I find parades, 'hikes,' etc. are not popular with the main body of the people. I am afraid the suffragists are doing too much of those things to please the judgment of the plain people, who are largely in the majority, and whose votes will decide our question." This was an area in which trends had passed Clay by: these tactics gained public attention, and the majority of the suffragists, as her friend Kate Gordon admitted, found them "exhilarating experiences."[15]

Laura Clay's participation in more orthodox suffrage activities continued. Upon leaving the presidency of the ERA, she was elected corresponding secretary and thereupon became Breckinridge's trusted and dutiful lieutenant, careful not to invade Breckinridge's authority and deftly deferring to her when correspondents forgot that she was no longer president of the ERA. When someone was needed to update an information brochure, to pick up a responsibility that another officer had not carried out, or to give counsel, Breckinridge turned most often to Clay.[16]

Despite her sixty-four years, Laura Clay worked harder and with better direction within Kentucky than she had at any time during the fifteen years she was a national officer. With the proud claim that she was accustomed to speaking "three or four times a day," she undertook tours in the spring and fall of 1913. Depending upon the town and the temper of the people, she would appear as an officer of the WCTU, the Kentucky Federation of Women's Clubs, or the ERA, as the situation demanded. Regardless of the sponsoring body, her subject in the twenty-eight places she visited was always the same—woman suffrage—and she organized leagues and gathered names as she went. It was not unusual for her addresses to last ninety minutes, and reportedly she could hold "the close attention of the audience" for the entire time. By early September she was writing, "I am perfectly overwhelmed with work and hot weather."[17]

On the fall tour, both she and Breckinridge directed their efforts toward the teacher education institutes which were held in the county seats. Breckinridge's method of organizing suffrage leagues at these meetings was a combination of audacity and finesse. After some of those present had signed the ERA's non-dues-paying membership cards, she advised Clay to "simply state that a league will be formed, and ask for a motion that one shall be formed. It is usually best to get someone beforehand to promise to make the motion. Then I say that until such a time as the organization is completed and officers elected I will appoint a County Chairman. Then I circulate and take up the membership cards. Of course, you have to have the permission of the County Superintendent, who is the boss of the institute to do this, but I find if you just assume that you can get it, it is usually granted."[18] This method avoided the risk that the organizer would have to leave with only a few membership cards and no local person to whom to send literature and prod into further activity.

Some of the newly formed organizations had little more than a paper existence and, as corresponding secretary, Laura Clay was expected to stay in touch with them and inquire about their progress. Some of her letters to local workers drew unenthusiastic replies, as the following from Tompkinsville. "Madam, yours of the 4th inst. to hand and in answer to same I will say I have done nothing except hand out a few papers sent to me. I am a lawyer and am trying to make a living. I have no time to work at your business as I have told you once before . . . . I am for woman suffrage but that don't make a living for me. I am police judge for our city and my duty there and my law practice keeps [sic] me busy." Clay assured her correspondent that she only wanted him to name a new chairman from the thirty-nine members of the ERA in his town. A woman in Harlan County reported that, aside from distributing literature, she had been too busy to do anything: "I am now Superintendent of Sunday School, Guardian of Camp Fire Girls, Vice-President of the County W.C.T.U., Secretary of the

Ladies League, and teach nine month [sic] in [the] year. result [sic] nervous breakdown and am banished to the country by [the] doctor. I am greatly interested in woman suffrage but hope you can find a more worthy chairman." Responding that she and the other officers were "also in a hard place," Laura Clay requested the woman not only to retain the chairmanship but also to suggest ways to gain subscribers for the *Woman's Journal* as well.[19]

During Breckinridge's first three years as their president, Kentucky women suffered many frustrations and a few defeats, which, however, were eclipsed by their victories and the amazing growth of their organization. Defeat came at the hands of the politicians in 1914, when a bill for full suffrage failed to come to a vote in the legislature and, in the following year, when the Democrats refused in their state platform to support a woman suffrage referendum. Politicians also gave some cause for optimism. According to Breckinridge, the most important accomplishment of 1915 was the Republicans' acceptance of a suffrage plank in their state platform. Similar planks were also secured from the Prohibitionist, the Socialist, and the Progressive parties.[20]

"There is no reform in Kentucky more popular than woman suffrage," Laura Clay boasted in 1915. The Kentucky Federation of Women's Clubs, representing some 1,700 women, along with the Grange, the WCTU, and the state AF of L gave their full endorsement to the movement. All the clergy of the state, Protestant, Catholic, and Jewish, were asked to preach one sermon in behalf of woman suffrage and to use their moral influence for the cause. Many sent encouraging replies and some asked for additional literature. Most encouraging was the growth of suffragists in numbers and the increase in their activities. Membership rose from 1,799 in 1912 to 15,557 in 1915, and the number of delegates attending the state convention increased from thirty-eight in 1913 to 100 in 1915. Prizes for oratorical and essay contests created interest among young people in the state's colleges and universities, while legislators and newspapers were subjected to a barrage of news material.[21]

As Kentucky suffragists gathered for the ERA convention at Lexington in November 1915, their prospects were bright. Growing in numbers and gaining in public favor, they planned a vigorous campaign for full suffrage in 1916. Since the constitutional limitation kept Breckinridge and Clay from serving again in their respective posts, both accepted election to new positions. Breckinridge, who was replaced as president by Elizabeth ("Elise") Smith, a daughter of Sallie Clay Bennett, was chosen legislative chairman, to direct the effort at Frankfort, and Laura Clay became the ERA's representative on the executive committee of the NAWSA. Both offices afforded their holders votes on the ERA's executive committee.[22]

During even her most active periods of work in her own state, Laura Clay was never unmindful of suffrage developments elsewhere. Despite her defeats in the 1911 elections, she had continued to cooperate with the NAWSA and remained one of the most popular suffrage lecturers in the country. For two years following her expulsion from the Official Board, she served as the chairman of the NAWSA Membership Committee, working closely with some of the officers who had defeated her in 1911. Much of the work of this committee was routine, but it required a considerable amount of correspondence on her part. During the first year alone, sixteen organizations, representing at least 55,000 women, joined the NAWSA.[23]

One interesting case in her work arose when the Pennsylvania Limited Suffrage League applied for membership. In an effort to exclude "the criminal and illiterate of both sexes" from the ballot box, this society had written tax and educational qualifications into its constitution. Clay led the committee in rejecting the application. While noting that she had "no objection to an educational qualification where states provide public education," she asserted that tax qualifications were against her principles.[24]

Before the federal amendment captured most of the suffragists' attention, Laura Clay continued to aid various state organizations. She seldom refused her services, working from two to six weeks in Ohio and Kansas in 1912, Michigan and Wisconsin in 1913, West Virginia in 1915, Iowa in 1916, and Rhode Island and New York in 1917.[25] In addition to these campaigns, where it was her habit to contribute her own expenses as well as a generous donation, she was a principal speaker at eight state conventions between 1913 and 1917.

In the spring of 1912 she spent more than a month in Ohio, speaking in about twenty towns as she worked her way across the southern half of the state. When a clerical error gave her more appearances than she had agreed to make, she filled all the engagements. Commenting on Laura Clay's perseverance, Harriet Taylor Upton wrote: "you once told me . . . a bull dog did not let go . . . because it could not let go and I suppose that was the reason you were hanging on to the last town." Preparing herself for the defeat that came in the fall, Clay reasoned, "If we win, I shall always feel proud that I had a share in it. If we lose, I shall anyway rejoice that we made a good fight."[26]

By the time the news of the Ohio defeat reached her in September 1912, she was already campaigning in Kansas, where she traveled more than a thousand miles by automobile and spoke more than one hundred times, much of the time in more rain than Kansas had experienced in twenty-six years. Her health and stamina were amazing for a woman in her mid-sixties. She found the automobile, used for the first time in her campaigns, a very useful means of getting to the people and was impressed with the use Kansas made of the telephone. A call ahead to the telephone operator in a town of 300, she claimed, would often produce a crowd of 600 by the time the suffragists arrived. When the woman suffrage amendment to the Kansas constitution carried by 175,246 to 159,197 votes on November 5, it was the first time Laura Clay had participated directly in a full suffrage victory.[27]

Her message over the years had changed little. She tended to use the argument of expediency—that suffrage was practical, both for the political parties and the good of the country—more often than the argument of justice—that suffrage was right and women deserved it on legal, moral, and religious grounds. But the Progressive Movement and the outbreak of war in Europe combined to produce variations in her suffrage speeches.

The influence of the Progressive Movement was evident in her lecture "Woman Suffrage and the Home," in which she excoriated the government for paying "more attention to the care of colts and calves than to its children." The Department of Agriculture, she charged, spent $3 million annually to investigate the diseases of pigs, while the Children's Bureau, which women worked years to establish, had to beg for its appropriation of $30,000. Sanitary sewage systems, pure water, safe canned food, and the abolition of child labor were among the reforms that woman suffrage could be expected to help effect.[28]

Soon after the outbreak of the First World War, Laura Clay joined the Woman's Peace party, which had been founded by Jane Addams and others early in 1915, She was appointed party chairman in the Seventh Congressional District of Kentucky and spoke to the state Federation of Women's Clubs on "Peace" in May 1915. Attacking the forces of "imperialism, militarism, and commercialism," upon which she blamed the war, she rebuked those who were preaching military preparedness. The "stricken humanity" of Europe was a result of the preparation for war; America must prepare for peace. To prevent such conflicts in the future and to guard America's sanctity, she advocated "the substitution of law for war in the affairs of nations" and the "humanizing of government." Believing that woman's voice would bring "justice and reason" to the front in international affairs, she urged the early enactment of woman suffrage.[29] From 1915 until early 1917 she gave this speech often, always stressing that woman suffrage was the keystone of the Woman's Peace party.

After Germany announced the resumption of unrestricted submarine warfare in January 1917, although "not much good at sewing," she joined the Fayette County Red Cross Society and helped make hospital supplies, which were to be given to the government or to the Allies if America remained neutral. As President Wilson took a stronger line, she supported him and disagreed with the Woman's Peace party's call for a referendum on war, because "the constitution says plainly that the Senate and President alone have the power to declare it."[30]

Soon she was wrestling with the problem of pacifism versus patriotism amid a growing war hysteria. The proposed referendum, she wrote, related to one question she could not put to a popular vote, "when I know that so many of our so-called citizens are more interested in some foreign country than in our own." Her own patriotism came under attack when she innocently used the old suffragist argument that it was a strange thing that citizenship was taught in the public schools of America by those deprived of its benefits. What was earlier a harmless point to seal an argument for woman suffrage was fast becoming an attack on the country in 1917.[31]

When the United States declared war on April 6, Laura Clay, like most of the members of the Woman's Peace party, entered wholeheartedly into the war effort. While continuing to profess pacifism, she stated that she had never "thought war as great an evil as surrender of national rights and national independence." Believing that the Woman's Peace party was no longer guided "at all times by a clear-cut American policy," she asked that her name be dropped from its membership roll.[32] Her growing concern about enemies and aliens in the United States not only mirrored the times but was also a contributing factor to her own attitudes in the final months of the drive for woman suffrage. Her reactions as the country's mood changed from neutrality to war indicate that her pacifism was shallow and suggest that civil liberties in wartime were not part of her reform program.

Until 1916 it appeared that the woman suffrage movement would continue in the direction it had followed for twelve years, though at an accelerated rate of speed. Hard-fought campaigns would be waged at the state level, victories would more frequently relieve the long list of defeats, and the NAWSA would continue to serve more symbolically than factually as the coordinator of its many state auxiliaries. Under Anna Howard Shaw's leadership, the suffragists were like a body without a head. Dissension among the leaders had persisted after 1911, and dissatisfaction with Shaw had grown.[33]

In light of these circumstances at the national level, it is not surprising that the suffrage movement spawned two new organizations in the last years of Shaw's administration. Ironically, both started as protest movements against the NAWSA's attitude toward the federal suffrage amendment: the Congressional Union (CU), because its members believed the NAWSA was giving too little attention to the amendment; and the Southern States Woman Suffrage Conference (SSWSC), because it feared the NAWSA was giving it too much.

The CU, later renamed the Woman's party, is best remembered as the semimilitant branch of American feminism. Its members

were called "suffragettes," and they are the only part of the movement which can correctly be given that title. The CU was founded
late in 1913 by Alice Paul and Lucy Burns, who were unhappy in
the NAWSA because they thought it was giving too little effort
to securing the Anthony or federal woman suffrage amendment.
Their plan called for a complete abandonment of state campaigns
and total concentration on Congress to force the adoption of a
woman suffrage amendment. It was this group that attempted to
defeat representatives of "the party in power," from president
through the Congress, in 1914 and 1916, copying a tactic employed
by the Pankhursts in England. Mrs. Oliver H. P. Belmont, who
had recently been Shaw's benefactor, became an officer of the CU
and its main financial support, when it was refused affiliation with
the NAWSA and went its separate way in 1914.[34]

The SSWSC was the creation of Kate Gordon of New Orleans,
one of the best known southern suffragists and a narrow states'
rights advocate. Her opposition to the federal amendment was
long-standing and consistent. She had resigned as the corresponding secretary of the NAWSA in 1909, because of her opposition
to Catt's Great Petition, which asked Congress for federal suffrage
legislation, and, as early as 1912, she was trying to organize a southern suffrage association. She redoubled her efforts during the next
year when she began to fear that the rise of the CU was about to
capture suffrage interest for the federal amendment.[35]

Laura Clay was lukewarm toward a sectional suffrage society.
She had never shared Gordon's fear of the federal amendment;
indeed, she had loyally worked hard at the task of gathering signatures for the Great Petition in Kentucky. Later, at the Mississippi
Valley Suffrage Conference in 1913, she suggested a resolution
asking President Wilson to incorporate woman suffrage in his
annual message to Congress. In her opinion, work for the federal
amendment was useful "agitation" to gain publicity but was nothing more, since the southern states would block its ratification even
in the unlikely event that Congress passed it. As a consequence,
there was no need to worry about the amendment unless the
NAWSA gave it so much attention that suffragists were diverted
from more practical work in the states. In short, she never believed that the situation which she faced in 1919 would come

about: accepting the federal amendment or opposing her own enfranchisement. In the meantime, her position down to 1919 was that, although "it would be a misfortune to have suffrage come by a Federal Amendment," she "would rather it should come that way than not at all."[36]

In November 1913 representatives from eight states met in New Orleans to discuss Gordon's ideas and there decided to form the SSWSC. Although Laura Clay was not present, she was elected vice-president-at-large of the new organization, having declined to consider its presidency. The announced purpose of the SSWSC was to aid the NAWSA as a "flank movement" in the drive for woman suffrage. Most of the women at New Orleans wanted to make it clear that the new organization was not a rival of the NAWSA, nor was its purpose exclusively for states' rights. Kate Gordon was, despite some protestations to the contrary, the leading advocate of a purely states' rights position. Her continuing insistence on this point and her enmity toward the federal amendment later drove some prominent southern suffragists from the SSWSC. No figures are available on its membership, but the SSWSC continued in existence until suffrage was won in 1920, although it was little more than a paper organization after May 1917. Its most active period was from October 1914, when the first issue of its monthly publication, New Southern Citizen, appeared, through the Democratic national convention of 1916, when it claimed that its goal had been achieved: a states' rights woman suffrage plank in the platform.[37] The last issue of its publication came in May 1917, after which time the magazine quietly folded.

The money for financing the operations of the SSWSC, which cost $6,000 per year, came from a secret donor, whose identity would have surprised the country's suffragists. Until early April 1914, Gordon was frantically searching for funds, but her efforts had accumulated only $4,000 in donations and pledges. On April 8 she sent Laura Clay a piece of correspondence which had rendered her "numb for several days." After telling Clay to read it, if she could keep a secret, Gordon asked her to write the donor, Belmont, a letter of appreciation for the $10,000 gift to the SSWSC. This large donation (the same person had given $1,000 earlier) was not made public until after the demise of the SSWSC. This secrecy left Gordon in a quandary in regard to paying herself a salary out of the treasury. Ordinarily that question would have been decided by the SSWSC officers, she wrote, "if I was at liberty to say we had the $10,000, . . . but Mrs. Belmont seems very positive about not having this known."[38]

It is strange that Belmont was at one time the great patroness of both the CU, which was bending every effort toward the federal amendment, and the SSWSC, whose president stood for a dogmatic states' rights policy. And it is revealing of the Progressive mind that the same Belmont, known for her philanthropy in behalf of Negroes in New York, wrote Laura Clay in regard to the SSWSC that she "fully understood the necessity for 'eternal vigilance' [on the race problem] in the southern suffrage movement."[39]

Gordon continued to clash with some other members of the SSWSC over the objectives of the organization. Most of her opponents were willing to admit that state action was preferred, but they were not willing to forgo opportunities for enfranchisement at the federal level. During the annual convention of the SSWSC at Chattanooga in November 1914, a majority of the delegates, including Clay, defeated Gordon's attempt to put the organization on record for exclusively states' rights action. Clay tried to dissuade her from entering into a controversy with the NAWSA over its activities in the South, which Gordon took to be her own special domain, and to impress upon her the need for some work on the federal level. Laura Clay's argument was that southern women were going to do some sort of federal work, whether Kate Gordon liked it or not, and should be guided toward efforts which would not be antagonistic to states' rights. To meet the problem she recommended that the SSWSC work for a bill which she proposed, a measure that would provide a goal at the national level and at the same time not be antagonistic to states' rights.[40]

Clay's bill was a variation of a proposal which her sister Sallie Clay Bennett had been sending to the Congress since the 1890s. Citing the Fourteenth Amendment, Bennett maintained that Congress had the power to give women the vote in congressional and presidential elections. Although she had been at first the butt of some ridicule among suffragists, by the second decade of the century her ideas had become the subject of serious consideration among suffragists and a few congressmen.[41]

Laura Clay had been slow to take up her sister's cause. She seems to have first given the matter serious consideration in 1911, when Sallie Bennett sent a memorial to Congress asking it to include women in the proposed amendment for the direct election of senators. By 1913 Clay considered federal suffrage as an alternative to the federal amendment and in 1914 drew up her own proposal, the United States Elections bill, which differed from her sister's in basing its justification on the Preamble and Article I, section 2, of the Constitution and in claiming the franchise in congressional elections only. Clay argued that "the people" of the Preamble were the same "people," women and men, of Article I, section 2, who were designated to choose members of the House and (after the Seventeenth Amendment) of the Senate.[42]

There was some hope for the United States Elections bill during 1914 and 1915, the last two years of the Shaw administration, when the affairs of the NAWSA were in an especially muddled state. With the CU from the one side demanding that the NAWSA devote all its efforts to the federal amendment and Kate Gordon and other states' righters, from the other, claiming that southern opposition made such a course impossible, the national organization was ready to consider alternatives. Laura Clay believed that her bill was a compromise option on which all suffragists could unite. States' rights supporters should find it acceptable, because it dealt only with federal elections and left the qualifications for voters, aside from sex, in the hands of the states. With the political leverage won in congressional elections, women could soon obtain state amendments that would extend suffrage in all other elections, "with such qualifications and restrictions as sectional problems might seem to demand." An added advantage of her proposal, as she pointed out to Gordon, was that it would hold southern suffragists loyal to the SSWSC by giving them work to pursue in the "imposing . . . arena" at Washington.[43]

The United States Elections bill should appeal to the supporters of federal legislation, Laura Clay believed, because it offered a quicker route to enfranchisement than the Anthony amendment.

She saw the way to the latter as long and hazardous, even imagining that no state would ratify it unless it already had woman suffrage. The great stumbling block was the South. "I have no expectations that the Susan B. Anthony amendment will ever assist our cause," Clay wrote in 1916; "Congress may submit it to get rid of them [the suffragists] but the difficulties of ratification are insuperable." Her belief is more understandable when one remembers that many statesmen, including President Wilson and Senator William E. Borah, saw suffrage as a states' right. Later Wilson began to support the federal amendment under the pressure of a growing female constituency; but Borah, who supported the reform and represented an equal suffrage state, did not. Borah declared that it was impossible to get the vote for women by a federal amendment, because the issue "was loaded down with the Negro, Japanese and a dozen other States' Rights Problems."[44]

With endorsements of her bill from both the conventions of the SSWSC and the NAWSA, Clay spent the early part of 1916 lobbying for it in Washington. Aided by Ida Husted Harper, she interviewed a number of congressmen about their general attitudes on suffrage and her bill in particular. Senator Robert L. Owen, an old acquaintance from the Oklahoma campaign, introduced the measure on February 3. It was referred to the Committee on Privileges and Elections, and never emerged.[45]

The United States Elections bill was never popular among suffragists. The NAWSA never threw its political strength behind it. Carrie Chapman Catt had become president of the NAWSA just before the effort was made to influence Congress, and her grand design for winning woman suffrage did not include the United States Election bill. Moreover, like the Shafroth amendment, it was a halfway measure which did not excite the imaginations of the suffragists, as even Clay had to admit. Although she continued to agitate for the bill, and Catt, in a generous, though meaningless, gesture, had the convention of 1916 endorse it, as well as the Bennett bill, federal suffrage was a dead issue.[46] For all practical purposes, Catt and the NAWSA leadership had assigned it, like the Shafroth amendment, to the limbo of lost suffrage causes. With Catt at the helm, all efforts of the national organization were turned to winning the federal amendment in 1916.

IX

A QUESTIONABLE VICTORY

1916-1920

SPEAKING TO THE forty-eighth annual convention of the NAWSA at Atlantic City in 1916, President Wilson gave the suffragists great hope that their long struggle would soon be over. He reiterated his support of woman suffrage and, more importantly, indicated that he was no longer opposed to federal legislation as a method of achieving it: "I get a little impatient sometimes about the discussion of the channels and methods by which it is to prevail. It is going to prevail . . . . We feel the tide; we rejoice in the strength of it, and we shall not quarrel in the long run as to the method of it."

Wilson undoubtedly spoke the sentiments of the vast majority of suffragists and realized that his words would receive the approbation of the Progressive Movement which had engulfed the country. To win another term, the president knew that his minority party must win, even at the risk of some unhappy rumbling from the South, a good share of the northern and western votes, which had gone to the Progressive party in 1912. The declaration was in keeping with the transition occurring in Wilson's thinking, for during the last months of his first term he had become convinced that the federal government had to play a more active role in effecting reforms. This shift from the program of the New Freedom to that of the New Nationalism was prompted in part by the knowledge that he faced defeat in the upcoming presidential election unless he came out wholeheartedly for reform. The Democratic party platform, written by Wilson and adopted only two months earlier in Saint Louis, embodied the objectives of advanced progressivism, including woman suffrage.[1] Since the plank recommended extension of suffrage by the states, it was a disappointment to the NAWSA's leadership, but at Atlantic City the president made clear that the means of achieving the reform were not vital considerations to him.

The suffragists had other reasons to take heart. A few months earlier they had regained, in the person of Carrie Chapman Catt, a leader who had both a plan for winning suffrage and the financial support to wage the campaign. Catt intended to undertake simultaneous efforts in the states and in Congress. Campaigns would be waged in order to increase the number of congressmen from woman suffrage states; at the same time pressure would be maintained at Washington to force the passage of the federal woman suffrage amendment.[2] Although no plan and no leader could have united all factions of the suffrage movement, Catt, who possessed an abundance of skill, tact, and patience, came as close to bringing the suffragists together as was humanly possible.

Catt also had the financial means to carry out her plan. In 1914 Mrs. Frank Leslie, heiress of a publishing house fortune, left about two million dollars to the cause of woman suffrage, designating Catt as the sole legatee. Although the legacy would not be immediately available, its very promise gave Catt, who was well-to-do in her own right, a power and financial independence that no NAWSA leader before her had enjoyed. In the meantime the delegates at Atlantic City proved they were willing to finance their own enfranchisement by pledging $800,000 to the cause.[3]

The great wars of the twentieth century have accelerated changes in the traditional role of women, as the First World War graphically demonstrates. Although it had not reached America in the summer of 1916, no one could ignore the part women were playing in the conflict in Europe. Their work in factories and hospitals, on farms and police forces, and with army auxiliaries was proving to the world that they could perform many of the traditional tasks of men. As the service and sacrifices of women mounted, opposition to their full citizenship melted. Great Britain and Canada granted partial suffrage while the war was still going on. Could America do less for her women? The question became even harder to answer negatively after April 6, 1917. The war was "the chance of a lifetime" and Catt quickly seized it.[4]

Laura Clay eventually set herself against a rejuvenated NAWSA, a growing support of its goals among politicians, and the social and economic changes of the war which were pushing the country toward an early and full acceptance of woman suffrage. In the first half of this last period of her suffrage activity, she remained loyal to the mainstream of the movement. Catt's plan allowed for state work, and Clay put her hand to it with a willing heart, contributing to the important victories in Rhode Island and New York during 1917. But as a sufficient number of states were won to make passage of the federal amendment a possibility, the emphasis of the movement shifted first to Washington and then to the struggle for ratification. In effect, this put Clay, a states' right suffragist, and the vast majority of her old comrades on a collision course.

The Kentucky ERA had continued to grow in the year after Madeline Breckinridge relinquished the presidency. Its only disappointment in 1916 was the failure of the state legislature to pass the association's bill for full suffrage. Even here there was hope because the Republicans had backed the bill solidly; it had passed the senate with the required two-thirds majority, and only the opposition of Governor A. O. Stanley had kept it in committee in the house.[5]

The setback did not dampen the enthusiasm for the movement or slow its numerical and financial growth. Increasing public endorsement was evident at Lexington where "the biggest suffrage parade ever held in Kentucky" was staged in May. By the end of 1916, some 19,590 Kentuckians were registered as suffragists and over $5,000 was spent in support of the movement. The Kentucky suffragists had come a long way since 1903, when they numbered 248 persons and operated on a budget of $359.[6]

As Kentuckians optimistically looked forward to 1917, there were evidences that Laura Clay's influence was waning in the ERA, which was leaning toward acceptance of the Catt plan and the accompanying direction of the NAWSA. Led by Christine Bradley South, who had been elected to fill the unexpired term of Mrs. Thomas Jefferson Smith, the new board had a strong Louisville and Republican flavor. South and three other officers were Republicans and, along with a majority of the association, did not share Clay's aversion to the federal amendment. Nonetheless, Laura Clay had voted for these officers, as she said, "cheer-fully, believing that their good sense and understanding of the situation in Kentucky will prevent them taking any steps that will give our enemies a political advantage."[7]

The allegiance of these new leaders was a crucial factor in de-termining the course of the ERA in the months that lay ahead. When Catt expressed the fear that a state campaign in Kentucky would be a mistake, the association was torn between following her plan or the state work advocated by Clay. If it opted for the latter course, as Catt made clear, it would be without the blessing or the financial support of the NAWSA.[8]

During much of 1917 Kentucky suffragists were occupied in war work. Laura Clay, still very active at sixty-eight, was no ex-ception. Her backyard at Second and Mill streets in Lexington was plowed up and made into an "emergency garden." "We are all imbued with the food conservation idea," she wrote to Rhode Island friends, challenging them to a contest to see who could grow the most vegetables.[9]

In addition to patriotic work on farms and in factories, the Kentucky suffragists raised over $1,000 for the Overseas Hospital, which was sponsored by the NAWSA. Behind the leadership of Mrs. E. L. Hutchinson of Lexington, money was raised to buy an ambulance, which was named in honor of Laura Clay and turned over to the Red Cross.[10] As events were soon to prove, the suffrag-ists were more willing to honor Clay than to follow her in a 1918 campaign.

All seemed well between Laura Clay and her colleagues at the outset of 1918, since the ERA convention had recently voted to work at Frankfort for the submission of a state woman suffrage amendment. Hardly had the decision been made, however, when the NAWSA asked the Kentuckians to abandon their plans.[11] The national organization's request was in keeping with its plan to concentrate all efforts on a few state campaigns where there was the greatest probability of winning.

Carrie Chapman Catt had gone to some lengths to explain to Clay the reasons why this NAWSA policy was necessary. First, she claimed that "frauds and irregularities" in the voting were common in state referendums. Such practices had recently cost the suffragists victories in West Virginia, Iowa, and South Dakota, she asserted, and would be "rampant in a whisky state like Kentucky," making a favorable outcome impossible. Furthermore, she asserted that in a number of states enemies of woman suffrage were planning to submit the question to the people, without the concurrence of the suffragists, with the purpose of working for the amendment's defeat and thereby discrediting the suffragists' claim of public support. Finally, she argued that the ERA could expect no outside help, since the NAWSA had all the commitments to state campaigns it could handle.[12]

The most helpful role the ERA could play, according to Catt, was to await congressional submission of the federal amendment and then throw all resources into the ratification effort. When President Wilson, himself a onetime states' rights suffragist, came out for submission of the amendment, Laura Clay was won over. "It is futile for me to hold out opposition on account of States' Rights," she wrote, "when a great statesman and head of the Democratic party contends that it is not an infringement of States' Rights."[13]

On January 10, 1918, the day after Wilson's endorsement, the House of Representatives gave the woman suffrage bill the necessary two-thirds vote. Even though early Senate approval seemed possible, Clay still insisted on working for a state bill, in case the amendment was defeated. This would give Kentucky women two chances for their enfranchisement and would be creating sentiment for the cause at the same time.[14]

She believed that there was little chance for defeat in the Democratically controlled state legislature because the major parties were vying for the credit of passing woman suffrage. If it came in a federal amendment, she thought that the reward would belong to the Republicans, whom she regarded as the advocates of federal legislation; if the states extended it, then credit and votes would belong to the Democrats, the party of states' rights. She was illogically obsessed with this idea, even after a number of prominent Democrats, including Wilson and seven of Kentucky's eleven congressmen, had switched to support of the federal amendment. "The success of the Federal Amendment will be a great Republican victory," she maintained, "and if woman suffrage proves as potent a factor in politics as Negro suffrage, such a result will mean the defeat nationally of the Democratic party for a generation." She could not believe that the Democrats, "having the game" [chance for state action rather than federal amendment] were going "to give it away to the Republicans in this obvious way." Clay was right in believing that both parties were then anxiously jockeying "for the expected advantage of women's support," but she was wrong in thinking that the method of enfranchisement would be a decisive partisan issue.[15]

Despite Clay's earnest pleading, the executive board of the ERA refused to lobby for a state woman suffrage amendment in 1918. Only one other member supported her position. Aside from the desire to cooperate with Catt, the board was prompted by the information that Governor Stanley, a known anti-suffragist, was behind the suffrage bill which had been introduced in Frankfort.[16] This information seemed to bear out Catt's contention that the antis were trying to inaugurate numerous ill-prepared state referendums to embarrass the suffragists and thwart the progress of the federal amendment.

When the Kentucky legislature adjourned, the federal amendment was still tied up in the Senate. Not only had the Kentucky suffragists lost the chance to act on the federal bill, they were too late to do anything about a state campaign. Laura Clay was understandably vexed. There were, as she pointed out, sound reasons for seeking the state bill: 1) there was a chance that the federal amendment would never be passed and ratified; 2) the state bill might enfranchise women before the federal amendment could complete its tortuous route through Congress and the states; and 3) even if the federal amendment were ratified, the word male would remain in Kentucky's constitution, a standing reminder to women that their enfranchisement came from without rather than by the men of their own state. Clay and a few other suffragists believed that their state had been made a sacrifice to NAWSA policy, and they resented it strongly. When she heard that Kate Gordon and the Louisiana suffragists had secured the submission of a state suffrage bill without help from the NAWSA, her belief that the Kentuckians had made a serious mistake was reinforced.[17]

She also was soon regretting her brief acceptance of the federal amendment. By the time Carrie Chapman Catt came to Lexington to deliver a speech in June 1918, Clay could no longer give silent support to the federal bill. She cast the only negative vote on a resolution asking the Kentucky senators to support and vote for its passage, declaring that she intended to keep up her "open opposition hereafter." She was temporarily persuaded from this design when a local editor asked her not to submit letters to the paper opposing the amendment, pleading that they would aid the antis and that his war-depleted staff could handle no more work.[18]

The breach that was developing between Laura Clay and the national leadership resulted partly from her belief that the NAWSA was "systematically suppressing" all work other than that for the federal amendment. She was annoyed that the chance for work in the state legislature had come and gone and that the NAWSA, despite its fruitless wait for action by the United States Senate, was no closer to abandoning the federal amendment than it had been when Wilson endorsed it at the beginning of the year. Clay's conviction that the NAWSA was departing from its constitutional obligation to work for both state and federal legislation and her disappointment at Catt's indifference to the possibilities of the United States Elections bill were laying the basis for her dislike, perhaps jealousy, of Catt.[19] The national president's power to direct the sentiment of Kentucky suffragists, long Clay's personal prerogative, must have been a bitter realization for the Kentuckian.

Despite her personal feelings, Laura Clay hoped to remain with the Kentucky ERA, realizing that a break in the ranks would imperil the suffrage movement in the state. Even so she was on the verge of resigning from the organization in October 1918, when the Kentucky suffragists threatened Senate candidate A. O. Stanley with public censure if he did not announce his support of the federal amendment. Clay termed this a partisan action, since a negative answer could help Stanley's Republican opponent. The resignation, which she had actually submitted, was withdrawn when Stanley's compliance made it possible for the suffragists to avoid any public action and thus conceal Laura Clay's minority viewpoint. The board of officers unanimously urged Clay to return to her place in the organization.[20]

Undeterred by the news that the Louisiana suffragists had lost the campaign which Kate Gordon expected to be a "walkover," Clay again tried to win the ERA to support a state bill in 1919. She hoped that the failure of the Senate to pass the federal amendment, despite Wilson's personal plea, would convince her fellow Kentuckians that their only alternative was to return to state work. But when the ERA convened at Louisville in March, Clay once more found herself in a minority. The Louisville delegation, the largest at the convention, was bent on working for the federal amendment and opposed a state campaign. Breckinridge, who was elected president for a second term, joined Clay in a plea for a state bill, but the convention voted to consult the NAWSA and proceed to a state campaign only if it did not object.[21] Although this was less than Clay had hoped for, the possibility was kept alive that the Kentuckians would launch their own campaign during the legislative session of 1920.

While the Kentuckians were trying to determine their course, the United States Senate in February 1919 again rejected the federal amendment. Clay hoped that the "spell" of federal work over the NAWSA had been broken and "more reasonable measures," such as renewed efforts in the states, would now be pursued. Thus when Laura Clay went to the Saint Louis convention of the NAWSA in March 1919, she had two specific goals in mind: 1) gaining consent for a state campaign; and 2) convincing the convention that the defeat of the federal amendment indicated the need to seek a new sort of bill in Congress. She suggested amending the Constitution by striking the word male from section 2 of the Fourteenth Amendment, which specified that a state's representation in the Congress would be reduced if it denied the right to vote to any qualified male inhabitants. The effect of her proposal would have been to penalize, in a like manner, any state that did not enfranchise women. By leaving the option to the states, she believed that the states' rights faction which had blocked the Anthony amendment could be won to her design.[22] Since the threat contained in section 2 of the Fourteenth Amendment had never been invoked in the Negroes' behalf, Laura Clay's proposal appears to have been a futile rearguard effort to head off the Anthony amendment rather than a viable alternative to it.

At the Saint Louis convention, advocates of the federal amendment, who had been within one Senate vote of victory, confidently expected their bill to go through when the Sixty-sixth Congress met in the spring. In no mood for compromises, the convention overwhelmingly rejected all alternatives to the original amendment, including Clay's which received only three votes. The defeat of her proposal called national attention to her position. As she explained later, the heart of her complaint about the federal amendment was its second, or, as she called it, the "enforcing clause," which read: "Congress shall have power to enforce this article by appropriate legislation." She believed that this clause would provide the Congress with an ever-ready excuse for intervention in state affairs, not only in disputes involving woman suffrage but in any situation where a partisan majority in Congress might wish to force its will on some state or section. The best examples of such possibilities, to her mind, were the Force Acts of 1870 and 1871, which she believed were used for the advantage of the Republican party, rather than for the protection of the freedmen.[23]

Whenever Clay used this argument it was always assumed that her sole fear was that the federal government would force the southern states to let Negro women vote. On more than one occasion she vigorously and directly denied that this assumption was correct. One such situation arose during the Saint Louis convention, when the *New York Times* reported that she had proposed changing the federal amendment, "with particular reference to those parts that would permit enfranchisement of Negro women of the South."[24]

Clay bluntly denied the accuracy of this story. "My remarks were necessarily extemporaneous," she wrote to the editor of the *Lexington Leader*, "but I should be ashamed of myself if even in the impulsiveness of such remarks I had abandoned my consistent stand for equal rights for women of every race and section. But I did not. It was a mere assumption of the reporter because I objected to a repetition of the enforcement provision of the Fifteenth Amendment in the Anthony Amendment." She admitted warning the convention in Saint Louis that the Fifteenth Amendment had led to federal interference in state elections, "inaugurated

ostensibly for the protection of the freedmen but . . . used practically as an instrument for partisan advantage." And this interference had brought on the subterfuges designed to keep Negroes
from the polls and resulted in "a disastrous lowering of the public
conscience towards the sacred right of the franchise." She believed
the new amendment to be even more dangerous than the old.
Since women were in every state, the enforcement clause might
be employed against any state or any section by either party, as
partisan advantage dictated.[25] Since publication of her denial was
limited to the local press, it is understandable that most suffragists
continued to believe that her objections were based entirely on
the race problem. In short, Clay was not denying that the South
had a race problem, but she wanted it understood that her objections to the federal amendment were based on the principle of
federal-state relations.

Clay's plan for a campaign in Kentucky again failed to materialize. At Saint Louis the leaders of the NAWSA agreed to support
a campaign if it had the solid support of the Kentucky officers.
A follow-up meeting of the ERA officers in Louisville showed
little enthusiasm for a state bill. By early May 1919 it was obvious
that the majority of Kentucky suffragists were opposed to Clay's
proposal. Their decision was to wait. If the special session of Congress passed the federal amendment, most of them believed, a
state amendment would be superfluous.[26] It had become clear
that if Clay wanted a state amendment submitted, she would have
to secure it without the aid of the major body of suffragists, who
did not share her fear of the federal amendment or her aversion
to the fact that even its successful passage would not remove the
word male from the Kentucky constitution.

When the United States Senate approved the federal amendment on June 4, Laura Clay immediately resigned from the Kentucky ERA, claiming that success in the Senate had committed the
organization to work solely for ratification of the federal amendment. Believing as she did, she said, she could not remain in the
old ranks. She expressed opposition to a majority of the states
forcing their will upon a smaller number and feared that moves in
that direction would cause the states "to be administrative units,
not self-governing units." The atmosphere of the times strength-

Portrait of Laura Clay by Laura Bruce
Courtesy of White Hall State Shrine (photograph by Tom Woods)

Mary Barr Clay

From Elizabeth Cady Stanton
et al., eds., *The History of
Woman Suffrage*, vol. 3

Mary Jane Warfield Clay

Courtesy of White Hall
State Shrine (photograph
by Tom Woods)

The officers of the NAWSA in 1900, meeting in executive
session at the Anthony home in Rochester, N.Y.
Pictured l. to r. front row: Harriet Taylor Upton, treasurer
(seated); Anna Howard Shaw, vice president;
Susan B. Anthony, retiring president; Carrie Chapman
Catt, president-elect. Back row: Rachel Foster
Avery, corresponding secretary; Mary Anthony (co-hostess
for meeting); Alice Stone Blackwell, recording secretary;
Laura Clay, auditor; Catherine Waugh McCulloch
(partially hidden), auditor.

Josephine K. Henry
Courtesy of Margaret I. King Library,
University of Kentucky

Madeline McDowell Breckinridge
From Sophonisba Breckinridge,
Madeline McDowell Breckinridge

Representatives of the Kentucky ERA at the Democratic National
Convention in Saint Louis, 1916. Laura Clay is in
the center holding an umbrella.

FOR
STATE SENATE

LAURA CLAY
Of Madison County

Democratic Candidate from the 29th District

ESTILL, JACKSON, MADISON, OWSLEY AND ROCKCASTLE COUNTIES

Campaign poster from Clay's unsuccessful
Kentucky Senate race in 1923

Courtesy of Margaret I. King Library,
University of Kentucky

Governor Ruby Laffoon presenting the gavel to Laura Clay, who served as temporary chairman of the Kentucky convention to ratify the Twenty-first Amendment, November 27, 1933.

Courtesy of Margaret I. King Library, University of Kentucky

Laura Clay as photographed in 1923
Courtesy of White Hall State Shrine

ened her antipathy to the federal amendment. The rise of Bolshevism in Europe and the growing Red Scare in the United States seem to have transformed her constitutional opposition to the Anthony amendment into an almost irrational fear of it. She wrote Kate Gordon about the dangers of enfranchising twelve to fifteen million untrained voters "in this time of world revolution" and warned another correspondent that the newly enfranchised women would be especially susceptible to the radicalism of the "agitators swarming the United States."[27] Her fears served to reinforce her belief that the right of suffrage was best left to the states, where it could be extended at their discretion.

Although she had severed suffrage ties of more than thirty years standing, Laura Clay had no intention of stopping her work for the ballot. She was convinced that the only way the federal amendment could be stopped was through the rapid success of a number of state woman suffrage amendments. This would prove that there was no need for the federal measure and, consequently, state legislatures would not ratify it. She believed, however, that woman suffrage was a certainty, through one method or the other. These ideas were behind the formation of the Citizens' Committee for a State Suffrage Amendment, which she and a few like-minded suffragists organized after leaving the Kentucky ERA.[28]

As its name indicates, the main purpose of this new group was to push for the state amendment. Opening headquarters in Lexington, the Committee issued an "Open Letter to the Public," which was mailed to all legislative candidates in Kentucky. Questioning whether the suffrage organizations demanding a federal amendment spoke for the majority of women, the "Letter" called for a state referendum as the best determinant of the attitudes of Kentuckians on the suffrage issue. A more accurate expression of the women's wishes, declared the "Letter," had been voiced in the platforms of the two major political parties in 1916, which called for extension of the franchise by state action. Although expressing Clay's fear that the states' control of their own elections was threatened and that the power of the national government would be vastly increased, the "Letter" did not express fear of the Negro vote. In addition to distributing literature, the Citizens' Committee carried its appeal for state suffrage to the convention of the Kentucky Democrats. The *Lexington Herald* reported that Laura Clay was being considered as a delegate to the convention, the first woman to be so honored by a major party in Kentucky. She declined final selection, however, in order to represent her new organization before the Democratic gathering. The delegates were urged by President Wilson to endorse the federal amendment and assured by Congressman James C. Cantrill that its effect in the South would be "merely to add the white women to the voting population." The convention responded by promising to promote the federal amendment and to initiate a state bill if the amendment had not become law when the Kentucky legislature next met in January.[29] Though less than what Clay desired, the convention's promise of state action was a small victory for the Citizens' Committee.

While working for a state amendment, the Citizens' Committee carried on a campaign against the federal bill. Believing that the South needed no awakening to the dangers of federal interference, Clay decided that the crucial area in the battle would be the western states, and that there the states' rights suffragists must make their principal appeal against the federal amendment. She regarded the West as the natural ally of the South because of its agrarian economy, sparse population, and the fact that it, too, had "a race problem."[30]

The idea of a race problem in the West may have been suggested to her by the well-publicized views of California Senator James D. Phelan, although her own trips to Oregon, Washington, and Arizona had given her some knowledge of anti-oriental feeling in the West. Phelan, supported by Senator Borah, voiced strong objections to the Japanese request for a clause on "racial equality" in the discussions on the Covenant of the League of Nations then under way in Paris. Phelan saw the clause as another step in circumventing the efforts of states like California to protect themselves from "the Japanese menace" and "to preserve the soil . . . for the white race."[31]

Laura Clay spent much of the summer and fall of 1919 writing western congressmen about the dangers of the federal amendment. She explained that the enforcing clause of that measure might enable the Japanese in the western states to achieve through the interference of the federal government what they had not been able to gain through state laws. She pictured the Japanese government, working through a lobby or in regular diplomatic channels, securing treaties and federal laws to overturn anti-oriental legislation in the West. The clause, in other words, was an opening for a vast extension of federal control over state affairs. This was a novel attack on the federal amendment, but it elicited little, if any, support. Those who bothered to respond either did not understand the distinction she was making in how suffrage should be achieved or else believed she was prompted entirely by the question of the Negro vote.[32]

Despite the pleadings of friends and lack of success in her efforts, Laura Clay maintained her course. Ida Husted Harper, who was editing the final two volumes of the *History of Woman Suffrage* at the NAWSA headquarters in New York, sympathized with her position, but warned that Clay was not in good company. Harper assured Clay that her fears of federal intervention would not be realized. Prominent women in Kentucky who had always looked to Laura Clay for guidance on the suffrage question were disturbed and bewildered to find themselves in another camp. "I often wonder if I really have your argument in full," wrote Alice Lloyd, "or whether I have just enough of it not to understand." Whichever the case she could "scarcely realize" that she was openly differing with Clay after so many years. "You've always seemed the biggest part of the Kentucky E.R.A. to me," another pleaded, "couldn't you reconsider?" "How is it possible that you could break the tie which bound us together?" asked an ally from the earliest Kentucky campaigns. "Well! I thought you always favored the Susan B. Anthony Amendment."[33] Near the end of the long struggle, Clay had neither the sympathy nor the understanding of her old suffrage comrades.

Her effort to thwart the mushrooming support for the federal amendment and her hope for launching a formidable campaign for a state bill failed. The Citizens' Committee for a State Suffrage Amendment remained small and dependent upon her for financial support and public pronouncements. A leading Democratic newspaper claimed that Clay's group was hardly affording a challenge to the majority and had never assumed "a serious aspect." Congressman Cantrill of her district, a former foe but recently an avid sponsor of woman suffrage, promised to work hard for the ratification of the federal amendment, because he was convinced that it would "be suicide for the Democratic Party in Kentucky if such action is not taken."[34]

At NAWSA headquarters, where Carrie Chapman Catt had counted Kentucky among the states which the anti-suffragists could control in July 1919, there was confidence by October that the state would be won by the able Madeline Breckinridge and her efficient staff, who were pledging the vast majority of candidates for the state legislature to a prompt ratification of the federal amendment.[35]

On the eve of the convening of the Kentucky legislature in January, the Southern Woman's League for the Rejection of the Susan B. Anthony Amendment wrote Laura Clay for her advice on the feasibility of sending a representative to oppose ratification of the federal amendment at Frankfort. Clay made it clear that she was a strong advocate of woman suffrage and doubted if an anti-suffragist could find a single person to cooperate with her at the state capital.[36]

Clay then proceeded to lecture her correspondent on the reasons for the impending success of the federal amendment. She refused to blame President Wilson or the southern congressmen, as many opponents of the bill were doing. The chief responsibility, she declared, "must rest with the Southern States. They ought to have seen years ago that no Democrat or Republican in the Western States could resist woman suffrage." But the South had remained obdurate on the question with the result that southerners had "isolated themselves from national sympathy with their own peculiar social and racial problems.... White supremacy, as I have often told my Southern suffrage friends, is an issue of little or no importance to more than a half-dozen states, and the rest of the country will not consent to sacrifice great national issues and problems to the self-centered wishes of those half-dozen."[37] Now, it seemed to Clay, the Anthony amendment was almost certain to sweep aside opposition to suffrage and states' rights together. This exchange illustrates Clay's differences with deep South opponents of the federal amendment.[38] She sympathized with their race problem but the continued use of it as an excuse to thwart progressive legislation had worn her patience thin.

Perhaps because she saw the hopelessness of opposition to ratification, perhaps because she could not bring herself to oppose her own enfranchisement, Clay decided not to resist at Frankfort the federal amendment. The only business of the Citizens' Committee, she said, would be to ask the legislature for submission of a state amendment, claiming it as the promise of both the Republican and Democratic state conventions, regardless of the action taken on the federal woman suffrage bill.[39] But her hopes failed to materialize because most attention was riveted to the Anthony amendment.

Kentucky became the twenty-third state to ratify the amendment, large majorities carrying it in both houses. Amid the rejoicing of the suffragists at their victory convention in Lexington, Breckinridge remembered the past services of Laura Clay:

It is only proper that recognition should be given to Miss Laura Clay, who for a quarter of a century when the cause of woman suffrage seemed but an incandescent dream, labored, toiled, spoke, spent herself and her wealth to advance that cause. Due to her convictions about States' Rights she separated herself from the forces that led the fight in the past few years and have brought it to triumph. But in the future recollection of her separation will be forgotten, as it should be forgotten, by those who wish to give credit to the pioneers of this movement for the extension of human rights.[40]

Thus, 1920, the year that saw women enfranchised, was a bittersweet time for Laura Clay. Old friends continued to express regard for her and sought her counsel despite differences on the suffrage question. Her continuous prominence in the state was acknowledged by the Democratic party when it selected her as one of its eight delegates-at-large to the national convention in San Francisco. She enjoyed the trip to the West Coast, engaging Senator Thomas J. Walsh of Montana in a debate on the League of Nations while enroute. Although she failed to get a hearing before the Resolutions Committee on her opposition to the federal amendment, she was nominated for the presidency and "got a nice complimentary vote." It was the first time a woman had ever been nominated for the position at a major party convention.[41]

In the meantime, the federal bill moved steadily through the ratification process. With one more state's approval needed and only four states left which had not acted on the question, a crucial moment came in August 1920 when the Tennessee legislature met in special session to consider the amendment. While in San Francisco, Clay had been approached by a prominent anti-suffragist and asked to go to Nashville to oppose ratification. Wanting to see the amendment defeated, she had agreed to go. She had hardly returned from San Francisco, however, when she began having second thoughts about working under the opposition's banner. "I feel a great distaste to working with those who are avowedly opposed to suffrage," she wrote Kate Gordon, and decided that she would not go unless the states' rights suffragists decided to lobby for the defeat of the amendment. But a call came from Gordon, acting in the name of the defunct SSWSC, and Clay went to Nashville for a few days during the second week in August. She claimed that she and Gordon did not unite with either the antis or the federal amendment advocates in their unsuccessful fight against ratification. It was an artificial distinction, since their old suffrage friends saw them as part of the opposition and their old enemies saw them as allies. The result was that both friend and foe misunderstood Clay's mission in Nashville. As she was only one among a thousand men and women who had come to the city to work for or against the amendment, she made little impact on the proceedings. Aside from noting her presence as a lobbyist, the newspapers carried no information on her activities.[42]

Laura Clay had tried to sweep back the sea and lost. It is ironic and unfair that historians of the suffrage movement should remember her most often for this last ineffectual and misunderstood battle in the long campaign for woman's rights. She has been accused of joining with the most unscrupulous foes of woman suffrage and "appealing to Negrophobia and every other cave man's prejudice," but the charge is too severe. Although she shared the racism of her time, accepting without question the popular belief in Anglo-Saxon superiority, she was no different in this regard from the vast majority of suffragists, North and South, for and against the federal amendment. Her long record of service to the black Episcopal church in Lexington, her support of a Negro woman's club which wanted to affiliate with the NAWSA, her attempts to moderate the extremism of Kate Gordon and other southerners who could not see issues beyond the race question, all deny the charge that Clay was an extremist.[43]

In her attitude toward the Negro, Clay belonged to that advanced group of southerners who Guion Griffis Johnson called progressionist and paternalist.[44] Perhaps her major shortcoming in the area of race relations was her naive belief that the majority of southerners shared her interest in the Negro's advancement and her commitment to his just treatment.[45] She made "tactical concessions" to racism, as did virtually all the southern progressives. But in fairness to them, as Henry F. May has written, "one must remember the obstacles they confronted, the devastating poverty, the ever tightening and narrowing religious orthodoxy, the sensitivity to criticism, and underlying all, the racial dogmas that had grown more and more rigid since the tensions of the Populist times."[46]

X

OTHER CAUSES AWAITING

1920-1941

ALTHOUGH LAURA CLAY remained opposed to the Nineteenth Amendment, fearing that it had seriously altered the relationship between the states and the federal government, she was not embittered. She regretted the passage of what she termed a "needless and mischievous" law and continued to be concerned about what she believed was a trend toward the centralization of power in Washington. The strength of American government, she wrote a friend, "is the large measure of local self-government which is given to the people, and I am therefore jealous of any movement which endeavors . . . to diminish the people's watchfulness over the legislation which affects their own particular requirements." Believing that its philosophy came closer to satisfying her states' rights principles, she joined the Democratic party.[1]

However grave her concern for states' rights, Clay did not give way to bitterness or inactivity in the wake of the women's triumph. She was prominent in the formation of the Democratic Women's Club of Kentucky in 1920 and was in great demand as a speaker to its local branches. Although she was not happy about the way she had received the ballot, she did not hesitate to use it, voting a straight Democratic ticket in November in spite of some qualms about the League of Nations and her disappointment with the party's support of the Nineteenth Amendment.[2]

Any personal feelings she might have had during the heat of the last battle for the amendment quickly evaporated, for to an unusual degree, she could separate people from their stand on public questions. Late in 1921, she wrote Harriet Taylor Upton, a staunch Republican and one of Carrie Chapman Catt's chief aides in the ratification struggle at Nashville, that her vote for Governor James M. Cox had not made her "love her Republican friends the less." She also continued an affectionate correspondence with Catherine Waugh McCulloch, Alice Lloyd, Alice Stone Blackwell, and other advocates of the Nineteenth Amendment.[3]

Laura Clay had always viewed the effort for woman's rights as a multifaceted struggle, and she realized that there were yet victories to win after 1920. One area in which she had long been active and continued her efforts into the 1920s was church laity rights for women. A devout and lifelong member of Christ Episcopal Church in Lexington, she began in the 1890s to demand that "the miserable spectacle of severing labor and responsibility from honor and authority" in church government should end. The other ladies of the Woman's Auxiliary of Christ Church were not as bold as Laura Clay, however, and voted down her resolution to have women elected to the church's ruling body, the vestry. Her efforts were finally successful in 1905, when the church declared that women were eligible for election to the vestry.[4]

In 1911, despite her involvement in the NAWSA headquarters' dispute, Laura Clay found time to begin a drive to amend the canon laws so women could be elected to the next higher governing body, the Diocesan Council. In answer to the oft-expressed fear that men would quit working in the church if the role of women in its government was expanded, she answered, "I hardly know whether to say that it speaks too poorly of the men or too highly of the women." Disturbed that "some very worthy women" of the auxiliary opposed her design, Clay wrote an Episcopal friend who she was urging to make the same demand in her diocese, "Is it not wonderful how little trust women have in their own sex?"[5]

The Diocesan Council agreed to hear Laura Clay's arguments for female representation at its annual meeting in June 1911. Her speech, sounding very much like a suffrage talk, was commended as "able, thoughtful, and well-expressed," but the council refused to accede to its plea. With dioceses according women full rights in California, Washington, and New York, the pressure on the Lexington diocese to do as much grew until 1920 when it also acquiesced. The final step in Clay's efforts to elevate women in church government was achieved in 1924 when she was elected as a delegate to the Episcopal Synod of the District of Sewanee, the first woman in the church to be so honored.[6]

The admission of women to the University of the South, an Episcopal school at Sewanee, Tennessee, was another of her church-related goals. The Woman's Auxiliary of Lexington requested that the school's board of trustees make the school coeducational as soon as its million-dollar endowment drive was fulfilled in 1920. Implying that women's cooperation in the fund drive would be dependent upon a positive answer, Clay reminded the trustees that parents cared as much for their daughters' education as for their sons' and that the church should offer as good opportunities to women as to men.[7]

When the Auxiliary failed to get a favorable response, Clay determined to withhold her church contribution until she could be assured that no part of it would go to the University of the South. She apparently resumed her donations after the vestry passed a resolution recommending coeducation to the university and assured her that her money could in only the most indirect way aid Sewanee. Whether or not the protest of the Woman's Auxiliary was the motivating force cannot be determined, but a partial victory for their cause was won when the University of the South admitted women to its summer session for the first time in 1920.[8]

While Clay was not bothered, as were some of the suffragists, by the thought that young women took the franchise for granted, she was concerned because they did not use it more. With this concern in mind, she decided at seventy-four years of age to run for the state senate in 1923. Unchallenged in the Democratic party primary, she faced a hard fight in the Twenty-ninth Senatorial District, a Republican stronghold. In her rural area, where conservative views on drinking were strong and gambling, legal or otherwise, was regarded as sinful, Laura Clay's support of the pari-mutuel law, which had become the main issue in the campaign, probably contributed to her defeat in November. Nevertheless, she professed no regrets: "If I have indeed helped to arouse the women of Kentucky to take a stronger interest in their right of suffrage, I have already succeeded in my campaign, no matter what the result of the election . . . may be."[9]

The outcome of one other vote in the election must have been even more discouraging to her. An effort, financed by her and backed by the League of Women Voters, was made to strike the word male from the election clause of the state constitution. Clay led a committee to Frankfort which succeeded in getting the bill through the legislature without a single negative vote. When the people had their chance at the amendment, however, it was defeated, 45,308–56,441.[10]

Little attention had been given to the amendment by the political parties and it made no practical difference insofar as any concrete issue was concerned. But it did matter to Laura Clay, who believed that the general extension of suffrage belonged to the states, and who was, as one of her friends wrote, a "hard-headed" woman.[11] At least it was an action consistent with her convictions that the word male in the election clause was a standing reminder that the voters of Kentucky had not determined their own electorate.

Laura Clay's political activity continued through the 1920s as she often lent her speaking talents to the Democratic party. During the presidential campaign of 1928, she was a vigorous supporter of Governor Alfred E. Smith, making about twelve speeches in support of his candidacy. She endorsed his attack on the prohibition amendment, which she called a social and economic mistake. She contended that "wartime fervor" had been responsible for the passage of the amendment in the first place, and, while she watched it with hope at first, its results had proved it to be a "poor law." Although it is unlikely that any of her WCTU friends were aware of her reservations, she claimed that she had been "strong for temperance, but not for prohibition." She also defended Smith on the religious issue, asking the voters to be as oblivious to his Catholicism as the Constitution was to religious partiality. She condemned both the militant prohibitionists and religious bigots and asked her audiences to give Smith a chance to return the liquor question to the states.[12]

Although Smith failed to carry Kentucky, the campaign provided a closer examination of the prohibition issue and established Laura Clay as one of the prominent opponents of the "noble experiment." Five years later when Kentucky voted for the repeal of the Eighteenth Amendment, Clay was selected as a member of the ratifying convention which met in Frankfort. She was honored with the convention's temporary chairmanship and used the opportunity to reaffirm her states' rights convictions. Speaking in a voice "which rang clearly and was audible throughout the House Chamber," she said, "There is one governmental principle that is cardinal and sacred. That is the right of the states to govern their own internal and local affairs." [13]

At eighty-six, though retired from public speaking, Laura Clay struck a final blow for woman's rights. A recommendation of the Bureau of School Service of the College of Education in the University of Kentucky that male teachers be paid more than females in order to entice more men into public school education angered her. Coming to the defense of the concept of equal pay for equal work, Clay claimed that it would be a travesty to have injustice prevail where citizenship was taught and asked what the costs to a civilization would be if its children were led to believe that men were superior to women. [14]

During the 1930s, Laura Clay made fewer and fewer public appearances. A lover of contract bridge, she played regularly with a circle of friends in her home at 193 Mill Street and in Richmond where she frequently visited with her brother Brutus or her sister Sallie. Age finally required her to rent out the farm that she had managed for nearly fifty years. Occasionally honored on her birthday by the Business and Professional Women's Club or the Democratic Women's Club of Fayette County, she slipped gracefully into old age, dying at ninety-two on June 29, 1941. [15] Until the last she remained, as she had been for longer than anyone could remember, the personification of woman's rights in Kentucky.

In her long and eventful career, Laura Clay had played three roles in the woman's movement. She was first of all a leader in the cause of reforming the laws of her own state relating to women and children. By and large, she was successful in this endeavor and at the end of her life Kentucky women claimed a wide range of legal protection and enjoyed a scope of opportunity which was unknown at her birth. Generally overshadowed by the later and more newsworthy struggle for the franchise, the early efforts to make the state laws more equitable were, perhaps, of greater practical benefit to women than the ballot. The legislation that gained equity in property rights between husband and wife (1894), the co-guardianship law (1910), and the great strides toward coeducation were of enduring value to Kentucky women and permanent reminders of their indebtedness to Laura Clay and other early feminists. While one might question whether or not woman suffrage has improved the quality of American politics, he cannot deny that a more equitable treatment of women has been of incalculable aid in the progress of the country, as well as an act of justice to more than one-half the population.

Laura Clay was the leader of the suffrage movement in Kentucky through 1912. After Madeline McDowell Breckinridge was elected president of the ERA, Clay continued to 1918 to render important services to the organization, but she was no longer vital to its continuation or its ultimate success. As she realized, younger women and innovative methods were needed as the suffrage movement began to grow rapidly, and she willingly stepped aside to give new leaders their chance. But her long service had won the respect and gratitude of Kentucky suffragists, which remained despite her dogged and, in their minds, pointless opposition to the federal amendment.

As a sectional suffrage leader and progressive southerner, Laura Clay's life is both interesting and instructive. Raised in an abolitionist family, she took pride in the destruction of slavery, but like many southerners she was caught in a dilemma over the new status of the Negro. She accepted the judgment that most freedmen were not prepared for the full responsibilities of citizenship and made concessions in her democratic philosophy for the sake of white supremacy and to win support for woman's rights. With the South in the hands of the whites, she expected that they would paternalistically lead the Negroes into full citizenship, as they became educated and dependable citizens. This was a naive expectation based on a dangerous philosophy. The mass of southerners were not prepared to give Negroes, regardless of their qualifications, an equal place in American life, and the racial gradualism propounded by Laura Clay and other paternalists simply provided a convenient excuse for the worst sort of discrimination. In a similar way, her advocacy of states' rights sometimes placed her in the camp of racists, blind to human justice, who used the ideology she cherished to deny Negroes their rights and block progressivism in general. In the end her ideas were rejected by both friends and foes of woman suffrage, and, in perspective, one can see that Clay's proposals did not offer a viable alternative to federal enfranchisement of women.

Clay's role in the national movement was also important. Although she does not belong with Susan B. Anthony, Elizabeth Cady Stanton, and Carrie Chapman Catt in the first rank of suffrage leaders, she made a substantial contribution to national developments. While her efforts as an unselfish and dedicated worker in several state campaigns from 1895 to 1917 deserve attention, her greatest service to the national movement probably came from her long tenure as an officer of the NAWSA. Her judicious mind and calm mastery of parliamentary skills was a steadying force in most of the years when Catt was not a member of the Official Board. Blessed with an ability to see another person's point of view and anxious to find good intentions in the actions of others, she was a noted compromiser in the conflicts that inevitably arose among the officers. When she broke with the mainstream of the suffrage movement in the unfortunate effort to prevent ratification of the Nineteenth Amendment, it was actually too late for any suffrage leader to turn back the national tide favoring the reform. Indeed, Laura Clay had played a significant role in creating the suffrage sentiment which swept her and other opponents of the federal amendment aside in 1920.

For the last fifty years of her life, Laura Clay was a persistent and able advocate of the equality of the sexes. Entering the woman's rights movement at a time when childbirth and family responsibilities took a heavy toll of feminists, she and a few others kept the agitation alive until the reform became a popular cause. Her long public career was spent in exposing sex discrimination, pleading for equal rights in all fields of endeavor, and seeking to convince other women that they could compete in most fields traditionally reserved for men. She realized that the removal of legal disabilities was only part of the task of achieving equality; the other, and equally important, part was removing the mental inferiority that women developed in a male-dominated society. In the final analysis, Laura Clay refused to let Americans, women as well as men, live in the complacent belief that theirs was a land of equality and freedom when over one half of its citizens shared in neither its full opportunities nor all of its rights. Her contributions to woman's rights were significant, and her vision of a land of sex equality was brought closer to realization by her patience, strength, intelligence, and courage.

Notes

Chapter 1

1. See David L. Smiley, *Lion of White Hall: The Life of Cassius M. Clay* (Madison: University of Wisconsin Press, 1962), for a full account of this fascinating figure. Smiley gives little attention to Clay's children and none to the feminist activities of the Clay women.

2. Ibid., pp. 152–53, 157, 217–18.

3. Laura was an infant during Clay's long convalescence at White Hall after he had killed Cymer Turner at a political rally in Foxtown, Kentucky, and had suffered wounds which almost took his life; ibid., pp. 141–42; Cassius M. Clay, *Memoirs* (Cincinnati: J. Fletcher Brennan & Co., 1886), 1:64–66; Smiley, *Lion of White Hall*, pp. 31–32; Clavia Goodman, *Bitter Harvest: Laura Clay's Suffrage Work* (Lexington, Ky.: Bur Press, 1949), p. xiii. This description of the Warfields is contained in the "Foreword" by Sophonisba P. Breckinridge, a Lexingtonian who knew the family well.

4. Mary Rogers Clay and Zachary F. Smith, *The Clay Family* (Louisville: John P. Morton and Company, 1889). For births and deaths of children who did not live into adulthood see a note in Laura Clay's handwriting in October 1903, Laura Clay Papers, University of Kentucky Library, Lexington (hereafter cited as Laura Clay Papers).

5. Before the war, Mary Jane Clay wrote to two of her daughters who were away at school: "Poor Negroes, miserable creatures! They cannot be relied on, therefore I find if I want a thing done, I must see it done. I am compensated for my attention by having 1 and 1/2 gallons of milk from cows at milking, that gave a quart before." She also reported that she had been able to double the amount of butter from a gallon of milk by "experimenting" with the churning process. To Mary Barr Clay and Sarah ("Sallie") Lewis Clay, n.d., Clay Family Papers, Filson Club, Louisville, Ky. (hereafter cited as Clay Family Papers).

6. Smiley, *Lion of White Hall*, p. 156; Mary Barr Clay, "Kentucky," in *History of Woman Suffrage*, ed. Elizabeth Cady Stanton, Susan B. Anthony, and Mathilda Gage (Rochester, N.Y.: Susan B. Anthony, 1886), 3:820.

7. See copy of an anonymous poem, "All But My Wife and Mother Advised Me to Yield," which celebrates Clay's bout with pro-slavery forces of Lexington in July 1845. The poem, written shortly after Clay's *True American* newspaper was suppressed, was sent to Laura Clay by Letitia W. Brosius, 16 March 1872, Laura Clay Papers. Smiley, *Lion of White Hall*, p. 93, mentions the courage and steadfastness of the Clay women.

8. Cassius M. Clay, Jr., to Slew [Tarleton], 14 March 1857, Laura Clay Papers.

9. Ibid.

10. Smiley, *Lion of White Hall*, p. 175.

11. Ibid., pp. 175–77, 177–78; Andrew H. Campbell to Laura Clay, 3 May 1906, Laura Clay Papers.

12. Smiley, *Lion of White Hall*, p. 180; James Rood Robertson, *A Kentuckian at the Court of the Tzars* (Berea, Ky.: Berea College Press, 1935), p. 110.

13. Smiley, *Lion of White Hall*, p. 184. Laura Clay later said: "one of the girls could not stand the rigors of the bitter climate." *Louisville Courier-Journal*, 4 February 1940.

14. Thomas D. Clark, *A History of Kentucky* (New York: Prentice-Hall, 1937), pp. 457–64; J. Winston Coleman, Jr., *Lexington during the Civil War* (Lexington, Ky.: Commercial Printing Company, 1938).

15. Mary Jane Clay to Laura Clay, 17 February 1863, Clay Family Papers; J. Winston Coleman, Jr., *A Centennial History of Sayre School, 1854–1954* (Lexington, Ky.: Winburn Press, 1954), pp. 9–11.

16. *Louisville Courier-Journal*, 4 February 1940; Diary of Laura Clay, 12 April, 10 June 1864, Laura Clay Papers (hereafter cited as Clay Diary).

17. Mary Jane Clay to Laura Clay, 23 May, 6 June 1864, Clay Family Papers.

18. Clay Diary, 29 July 1864; Clark, *History of Kentucky*, p. 464; Clay Diary, 29 July, 4 April 1864.

19. Cassius M. Clay to John G. Fee, 8 July 1855. Quoted in Robertson, *A Kentuckian at the Court of the Tzars*, p. 31. Mary Barr Clay to Laura Clay, 13 March 1865; Green Clay to Mary Jane Clay, n.d., Clay Family Papers.

20. Clay Diary, 25 April 1864.

21. Ibid., 17, 18 April, 17 May 1864.

22. To Mary Barr Clay, 21 December 1865, Clay Family Papers; Clay Diary, 7 May 1864.

23. See Anne Firor Scott, *The Southern Lady: From Pedestal to Politics, 1830–1930* (Chicago: University of Chicago Press, 1970), pp. 59–68. While Scott's comments are not very specific about what was taught at Southern female schools, she states that "not much could be said for the rigors of their curriculums or the qualifications of the teachers," p. 68. This is a decided contrast to Sayre Institute, where, aside from piano and voice lessons, the curriculum was almost identical to that of Transylvania University, a male college located nearby. It is possible that the two schools shared other faculty members, as was the case with Dr. Peter. (Interview with John D. Wright, Jr., who has a history of the college in manuscript, Lexington, Ky., 26 September 1971.) Coleman, *History of Sayre School*, pp. 8, 10.

24. Clay Diary, 3 April 1864, 19 July 1865, 15 May 1864.

25. Mary Jane Clay to Laura Clay, 17 April 1864, Laura Clay Papers; Cassius M. Clay to Mary Jane Clay, 26 December 1863, Clay Family Papers; Clay Diary, 30 May 1864; Church Record of Baptisms, Confirmations, Marriages, and Burials at Christ Church, Lexington, Ky., 20 November 1864.

26. Clay Diary, 4, 13 April 1864.

27. Coleman, *History of Sayre School*, pp. 12, 39. Sayre has no records of Laura Clay's grades nor the courses she took to fulfill the graduation requirement. Interview with Donn D. Hollingsworth, Headmaster, Sayre School, Lexington, Ky., 29 June 1970. Scott, *The Southern Lady*, p. 59.

28. Mary Jane Clay to Laura Clay, 18 October 1864, Cassius M. Clay to Mary Jane Clay, 26 December 1863, Clay Family Papers.

29. 9 December 1865, ibid.

30. Cassius M. Clay to S. Bowles, 11 February 1869; to Laura Clay, 20 December 1865, ibid.

31. Laura Clay to Mary Barr Clay, 21 April 1866, ibid.

32. J. Winston Coleman reports that White Hall as it now stands was built while Clay was in Russia from a design by Major Thomas Lewinski, a noted Lexington architect, and that John McMurtry was in charge of the construction. *Lexington Sunday Herald-Leader*, 21 August 1960. Letters from the period make it clear that Mary Jane Clay was overseeing the work. Clay wrote his wife that his only concerns were permanency and fireproofing. Cassius M. Clay to Mary Jane Clay, 26 December 1863, Clay Family Papers. Mary Jane Clay wrote Laura, "I keep three men and three vehicles, four horses, four mules and eight oxen all the time engaged hauling and at night you can see but little accomplished; and three Irishmen are waiting continually on the stone masons besides, so in all there are eight men engaged and sometimes nine." 27 April 1864, ibid.

33. 5 May 1866, ibid.

34. Smiley, *Lion of White Hall*, pp. 202–3.

35. Laura Clay to Mary Barr Clay, 21 December 1865, Clay Family Papers.

36. Goodman, *Bitter Harvest*, p. 18.

37. Aileen S. Kraditor, ed., *Up from the Pedestal* (Chicago: Quadrangle Books, 1968), p. 6.

Chapter 2

1. Clay, *Memoirs*, 1:540; Laura Clay to Mary Barr Clay, 31 January 1866, Clay Family Papers.

2. Cassius M. Clay to Mary Jane Clay, 2 October 1866, 21 January 1867, Clay Family Papers; *Lexington Herald*, 1 March 1935.

3. Cassius M. Clay to Mary Jane Clay, 21 January 1867; to Mary Barr Clay Herrick, 28 February 1868, Clay Family Papers.

4. Smiley, *Lion of White Hall*, pp. 205–8; Clay, *Memoirs*, 1:220; Robertson, *A Kentuckian at the Court of the Tzars*, p. 265.

5. Clay, *Memoirs*, 1:540.

6. Robertson, *A Kentuckian at the Court of the Tzars*, p. 267; Smiley, *Lion of White Hall*, pp. 218–20; Clay, *Memoirs*, 1:548.

7. Smiley, *Lion of White Hall*, p. 234. *Cincinnati Enquirer*, 29 March 1879. Quoted in Thomas D. Clark, *The Kentucky* (New York: Farrar and Rinehart, 1942), p. 292.

8. Clay, *Memoirs*, 1:541, 549; Smiley, *Lion of White Hall*, pp. 220–21, misreads Clay's rambling account of the marital rupture, writing that his wife had made two efforts to save the marriage when Clay is actually writing about the same incident in two different places. Order Book No. 58, Fayette County Circuit Court, Lexington, Ky., p. 87; *Cassius M. Clay vs. Mary Jane Clay*, Fayette Circuit Court, File 1732, 7 February 1878.

9. Clay, *Memoirs*, 1:548, 540 (italics added).

10. Ibid., pp. 541–43, 543–44; Mary Barr Clay, "Kentucky," *History of Woman Suffrage*, 3:820.

11. Interview with Esther Bennett of Richmond, Ky., great granddaughter of Cassius M. and Mary Jane Clay, 26 June 1968. Box 1889, Fayette County Court of Common Pleas, Lexington, Ky., 15 January 1887. The court action on this date

made Laura Clay the trustee for the property left to her mother by Elisha and Marie Warfield, a move necessitated by the death of the former trustee, Madison C. Johnson. The legal device used by the Warfields was the only way they could protect their daughter's inheritance from Clay's possession. This had to be done through a legal procedure creating a "separate estate, with power to will it at death." See clipping, Laura Clay, "Woman's Column," *Lexington Kentucky Gazette*, 25 January 1890, Laura Clay Scrapbook, University of Kentucky Library, Lexington (hereafter cited as Laura Clay Scrapbook).

12. Clay Diary, 26 July 1874. The evidence from her letters to friends who had known her for years gives no indication that she ever discussed her parents' marriage and divorce. Her attitude was apparently summed up in her answer to a newspaper reporter's queries about Clay: "My father wrote his own memoirs, and you can find out about him from his own words." *Louisville Courier-Journal*, 4 February 1940.

13. A copy of the agreement, giving the exact size and location of each plot, is in the Laura Clay Papers. It is of some interest, in light of the family difficulties, to note that the smallest acreage went to Laura and Annie, 275 acres each, and the largest to Green, who was the closest of the children to his father, 425 acres. Mary received the second largest plot of 384 acres and Brutus's share was 330 acres. It is possible, of course, that differences in the fertility and terrain of the plots tended to even them out in value. In 1876 each of the children received approximately fifty-eight acres on which the homestead was located. At the time this transaction was made, Green sold his share to his father and his half brother, Launey Clay, for the sum of $2,000. A copy of this second agreement is also in the Laura Clay Papers. Box 3758, deed dated 10 October 1876, Fayette County Circuit Court, Lexington, Ky.

14. Mary Barr Clay, "Kentucky," *History of Woman Suffrage*, 3:820.

15. Laura Clay to Minnie C. Van Winkle, 12 July 1917, Laura Clay Papers; Mary Jane Clay to Laura Clay, 24 May 1885, Clay Family Papers; Mary Jane Clay to Laura Clay, 8 November 1880, 2 May 1885, Laura Clay Papers.

16. Mary Barr Clay to Mary Jane Clay, 22 May 1885, Clay Family Papers; Clay, *Memoirs*, 1:541; Box 3158, deed dated 11 March 1873, Fayette County Circuit Court, Lexington, Ky.; *Louisville Courier-Journal*, 4 February 1940.

17. See Christopher Lasch, *The New Radicalism in America, 1889–1963* (New York: Alfred A. Knopf, 1965), pp. 3–37, for a good account of Jane Addams's search for a role which would satisfy her own dedication to Christian humanitarianism. "From 1881 until 1888," writes Lasch, "Jane Addams underwent a prolonged nervous depression, from which she emerged with the decision to found a social settlement on Chicago's west side" (p. 15). Clay, *Memoirs*, 1:137, 159, 341, 342, 346. Clay's *Memoirs*, published just as the Clay women were getting the Kentucky feminist movement under way, often depart from the subject under discussion to editorialize on woman's rights. For example, he wrote that Russian women have "a subdued manner, which our countrywomen so much need" and added that "our boasted liberty of the sex is leading to very tragical results" (1:341–42). Even his discussion of the wild horses he observed in Texas en route to the Mexican War elicited an analogy which must have been painful to the equal rights advocates: "here, as in all animal nature, the leadership is on the part of the males. Let the Women's Rights people take note" (1:137). Thomas D. Clark, who knew Laura Clay, told me that she related to him that she had once asked her father to attend

a lecture on woman's rights. Clay refused the invitation and carried to the grave his hostility to the movement.

18. Clay Diary, 15 July 1878.

19. Ibid.

20. Ibid.

21. Annie Clay to Laura Clay, 20 September 1879, Clay Family Papers.

22. Clay Diary, 19 July 1878; Anne Ryland to Laura Clay, 26 October 1879, Clay Family Papers; interview with Mrs. Anderson Gratz, Lexington, Ky., 20 August 1970. Gratz described Laura Clay as a person who had a wide circle of friends and was "a delight socially." She related that her husband regarded Clay as a prized dinner guest and would often invite her along with others to their home for an evening of conversation. Mrs. Cecil Cantrill, who also knew Clay well, described her in much the same terms. Interview, Lexington, Ky., 26 January 1969. Unlike the stereotyped suffragist who is frequently pictured as a man-hater, Clay seems to have liked men and enjoyed their company. At the end of her life, she attributed the gains made by women to Kentucky men's "sense of justice." *Louisville Courier-Journal*, 4 February 1940. There are numerous indications in her letters that she established cordial and mutually enjoyable relationships with husbands and other male relatives of her suffragist friends. Laura Clay to Harriet Taylor Upton, 26 June 1911; to Mrs. Lucy B. Johnston, 12 October 1912; to Mrs. Sara M. Algeo, 23 April 1917, Laura Clay Papers.

23. Clay Diary, 18 April 1880.

24. Ibid.; Susan B. Anthony to Mary Barr Clay, 20 October 1879, Clay Family Papers.

25. Clay Diary, 18 April 1880. See the Matriculation Records, 4 January 1886, University Archives, University of Kentucky, Lexington. Clay's signature was entered below a pledge to "acquiesce in the regulations of the Agricultural and Mechanical College and acknowledge our obligations to obey them." There are no records of her grades at Michigan or the Agricultural and Mechanical College.

26. Ron S. B. [   ] to Laura Clay, 18 January 1886, Clay Family Papers.

27. Manuscript speech by Laura Clay, n.d.; Laura Clay Papers. Written in her own hand, this speech briefly outlines the principal events in the Kentucky woman's rights movement down to 1894.

28. Mary's marriage to Major Herrick produced three children in rapid succession and then ended in divorce. She had the surname of two of the boys, Green and Francis, legally changed to Clay, leaving only Clay, who would have otherwise become to Clay Clay, with the name of his father. Jo Baily Brown to R. H. Hill, 31 July 1958, Clay Family Papers. This communication gives much information on the second child of the marriage, Francis Warfield Herrick Clay. Mary's unhappy marriage, ending during her parents' separation, was probably part of that "unhappy domestic life" which was opening Laura's eyes "to the unjust relations between men and women and the unworthy position of women." Clay Diary, 26 July 1874. Mary Barr Clay, "Kentucky," *History of Woman Suffrage*, 3:818–22.

29. Mary Barr Clay to Laura Clay, 5 November 1879, Laura Clay Papers; Susan B. Anthony to Mary Barr Clay, 20 October 1879, Clay Family Papers; Laura Clay, "Kentucky," *History of Woman Suffrage*, ed. Susan B. Anthony and Ida Husted Harper (Rochester, N.Y.: Susan B. Anthony, 1902), 4:311; *Richmond* (Ky.) *Register*, 21 November 1879. Describing Anthony, Mrs. Clay wrote: "I found her very pleasant in conversation; a homely woman of sixty years of age, very well satisfied

with herself and her doings. Her eyes disfigure her. They set as far from one another as the sockets will allow, worse than crosseyed! If it were not for that she would be good looking." To Laura Clay, 27 November 1879, Clay Family Papers.

30. Mary Barr Clay to Laura Clay, 5 November 1879, Clay Family Papers; Mary Barr Clay, "Kentucky," History of Woman Suffrage, 3:819.

31. Mary Jane Clay to Laura Clay, 29 December 1879, 15 March 1880, Clay Family Papers.

32. National Woman Suffrage Association, Proceedings of the Sixteenth Annual Convention . . . Held in Washington, D.C., March 4–7, 1884 (Rochester, N.Y.: Charles Mann, 1884), pp. 13–16.

33. Mary Barr Clay, "Kentucky," History of Woman Suffrage, 3:819.

34. Ibid.; Eleanor Flexner, Century of Struggle: The Woman's Rights Movement in the United States (Cambridge: Harvard University Press, 1959), pp. 182–86; Mary Earhart, Frances Willard: From Prayers to Politics (Chicago: University of Chicago Press, 1944). Flexner discusses the rapid rise of the Woman's Christian Temperance Union after its founding in 1874. It was soon the largest women's organization in the country. Under the leadership of Frances Willard, it became a multipurpose organization, creating "departments" to work for suffrage, prison reform, kindergartens, physical culture and hygiene, as well as temperance. During Willard's presidency, which lasted until her death in 1898, the Franchise Department was very active and provided the surest source of allies for the suffragists.

35. Louisville Courier-Journal, 26, 27 October 1881.

36. Ibid., 27 October 1881.

37. Manuscript speech by Laura Clay, n.d., Laura Clay Papers.

38. Ibid.

39. Chicago Tribune, 2 June 1880; Louisville Courier-Journal, 27 October 1881.

40. Susan B. Anthony to Mary Barr Clay, 17 December 1888, Clay Family Papers. For a discussion of the cause of the division among the feminists and the eventual reunification of their forces, see Robert E. Riegel, "The Split of the Feminist Movement in 1869," Mississippi Valley Historical Review 49 (December 1962): 485–96; Flexner, Century of Struggle, pp. 151–55, 219–20.

41. Lucy Stone to Mary Barr Clay, 8 September 1883, Clay Family Papers; NWSA, Proceedings . . . 1884, pp. 33–34.

42. Anthony and Harper, eds., History of Woman Suffrage, 4:406–7.

43. Clipping, Woman's Journal, 6 December 1884, Laura Clay Scrapbook.

44. Anthony to Mary Barr Clay, 29 October 1880, 23 February 1882, Lucy Stone to Mary Barr Clay, 10 February 1884, Clay Family Papers.

45. Louisville Courier-Journal, 1 March 1896; Caroline M. Brown [Chairman of Committee on Topics and Papers] to Laura Clay, 4 June 1886, Laura Clay Papers.

46. Louisville Courier-Journal, 23 October 1886.

47. New York Tribune, n.d., reprint by Association for the Advancement of Women, Clay Family Papers.

Chapter 3

1. Clipping, Minneapolis Times, 23 April 1901, Laura Clay Papers; Susan B. Anthony to Mary Barr Clay, 17 December 1888, Clay Family Papers; Lexington Herald, 28 February 1935. Sallie's children were Mary Warfield, Elizabeth, Helen, Laura Clay, and Warfield Clay. See note written by Laura Clay, 19 October 1903,

Laura Clay Papers. Four children, Mary Warfield, Fanny Graves, Spotswood Dabney, Jr., and Clay were born of the Crenshaw marriage, which ended Annie's active participation in the woman's rights movement. Laura Clay to Mary Warfield Bennett, 6 January 1910, Laura Clay Papers. The Laura Clay Scrapbook contains a number of the "Woman's Column" articles written by Clay for the Kentucky Gazette, as well as other information on the 1889–1895 period. Eaton, Freedom of Thought in the Old South (New York: Peter Smith, 1951), p. 318.

2. Manuscript speech by Laura Clay, n.d., Laura Clay Papers.

3. Lexington Kentucky Leader, 19 November 1889. See copy of the original constitution of the Kentucky ERA, Laura Clay Papers. This document was based on the ideas of the Fayette County ERA, which in turn drew heavily from the charter of the Kentucky WCTU. Clay was following a good example here, since the WCTU had been phenomenally successful in drawing women to its banner. Later day critics of the WCTU sometimes forget that the organization established thirty-eight different departments of work, appealing to a wide range of womanly interests, while continuing its well-known efforts for state and national prohibition. Flexner, Century of Struggle, pp. 183–84.

4. Manuscript speech by Laura Clay, n.d., Laura Clay Papers.

5. Lucy Stone to Laura Clay, 22 October 1888, ibid.; Laura Clay, "Kentucky," History of Woman Suffrage, 4:665–66.

6. Manuscript speech by Laura Clay, n.d., Laura Clay Papers.

7. Ibid.

8. Ibid.

9. Mary Barr Clay, "Kentucky," History of Woman Suffrage, 3:821. The Kentucky State Board of Pharmacy refused to license the female graduates of the school until forced to do so by a court order. Founded by Dr. J. P. Barnum, the school offered a three-year program and enrolled approximately fifteen students annually. In 1884 it was incorporated by the state legislature and became the Louisville School of Pharmacy for Women.

10. Zerelda G. Wallace to Mrs. H. B. Chenault, 1 April 1888, Laura Clay Papers. Wallace of Owen County, Ind., was the stepmother of Lew Wallace, a Union Civil War general and the author of the popular novel Ben Hur. Clipping, n.d., Laura Clay Scrapbook.

11. Ibid.

12. Andrew Sinclair, The Emancipation of the American Woman (New York: Harper and Row, 1966), p. 222. Both Sinclair, pp. 220–29, and Flexner, Century of Struggle, pp. 182–86, spend some time debating whether or not the suffragists should have allied with the temperance people. It is a meaningless point. In many areas, particularly in the South and West, the suffragists simply had no other choice. WCTU members were the only people the suffragists could turn to for help in organizing meetings and distributing literature. Until well after the turn of the century, it was the WCTU which had the better organization and greater numerical strength. By the 1880s the WCTU "had reached into every state in the Union, and claimed to speak for more than two hundred thousand women" (Flexner, p. 184). As late as 1893, the membership of the NAWSA was only 13,150. Aileen S. Kraditor, The Ideas of the Woman Suffrage Movement, 1890–1920 (New York: Columbia University Press, 1965), p. 7. At the time Clay was struggling to get the suffrage movement under way in Kentucky, the WCTU already had an organization in many of the most remote counties. Whether she was seeking help in circulating

a petition or planning a tour, she had to turn to the WCTU, which had enrolled most of the socially conscious women up to the turn of the century. The Laura Clay Papers contain countless letters to WCTU correspondents.

13. Emma Curry to Mrs. H. B. Chenault, 7 May 1888, Laura Clay Papers.

14. Mrs. Lucy Winslow to Mrs. H. B. Chenault, 7 May 1888, ibid.; Hubert Vreeland, ed., *Hand Book of Kentucky* (Louisville: Globe Printing Co., 1908), pp. 389, 680; Kate Whitefield to Mrs. H. B. Chenault, 20 April 1888; Fannie T. Harrison to Laura Clay, 1 September 1888, Laura Clay Papers; Vreeland, ed., *Hand Book of Kentucky*, p. 533.

15. 3 October 1888, Laura Clay Papers.

16. *Woman's Journal*, 27 April 1889; Clipping, 20 February 1889, Laura Clay Papers.

17. Kraditor, *The Ideas of the Woman Suffrage Movement*, pp. 57–58. Some prominent suffragists were temperance proponents before joining the suffrage ranks. These included Susan B. Anthony, Anna Howard Shaw, Carrie Chapman Catt, Catherine Waugh McCulloch, and Ella Seass Stewart. Laura Clay, "Kentucky," *History of Woman Suffrage*, 4:666. Clay noted that the franchise department was adopted in 1892 and gave the WCTU credit for proving "a faithful and valuable ally in educating public sentiment and obtaining desired legislation."

18. Clipping, letter to editor, *Southern Journal*, 5 March 1892, Laura Clay Scrapbook. Clay's letter to this organ of the Prohibition party in Kentucky was for the purpose of chastising the party for removing the woman suffrage plank from its 1892 platform. She closed, "Very sincerely yours for Prohibition and equal rights."

19. Clipping, *Richmond* (Ky.) *Register*, n.d., 1894, ibid.

20. *Lexington Kentucky Leader*, 6 July 1894; manuscript copy of speech, "Lexington Chautauqua Address," n.d., Laura Clay Papers.

21. Ibid.

22. Clark, *History of Kentucky*, p. 595.

23. *Louisville Times*, 5 July 1895.

24. Ibid.

25. Ibid.

26. Ibid., 6 July 1895.

27. Mrs. R. J. Lewis [Eubank, Ky.] to Laura Clay, 11 November 1889; Miss Anna Wilkinson [Paducah, Ky.] to Laura Clay, 2 December 1889; Mrs. N. C. Hamilton [Verona, Ky.] to Laura Clay, 1 June 1889; Mrs. Elar G. Franceford [Crab Orchard, Ky.] to Laura Clay, 27 April 1889; Mrs. Ruth A. Martien [Warsaw, Ky.] to Laura Clay, 25 March 1889, Obenchain to Laura Clay, 2 March 1889, Laura Clay Papers. In one of Obenchain's short stories, "Aunt Jane Goes A-Visiting," a suffragist named "Miss Laura" appears and Aunt Jane gives a long monologue on woman's rights. *Cosmopolitan* 43 (September 1907): 495–506. Sophia Lee, "Lida Calvert Hall" (M.A. thesis, George Peabody College, 1942).

28. Lucy Stone to Laura Clay, 6 January 1888, Laura Clay Papers; *Lexington Kentucky Leader*, 22 November 1889.

29. *Louisville Post*, 10 October, 10 January 1890; *Louisville Times*, 6 July 1895.

30. *Atlanta Constitution*, 21 January 1895.

31. Mary Barr Clay, "Kentucky," *History of Woman Suffrage*, 3:821–22; *Encyclopedia of the Social Sciences*, s.v. "Marital Property."

32. *Louisville Courier-Journal*, 10 January 1890.

33. *Acts of the General Assembly of the Commonwealth of Kentucky*, 1837

(Frankfort, Ky.: A. G. Hodge, 1838), p. 282; National American Woman Suffrage Association, *Victory: How Women Won It—A Centennial Symposium, 1840–1940* (New York: H. W. Wilson Company, 1940), p. 165; Mrs. Kate Trimble de Roode quoted in Mary Barr Clay, "Kentucky," *History of Woman Suffrage*, 3:822; *Louisville Courier-Journal*, 14 March 1894; Rembert W. Patrick, *The Reconstruction of the Nation* (New York: Oxford University Press, 1967), p. 148.

34. Clipping, *Louisville Commercial*, 10 January 1890, Laura Clay Scrapbook.

35. *Lexington Kentucky Gazette*, 30 November 1889; *Louisville Courier-Journal*, 11 January 1890.

36. *Louisville Courier-Journal*, 11 January 1890; Newspaper clipping, 10 January 1890, Laura Clay Scrapbook.

37. *Louisville Courier-Journal*, 11 January 1890; Newspaper clipping, 10 January 1890, Laura Clay Scrapbook. Clay apparently was not a vain woman. She kept the clipping even though the reporter had added nine years to her life.

38. *Louisville Courier-Journal*, 12 January 1890; Arthur Krock, ed., *The Editorials of Henry Watterson* (Louisville: Louisville Courier-Journal Co., 1923), p. 365.

39. *Lexington Kentucky Gazette*, 8 March 1890.

40. Ibid., 15 March 1890; Newspaper clipping, 12 May 1890, Laura Clay Scrapbook.

41. Clark, *History of Kentucky*, pp. 601–2.

42. Ibid., p. 602.

43. Newspaper clipping, October 1890, Laura Clay Scrapbook.

44. *Louisville Post*, 10 October 1890.

45. *Louisville Courier-Journal*, 10 October 1890.

46. *Louisville Times*, 12 December 1890, Laura Clay Scrapbook; Newspaper clipping, 12 December 1890, ibid.

47. Newspaper clipping, 12 December 1890, ibid.

48. Kentucky Constitutional Convention, 1890, *Proceedings and Debates in the Convention Assembled at Frankfort, on the Eighth Day of September, 1890, to Adopt, Amend or Change the Constitution of the State of Kentucky* (Frankfort, Ky.: E. Polk Johnson, 1890), 2:39.

49. Ibid., p. 40.

50. Ibid., pp. 39, 41.

51. *Louisville Times*, 13 December 1890; vita prepared by Laura Clay, 13 December 1923, Laura Clay Papers.

52. *Lexington Kentucky Gazette*, 20 December 1890, 17 January 1891.

53. Clark, *History of Kentucky*, p. 604; Kentucky Constitutional Convention, 1890, *Proceedings and Debates*, 4:6050–51.

54. Anthony and Harper, eds., *History of Woman Suffrage*, 4:666.

55. *Louisville Courier-Journal*, 10, 12 February 1892; Kentucky Senate Journal, 1892–1893, p. 274.

56. Laura Clay, "Kentucky," *History of Woman Suffrage*, 4:673–74; letter to the editor, *Louisville Courier-Journal*, 13 February 1894.

57. Laura Clay to E. W. Bagby, 18 June 1914, Laura Clay Papers. Bagby had requested Clay's version of the bill's passage, particularly information about which legislators deserved the credit for drawing it up and seeing it through the General Assembly. 15 June 1914, ibid. In light of their estrangement at that time, Clay's praise for Henry's work is an interesting note on the former's fairness and generosity.

58. Kentucky *Senate Journal*, 1894, p. 947; *Lexington Kentucky Gazette*, 24 March 1894; Laura Clay to E. W. Bagby, 18 June 1914, Laura Clay Papers.

59. Kentucky *House Journal*, 1894, p. 290; *Lexington Kentucky Leader*, 29 March 1894.

60. *Louisville Courier-Journal*, 25 March 1894.

61. Anthony and Harper, eds., *History of Woman Suffrage*, 4:670–71.

62. *Louisville Courier-Journal*, 25 March 1894; *Lexington Kentucky Gazette*, 24 March 1894.

63. Nell Whaley, "Women at Transylvania," *Transylvanian* 28 (April 1919): 20–23.

64. Minutes, Fayette ERA, 1888, Laura Clay Papers.

65. Whaley, "Women at Transylvania," p. 22.

66. Ibid.

67. *Lexington Kentucky Gazette*, 19 November 1892; Laura Clay, "Kentucky," *History of Woman Suffrage*, 4:677.

68. *Lexington Kentucky Gazette*, 12 March 1892, 2 December 1893; Clipping, *Lexington Press-Transcript*, 9 August 1895, Laura Clay Scrapbook.

69. Clipping, *Lexington Press-Transcript*, 9 August 1895, Laura Clay Scrapbook.

70. Ibid., 6 November 1895; Anthony and Harper, eds., *History of Woman Suffrage*, 4:675.

71. *Lexington Kentucky Gazette*, 26 March 1894.

72. Laura Clay to Anna Howard Shaw, 16 December 1906, Laura Clay Papers.

73. To Harriet Taylor Upton, 26 June 1906, ibid.

Chapter 4

1. Clipping, *Owensboro Inquirer*, n.d., 1913, Laura Clay Papers.

2. *Louisville Times*, 6 July 1895; *Louisville Courier-Journal*, 1 March 1896; *Woman's Journal* (Boston), 7 September 1907; Clipping, Virginia D. Young in *Varnville* (S. C.) *Enterprise*, 5 June 1895, Laura Clay Scrapbook.

3. Alice Stone Blackwell to Laura Clay, 12 April 1910, Laura Clay Papers; Clipping, *Warren* (Ohio) *Daily Tribune*, 26 September 1904, ibid.

4. Eaton, *Freedom of Thought in the Old South*, p. 378.

5. NWSA, *Proceedings*, 1884, p. 94; Albert D. Kirwan, *Revolt of the Rednecks: Mississippi Politics, 1875–1925* (New York: Harper and Row, 1965), p. 3.

6. C. Vann Woodward, *Origins of the New South, 1877–1913* (Baton Rouge: Louisiana State University Press, 1951), p. 321.

7. George B. Tindall, *South Carolina Negroes, 1877–1900* (Baton Rouge: Louisiana State University Press, 1966), pp. 88–89; Kirwan, *Revolt of the Rednecks*, p. 58.

8. To Mary Barr and Sallie Clay, n.d., Clay Family Papers. (Internal evidence indicates that Mary and Sallie were away at school at the time, which would put the letter in the pre-Civil War Period.) John G. Fee, *The Autobiography of John G. Fee* (Chicago: National Christian Association, 1891), p. 126. Laura Clay to Mary Jane Clay, 30 November 1870, Clay Family Papers; Laura Clay to Eugenia B. Farmer, 5 August 1907, Laura Clay Papers.

9. Clipping, *Lexington Kentucky Gazette*, n.d., 1890, Laura Clay Scrapbook. Since Clay mentions that the House of Representatives has just passed the Wyo-

ming statehood bill, an event of March 27, it is obvious that this communication was written no later than early April 1890.

10. Ibid.

11. Ibid.

12. Ibid.

13. Ibid.

14. Kirwan, *Revolt of the Rednecks*, pp. 64, 68; *Louisville Courier-Journal*, 22 August 1890.

15. National American Woman Suffrage Association, *Proceedings of the Twenty-Third Annual Convention . . . Held in Washington, D.C., January 16–19, 1893* (Washington, D.C.: Stormont and Jackson, n.d.), p. 79.

16. Woodward, *Origins of the New South*, p. 321; Kirwan, *Revolt of the Rednecks*, p. 69.

17. Mrs. Olivia F. Fitzhugh to Laura Clay, 24 April 1892, Laura Clay Papers. Fitzhugh reported that "our last Constitutional Convention . . . came near giving woman suffrage."

18. NAWSA, *Proceedings . . . 1893*, p. 76.

19. Letters to the editor, *Woman's Journal* (Boston), 10, 26 March 1892, Laura Clay Scrapbook; letters to Laura Clay from Virginia D. Young [Fairfax, S.C.], 18 March 1892; Caroline E. Merrick [New Orleans, La.], 20 March 1892; Caroline H. Miller [Sandy Spring, Md.], 3 May 1892; Belle H. Bennett [Richmond, Ky.], 2 May 1892, Laura Clay Papers. Bennett, a prominent Methodist churchwoman, was the sister of James Bennett, Clay's brother-in-law. As agent and treasurer of the Scarritt Bible and Training School (later Sue Bennett College), she had wide contacts among southern churchwomen. Her letter included the names of several prospective suffrage workers. Mrs. M. M. Snell to Laura Clay, 24 March 1892, Laura Clay Papers.

20. Mrs. Olivia F. Fitzhugh to Laura Clay, 24 April 1892; Mrs. Virginia D. Young to Laura Clay, 18 March 1892, Laura Clay Papers.

21. NAWSA, *Proceedings . . . 1893*, pp. 77–78.

22. Ibid., p. 79. Clay's exclusion of the large Negro population from her demand for a government based on the consent of the governed was common among the suffragists. Like the Progressives, they seemed to see no inconsistency in advocating reforms in the name of the people, while accepting antidemocratic proposals where the rights of Negroes and immigrants were concerned. Many reformers of the period simply did not include Negroes and immigrants in their definition of "the people." See Woodward, "Progressivism—For Whites Only," Chapt. 14, in *Origins of the New South*. NAWSA, *Proceedings . . . 1893*, pp. 77–78. Clipping, letter to the editor, *Woman's Journal* (Boston), 10 March 1892, Laura Clay Scrapbook.

23. Ibid.

24. Clipping, *Woman's Chronicle* (Little Rock), 25 February 1893, Laura Clay Scrapbook; *Lexington Kentucky Leader*, 12 February 1894; Mrs. Ella C. Chamberlain [Tampa, Fla.] to Laura Clay, 5 April 1894; Mrs. Elizabeth B. Dodge [Manassas, Va.] to Laura Clay, 12 April 1894, Laura Clay Papers.

25. Susan B. Anthony to Laura Clay, 13 March 1894, Laura Clay Papers. Anthony was seventy-four years old at the time.

26. Susan B. Anthony to Laura Clay, 21 September 1894; H. Augusta Howard to Laura Clay, 26 November 1894; Circular letter, printed by Laura Clay for the Southern Committee, 26 November 1894, ibid.

27. *Lexington Kentucky Leader*, 10 January 1895; *Lexington Kentucky Gazette*, 26 January 1895; Nellie N. Somerville to Laura Clay, 16 February 1895, Laura Clay Papers. Somerville of Greenville, who was later to achieve national prominence as a suffragist, wrote that she thought the meeting in her town was a success, but feared that Catt was not of the same opinion.

28. *Atlanta Constitution*, 21 January 1895.

29. A. Elizabeth Taylor, "The Woman Suffrage Movement in North Carolina," *North Carolina Historical Review* 37 (April 1961): 45–62. Like so many of the other early suffrage associations, the North Carolina ERA did not have a rapid or continuous growth. Despite speeches there by Belle Kearney, Frances Willard, Laura Clay, and other "prominent suffragists," only the Asheville association was still in existence at the end of 1895 and it had only forty members. National American Woman Suffrage Association, *Proceedings of the Twenty-Seventh Annual Convention . . . Held in Atlanta, Georgia, January 31–February 5, 1895* (Warren, Ohio: William R. Ritezel & Company, n.d.), pp. 18–20. *Atlanta Constitution*, 2 February 1895.

30. Mary Gray Peck, *Carrie Chapman Catt* (New York: H. W. Wilson Company, 1944), pp. 83–84; Kraditor, *Ideas of the Woman Suffrage Movement*, pp. 271–72.

31. NAWSA, *Proceedings . . . 1895*, p. 19; National American Woman Suffrage Association, *Proceedings of the Twenty-Eighth Annual Convention . . . Held in Washington, D.C., January 23–28, 1896* (Philadelphia: Press of Alfred J. Ferris, n.d.), p. 75.

32. Nellie A. Somerville to Laura Clay, 28 December 1897; Virginia D. Young to Laura Clay, 8 March 1898, Laura Clay Papers.

33. NAWSA, *Proceedings . . . 1896*, pp. 40, 41; Peck, *Carrie Chapman Catt*, pp. 83–84.

34. Tindall, *South Carolina Negroes*, pp. 73–74; for a discussion of the situation in South Carolina see Francis B. Simkins, *Pitchfork Ben Tillman: South Carolinian* (Baton Rouge: Louisiana State University Press, 1944), pp. 72–76, 284–88; and Simkins, *The Tillman Movement in South Carolina* (Durham: Duke University Press, 1926), pp. 203–4, 212–13.

35. *Atlanta Constitution*, 3 February 1895; Clipping, *Woman's Chronicle* (Little Rock), 25 February 1893, Laura Clay Scrapbook.

36. NAWSA, *Proceedings . . . 1896*, pp. 42–43, 157.

37. Ibid.

38. Ibid., p. 42.

39. Clipping, a Greenville, S.C., newspaper, 30 April 1895, Laura Clay Scrapbook.

40. Ibid.

41. Ibid.

42. Ibid.

43. Ibid.

44. Clipping, *Varnville (S.C.) Enterprise*, 5 June 1895; Clipping, *Charleston News and Courier*, 14, 8 May 1895, Laura Clay Scrapbook.

45. Ibid., 3 May 1895.

46. Mrs. F. Evans to Laura Clay, 22 October 1895; John R. Finley [Auditor, Laurens County] to Laura Clay, 23 October 1895; Mrs. M. A. Conley to Laura Clay, 28 September 1895, Laura Clay Papers.

47. Simkins, *Tillman Movement*, p. 212.

48. NAWSA, *Proceedings* . . . 1896, pp. 42–43, 157.

49. Clipping, n.d., Laura Clay Scrapbook; Simkins, *Pitchfork Ben Tillman*, pp. 298, 211–12; Clipping, *Columbia Daily Register*, 24 November, 28 September 1895, Laura Clay Scrapbook.

50. Clipping, Varnville (S.C.) *Enterprise*, n.d., 1895; Laura Clay Scrapbook.

51. Clipping, *Charleston News and Courier*, 25 September 1895, ibid.

52. Ibid.

53. Clipping, Varnville (S.C.) *Enterprise*, 25 September 1895, Laura Clay Scrapbook. The writer of this article was Virginia D. Young, the associate editor of the newspaper who was present at the hearing.

54. Clipping, *Charleston News and Courier*, 6 November 1895; Clipping, *Columbia Daily Register*, 24 November 1895, ibid.

55. Simkins, *Pitchfork Ben Tillman*, pp. 296–97.

56. Clipping, *Charleston News and Courier*, 23 October 1895, Laura Clay Scrapbook.

57. *Origins of the New South*, p. 325.

58. Ibid., pp. 335, 338, 339.

59. NAWSA, *Proceedings* . . . 1895, p. 147; Clipping, Letter to the editor, *Charleston News and Courier*, n.d., 1895, Laura Clay Papers.

60. Simkins, *Pitchfork Ben Tillman*, pp. 558–59; NAWSA, *Proceedings* . . . 1896, p. 158; Clipping, *Columbia Daily Register*, 24 November 1895, Laura Clay Scrapbook.

61. Clipping, *Woman's Journal* (Boston), 13 July 1895, Laura Clay Scrapbook.

62. NAWSA, *Proceedings* . . . 1896, p. 67.

63. *Washington Post*, 26 January 1896; NAWSA, *Proceedings* . . . 1896, p. 157.

64. NAWSA, *Proceedings* . . . 1896, p. 157. She was probably referring primarily to the association's current argument over Elizabeth Cady Stanton's *Woman's Bible*. This attempt at biblical criticism from a female viewpoint had caused the suffragists some embarrassment in the South Carolina campaign. This publication will be discussed in the next chapter.

65. Ibid., pp. 67, 75.

66. Ibid., pp. 81–82.

67. Ibid., p. 43.

Chapter 5

1. Clipping, 19 January 1892, Laura Clay Scrapbook.

2. Anthony and Harper, eds., *The History of Woman Suffrage*, 4:185; NAWSA, *Proceedings* . . . 1893, p. 49.

3. National American Woman Suffrage Association, *Proceedings of the Twenty-Sixth Annual Convention . . . Held in Washington, D.C., February 15–20, 1894* (Warren, Ohio: Chronicle Print, n.d.), pp. 101–2; Alma Lutz, *Susan B. Anthony: Rebel, Crusader, Humanitarian* (Boston: Branan Press, 1957), pp. 277–78; Flexner, *Century of Struggle*, p. 221; NAWSA, *Proceedings* . . . 1894, pp. 98–99. Not until 1914 did a serious argument develop among suffragists over the question of how the franchise could be most quickly won. By that date, one faction believed that the ballot would have to be gained through state constitutional amendments, holding that three-fourths of the states would never ratify a federal amendment. Another

faction maintained that state campaigns were useless and that only the federal amendment should be pursued. Throughout the long history of the movement, however, the majority of suffragists were willing to work in either type campaign, seeking the ballot any way they could get it and as quickly as possible.

4. For example, while total attendance was less by four delegates in Atlanta in 1895, the number of southern delegates was more than double that of the previous year. NAWSA, Proceedings . . . 1895, pp. 10–12.

5. Ibid., p. 101.

6. Kraditor, The Ideas of the Woman Suffrage Movement, p. 10.

7. NAWSA, Proceedings . . . 1893, p. 87.

8. Washington Post, 20 January 1893; NAWSA, Proceedings . . . 1893, p. 116.

9. Elizabeth C. Stanton et al., Woman's Bible. Part I: "Comments on Genesis, Exodus, Leviticus, Numbers, and Deuteronomy" (New York: European Publishing Company, 1895). Part II: "Comments on the Old and New Testaments from Joshua to Revelation" (New York: European Publishing Company, 1898). Copies of these volumes may be found in the Woman's Archives at Radcliffe College. One of Stanton's fellow commentators was Josephine K. Henry, a fact that may explain the growing estrangement between the two Kentuckians which developed at this time. By 1899 Henry, who had been vital in the early successes of feminism in Kentucky, had withdrawn from active participation. It is interesting that the rift over the Woman's Bible which threatened the Anthony-Stanton friendship seems to have ended that of Clay and Henry. By 1906 Henry had become disillusioned with the women she had struggled to liberate in the 1890s. "Poor things!" she wrote a friend, "many of them do not realize their subject position in life, and the majority hug their chains and love the noise of their clanking." To Eugenia B. Farmer, 30 July 1906, Laura Clay Papers. Alma Lutz, Created Equal: A Biography of Elizabeth Cady Stanton, 1815–1902 (New York: John Day Company, 1940), p. 300. Clipping, Lexington Observer, 30 November 1895, Laura Clay Scrapbook.

10. Manuscript copy of speech, "Lexington Chautauqua Address," 6 July 1894, Laura Clay Papers; Kraditor, The Ideas of the Woman Suffrage Movement, p. 82. NAWSA, Proceedings . . . 1894, p. 160.

11. Clipping, Greenville Daily News, 23 November 1895, Laura Clay Papers; A. Viola Neblett to Laura Clay, 23 November 1895, ibid.; Peck, Carrie Chapman Catt, p. 87.

12. Washington Post, 29 January 1896; NAWSA, Proceedings . . . 1896, p. 91.

13. Lutz, Susan B. Anthony, pp. 280, 279; Susan B. Anthony to Elizabeth Cady Stanton, quoted in ibid., p. 280.

14. Kraditor, The Ideas of the Woman Suffrage Movement, p. 85.

15. Laura Clay to Flora Dunlap, 5 April 1916, Laura Clay Papers.

16. The Celebrated Trial of Madeline Pollard vs. Breckinridge (n.p.: American Printing and Binding Company, 1894). This account of the day-to-day details of the case is an obvious attempt to capitalize on the sensation it had created across the country. The book includes brief sketches of the two principal figures and lengthy excerpts from the testimony given during the trial. Pollard claimed that Breckinridge had promised to marry her in the period between the death of his second wife in 1892 and his marriage to Louise Wing of Louisville in 1893. Louisville Courier-Journal, 14, 15 April 1894. In this newspaper, as in others across the country, details of the trial were front-page news.

17. Louisville Courier-Journal, 26 March 1894.

18. Ibid., 5, 6 May 1894.

19. Ibid., 6, 14 May 1894.

20. Martha W. Fairfield to Laura Clay, 5 April 1894, Laura Clay Papers; *Louisville Courier-Journal*, 10 June 1894.

21. *Louisville Courier-Journal*, 18 September 1894. "The women defeated Mr. Breckinridge. There is no doubt about that," the paper reported after the primary. Anthony and Harper, eds., *History of Woman Suffrage*, 4:667. *Lexington Kentucky Leader*, 25 October 1894. *Atlanta Constitution*, 3 February 1895.

22. Rachel Foster Avery to Catherine Waugh McCulloch, 9 April 1901, Dillon Collection, Schlesinger Library, Radcliffe College, Cambridge, Mass. (cited hereafter as Dillon Collection).

23. Lutz, *Susan B. Anthony*, p. 290.

24. Ibid., pp. 291, 292, 293. Blackwell was the only man who regularly attended the annual conventions of the NAWSA. His wife, Lucy Stone, who had died in 1893, was a pioneer in the fight for women's rights. Their only child, Alice Stone Blackwell, continued in the cause her parents had adopted and became the editor of their paper, *Woman's Journal*.

25. Anthony to Clay, 8 August, 15 April 1900, Laura Clay Papers.

26. 3 August, 25 July 1900, ibid.

27. Carrie Chapman Catt to Laura Clay, 13 January 1899, ibid.

28. Harriet Taylor Upton to Catherine Waugh McCulloch, 9 July 1900, Dillon Collection. As late as July, Upton was expressing dissatisfaction with Catt's efforts to organize Ohio and her leading lieutenant's money-raising efforts. She complained that the new president had planned "four or five times as much work as could possibly be well done. Then she trusted to luck to help her out. I was disappointed in her in this regard and I was disappointed in Miss Hay's ability to raise money." Lutz, *Susan B. Anthony*, pp. 293–94.

29. NAWSA, *Proceedings . . . 1894*, p. 111.

30. Ibid.

31. NAWSA, *Proceedings . . . 1896*, p. 109; National American Woman Suffrage Association, *Proceedings of the Thirty-Fourth Annual Convention . . . Held in Washington, D.C., February 14–18, 1902* (Warren, Ohio: Press of Frank W. Perry, n.d.), pp. 45, 43; National American Woman Suffrage Association, *Proceedings of the Thirty-Fifth Annual Convention . . . Held in New Orleans, Louisiana, March 15–25, 1903* (Warren, Ohio: William Ritezel and Company, n.d.), p. 40. Clay's interest in the "argument of numbers" had undoubtedly been intensified during the previous year, because a principal argument of one of the legislators responsible for taking school suffrage from the women of Kentucky had been that most women did not want to vote. State Senator J. Embry Allen to Mrs. Eugenia D. Potts, 31 January 1902, Laura Clay Papers. This episode is discussed in this chapter.

32. NAWSA, *Proceedings . . . 1903*, pp. 40, 41.

33. Ibid.

34. Ibid., pp. 42, 43.

35. National American Woman Suffrage Association, *Proceedings of the Thirty-Sixth Annual Convention . . . Held in Washington, D.C., February 11–17, 1904* (Warren, Ohio: William Ritezel and Company, n.d.), pp. 57–58; Mrs. Mary J. Coggeshall to Laura Clay, 27 April 1904, Laura Clay Papers.

36. NAWSA, *Proceedings . . . 1904*, p. 58; *National American Woman Suffrage*

Annual Convention . . . Held in Portland, Oregon, June 28–July 5, 1905 (Warren, Ohio: Tribune Company, n.d.), pp. 71–89; Kraditor, *Ideas of the Woman Suffrage Movement*, p. 7; NAWSA, *Proceedings* . . . 1905, p. 72.

37. National American Woman Suffrage Association, *Proceedings of the Thirty-Ninth Annual Convention . . . Held in Chicago, Illinois, February 14–17, 1907* (Warren, Ohio: Tribune Company, n.d.), pp. 55–56; Newspaper clipping, 19 February 1907, enclosed in a letter, Grace Sherwood to Laura Clay, 25 March 1907, Laura Clay Papers.

38. Laura Clay to Harriet Taylor Upton, 20 November 1907, Laura Clay Papers.

39. Laura Clay to Anna Howard Shaw, 10 May 1907; to Harriet Taylor Upton [President of the Ohio Woman Suffrage Association], 20 November 1907; to Ella S. Stewart, 13 October 1910, ibid.

40. NAWSA, *Proceedings* . . . 1907, pp. 31–32; Flexner, *Century of Struggle*, pp. 248, 254; NAWSA, *Proceedings* . . . 1907, pp. 55–56.

41. Laura Clay, "Kentucky," *History of Woman Suffrage*, 4:672. "The result of the trial of women in this capacity," Laura Clay reported in 1899, "has been most successful." See National American Woman Suffrage Association, *Proceedings of the Thirty-first Annual Convention . . . Held in Grand Rapids, Michigan, April 27–May 3, 1899* (Warren, Ohio: Press of Perry the Printer, n.d.), p. 97. NAWSA, *Proceedings* . . . 1907, p. 72; Newspaper clipping, 1893, Laura Clay Scrapbook.

42. Laura Clay to Harriet Taylor Upton, 17 September 1906, Laura Clay Papers.

43. James F. Hopkins, *The University of Kentucky: Origins and Early Years* (Lexington: University of Kentucky Press, 1951), pp. 136–42, 278.

44. Letter to the editor, *Lexington Daily Leader*, 17 February 1896.

45. Ibid.

46. Ibid.; there were seventeen men on the board of trustees in 1896. Two of them, Governor William O. Bradley and James K. Patterson, were ex-officio members. See *Catalogue of the Officers, Studies, and Students of the State College of Kentucky, . . . Session ending June 4, 1896* (Louisville: John P. Morton and Co., 1896), p. 6.

47. Letter to the editor, *Lexington Daily Leader*, 7 February 1896.

48. Ibid., 20 February 1896. The feminists' demand for representation was not realized until Mrs. Paul G. Blazer was appointed to the Board of Trustees in 1939. See Minutes of the Regular Meeting of the Board of Trustees of the University of Kentucky, 4 April 1939, Archives of the University of Kentucky, Lexington.

49. Pamphlet, "What the Kentucky Equal Rights Association Has Done and What It Proposes to Do," Laura Clay Papers. *Lexington Leader*, 5 March 1902. Whereas male students were provided dormitory rooms, female students were expected to find lodgings in Lexington which were usually more expensive than the college housing. Letter to the editor, *Lexington Herald*, 6 June 1901. Minutes of the Regular Meeting of the Board of Trustees of the University of Kentucky, 10 June 1904, 31 May 1905. Archives of the University of Kentucky, Lexington.

50. E. Merton Coulter, *The Civil War and Readjustment in Kentucky* (Chapel Hill: University of North Carolina Press, 1926), p. 243. Coulter writes that Negroes were drifting to urban centers in Kentucky and becoming a majority of the population in many of them as early as 1870. To meet what was regarded as a growing problem, "Lexington secured a change in her charter, moving forward the time of her elections to February and lengthening the term of office to three years. As the Fifteenth Amendment was not proclaimed until March 30 [1870], the new city gov-

ernment would be elected before that time, and the spectre of Negro domination removed for three years."

51. *Lexington Herald*, 6 November 1901.

52. *Lexington Leader*, 5, 22 January 1902. Klair's figures are questionable, although his primary contention that more Negro than white women registered is probably accurate. As explained below, closer to 800 white women registered as Democrats, and Klair fails to mention that some white women were among the 1,900 who registered as Republicans.

53. *Lexington Herald*, 5, 22 January 1902, *Frankfort Morning Democrat*, 20, 25 January 1902.

54. *Lexington Leader*, 26 January 1902. This is the only instance in which Laura Clay was ever reported as close to tears.

55. Ibid., 6 February 1902.

56. Ibid., 11 March 1902.

57. J. Embry Allen to Mrs. Eugenia D. Potts, 25, 31 January 1902, Laura Clay Papers; *Lexington Leader*, 17 April 1902.

58. *New York Sun*, quoted in *Lexington Leader*, 17 April 1902.

59. Letter to the editor, *Woman's Journal* (Boston), 19 March 1902.

60. *Louisville Courier-Journal*, 1 March 1896; *Lexington Herald*, 27 January 1902; NAWSA, Proceedings . . . 1902, pp. 43–45.

61. Newsletter, Kentucky ERA, October 1903, Laura Clay Papers. The Fayette County ERA delegation to the Kentucky ERA convention carried a resolution which stated: "Recognizing the menace to good government of our present illiterate vote, we recommend to the State E.R.A. that it hereafter asks for the suffrage for women with an educational qualification." Ida Husted Harper, ed., *History of Woman Suffrage*, 6 vols. (New York: NAWSA, 1922), 6:209. *Woman's Journal* (Boston), 1 September 1894; Catt's presidential address of 1904 was devoted to the dangers of the illiterate immigrant vote and to the advocacy of a national educational qualification for all suffrage. Harper, ed., *History of Woman Suffrage*, 5:88–89. In a speech in Richmond, Virginia, on the same subject, Catt charged that the United States had become "drunk on democracy." Clipping, *Richmond Dispatch*, 5 October 1901, Laura Clay Papers.

62. Sophonisba P. Breckinridge, *Madeline McDowell Breckinridge: A Leader in the New South* (Chicago: University of Chicago Press, 1921), p. 54.

63. Clark, *A History of Kentucky*, p. 617.

Chapter 6

1. William L. O'Neill, *Everyone Was Brave: The Rise and Fall of Feminism in America* (Chicago: Quadrangle Books, 1969), p. 150.

2. *Woman's Journal* (Boston), January, 1904; Anna Howard Shaw to Laura Clay, 29 July 1904, Laura Clay Papers. Shaw wrote of Catt's continuing headaches and added, "I hope she may soon find relief from her troublesome head."

3. Kraditor, *The Ideas of the Woman Suffrage Movement*, p. 12–13.

4. *Lexington Herald*, 23 June 1904; Mrs. Mary J. Clay to Laura Clay, 29 December 1879, 26 April 1884, Laura Clay Papers; Laura Bruce to Laura Clay, 20 November 1885, ibid.; *Lexington Herald*, 23 June 1904; Laura Clay to Harriet Taylor Upton, 2 April 1910, ibid. Although Clay had faithfully nursed her friend through the fatal illness caused by uremic poisoning, she knew nothing of her in-

heritance until the will was read. Box 3386, Final Order in the Bruce Legacy Case, 7 May 1906, Fayette County Circuit Court, Lexington, Ky.; NAWSA, *Proceedings . . . 1905*, p. 38. The national treasurer reported that "Within the year Miss Clay paid the Treasury $70 on this account [Bruce legacy], $10.95 of which was paid out for water, rent, agent's commission and repairs, so that $59.05 of this bequest has been received."

5. Final accounting of the Laura Bruce legacy, 7 August 1925, Laura Clay Papers. Clay was a meticulous accountant, especially where the Bruce money was concerned. She regarded it as a near-sacred trust, always requiring receipts for the smallest expenditure and giving a scrupulous accounting to the NAWSA. The Laura Clay Papers are replete with evidence of her close guardianship of her friend's trust.

6. Flexner, *Century of Struggle*, p. 273. Leslie's will was also contested, and it was 1916 before Catt began to receive payments from it which eventually amounted to approximately $1 million. See Ida Husted Harper to Laura Clay, 9 February 1917, Laura Clay Papers.

7. Harper, ed., *History of Woman Suffrage*, 5:93.

8. Shaw's exhausting and sometimes exasperating experiences as the country's most popular female lecturer are fully documented in her many letters to her close friend, personal secretary, and companion, Lucy Anthony. Unfortunately, only excerpted portions of these letters are available and their historical value suffers thereby. See Anna Howard Shaw to Lucy Anthony, 3 December 1903, 11 December 1905, August n.d., 1907, Dillon Collection.

9. Carrie E. Kent to Laura Clay, 9 December 1904, Laura Clay Papers; Elizabeth Hauser to Mary Gray Peck, 24 July 1910, Hauser Letters, Library of Congress, Washington, D.C.; Laura Clay to Harriet Taylor Upton, 26 June 1911, Laura Clay Papers.

10. Despite their great faith in the judgment of the people, the suffragists won only two of their first seventeen referendums. In the final analysis it was the lawmakers, rather than the people, who gave full suffrage to all women. In effect, the Nineteenth Amendment was a way of evading the direct action of the people and that was exactly what most of the suffrage leaders were trying to do by 1918, trusting in the legislators at Washington and in the state capitals to enfranchise women. Carrie Chapman Catt to Laura Clay, 22 January 1918, Laura Clay Papers. Contrary to the early belief of the suffragists, the lawmakers usually proved to be more liberal than the people. In both Ohio and Texas, for example, the legislators ratified the Nineteenth Amendment only a few months after state amendments for woman suffrage had been defeated by the people.

11. Laura Clay to A. H. Campbell, 1 May 1908, Laura Clay Papers. Clay was not an absentee owner in the usual sense of the term, nor did she sharecrop her land. Her instructions to Bush indicate that she knew farm management and had a thorough knowledge of her own land, its problems, and its potential. Laura Clay to Howard Bush, 18 November 1912, ibid.; Harper, ed., *History of Woman Suffrage*, 5:117–18.

12. NAWSA, *Proceedings . . . 1905*, pp. 89–90; To Sallie Clay Bennett, 14 September 1905, Laura Clay Papers; Laura Clay to Eugenia B. Farmer, 29 December 1905; Laura Clay Vita, 23 December 1923, ibid.

13. Laura Clay to Eugenia B. Farmer, 29 December 1905, ibid.

14. Anna Howard Shaw, *The Story of a Pioneer* (New York: Harper and Broth-

ers, 1915), p. 291; Laura Clay to Anna Howard Shaw, 4 February 1910, Laura Clay Papers.

15. Shaw, *Story of a Pioneer*, p. 291; Laura Clay Vita, 23 December 1923, Laura Clay Papers. The campaign was expensive as well as strenuous. The NAWSA spent $18,075 in the effort, a sum equal its average annual income. See Harper, ed., *History of Woman Suffrage*, 5:211.

16. Clara Bewick Colby quoted in Eugenia B. Farmer to Laura Clay, 21 December 1905; Mrs. T. J. Turnbull to Laura Clay, 26 January 1905, Laura Clay Papers.

17. NAWSA, *Proceedings . . . 1907*, p. 72; Handbill, Kate H. Biggers, "Combine against Woman's Suffrage," Laura Clay Papers; Manuscript speech on the Oregon campaign, n.d., ibid.; Alice Stone Blackwell to Laura Clay, 17 June 1906, ibid.

18. To Harriet Taylor Upton, 26 June 1906, ibid. The following letters, drawn from many in the Laura Clay Papers which would illustrate the point, indicate the breadth of intrasuffragist dissension. The states involved are shown in brackets. Anna Howard Shaw to Laura Clay, 25 August 1910 [South Dakota]; Anna Howard Shaw to Official Board, 23 September 1910 [Washington]; Laura Clay to Hannah J. Price, 5 June 1914 [Tennessee]; Anna Howard Shaw to Official Board, 12 June 1911 [Wisconsin]; Maryland WSA to "Dear Friend," 12 October 1911 [Maryland].

19. To Harriet Taylor Upton, 26 June 1906, ibid.

20. Abigail Scott Duniway, *Path Breaking: An Autobiographical History of the Equal Suffrage Movement in the Pacific Coast States* (Portland, Ore.: James, Kerns and Abbot Company, 1914), p. 46. This thin volume does not fulfill its subtitle, and, while more frank than most personal accounts of the suffragists, it hardly scratches the surface of the strong animosities which existed between the author and most other suffrage leaders. Laura Clay to Harriet Taylor Upton, 3 May 1907; to Anna Howard Shaw, 3 May 1907, Laura Clay Papers.

21. Anna Howard Shaw to Business Committee, 13 May 1907; Harriet Taylor Upton to Laura Clay, 18 May 1907, ibid.; To Lucy Anthony, July n.d., 1907, Dillon Collection.

22. Laura Clay to Kate Gordon, 4 February 1908; Laura Clay to Henry Waldo Coe, 17 May 1908; Harriet Taylor Upton to Laura Clay, 7 February 1908, Laura Clay Papers.

23. To Laura Clay, 26 February 1908, 27 October 1912, ibid.

24. Dr. Jeffreys Myers to Laura Clay, 16 January 1911, ibid.

25. Laura Clay to Mrs. Henry Waldo Coe, 5 October 1908, ibid. In fairness to Clay, it should be pointed out that there is no evidence that she expected educational qualifications to be applied only to Negro women, although there can be no doubt that the requirement was a concession to Democratic politicians who wanted to keep them from voting. During her chairmanship of the NAWSA Membership Committee, Clay voted against the admission of suffrage societies which advocated tax qualifications and favored those with an educational qualification only if they were from states that provided free education. See Laura Clay to Mary Winsor [President of Pennsylvania Limited Suffrage League], 8 November 1912; to members of NAWSA Membership Committee, 12 February 1912, Laura Clay Papers.

26. Grant Foreman, *A History of Oklahoma* (Norman: University of Oklahoma Press, 1942), p. 313.

27. Extracts from letters, Marie Jenny Howe to Harriet Taylor Upton, enclosed in Mrs. Upton to Business Committee, 27 May, 12 June 1907, Laura Clay Papers.

28. Carbon of typed letter to the *Oklahoma Post*, 10 January 1907, ibid.

29. Harper, ed., *History of Woman Suffrage*, 6:522; To Harriet Taylor Upton, 8 April 1908, Laura Clay Papers. William Henry ("Alfalfa Bill") Murray was president of the constitutional convention and later United States congressman (1913–1917) and governor of Oklahoma (1931–1935). *Biographical Directory of the American Congress, 1774–1949* (Washington, D.C.: Government Printing Office, 1950), p. 1605.

30. Harper, ed., *History of Woman Suffrage*, 6:522–23. Mrs. Upton to Laura Clay, Alice Stone Blackwell, and Mrs. Florence Kelley, 19 March 1908; Miss Shaw to Business Committee, 31 March 1908, Laura Clay Papers.

31. Laura Clay to Mrs. Upton, 2 April 1910, ibid. Emmeline G. Pankhurst was an English suffragist who helped organize the National Women's Social and Political Union in 1903. She and her two daughters, Christabel and Sylvia, were more militant than the traditional suffragists and were soon given the name "suffragettes," to distinguish them from their less radical sisters in England and America. Before she and her followers began their violent demonstrations, breaking windows and stoning members of Parliament, Pankhurst visited the United States in 1910 on a speaking tour. Pankhurst made an impression on many American suffragists with her notion that the franchise would come when it was politically expedient, not when men's sense of justice had been touched. Constance Rover, *Women's Suffrage and Party Politics in Britain, 1866–1914* (London: Routledge and Kegan Paul, 1967), pp. 20–24; Sinclair, *The Emancipation of the American Woman*, pp. 384–88. Laura Clay to Kate H. Biggers [president of the Oklahoma WSA], 4 February 1910; to Henry B. Blackwell, 27 September 1907; to Miss Shaw, 3 July 1907, Laura Clay Papers.

32. Miss Gordon to Laura Clay, 7 May 1909, ibid.; Harper, ed., *History of Woman Suffrage*, 6:524. Mrs. Upton to Misses Clay, Gordon, Blackwell, and Kelley, 19 March 1908; to the Official Board, 4 January 1910, Laura Clay Papers. Boyer countered that it took money to win a campaign. The Anti-Saloon League had spent $50,000 in 1906 alone in its successful effort to write prohibition into the state constitution. The trouble, she claimed, was that the suffragists had "a bean shooter and the other fellow has gatling guns." Ida Porter Boyer to Harriet Taylor Upton, 11 January 1910, ibid. The title of the board of officers was changed from the Business Committee to the Official Board at the convention at Seattle in 1909. Laura Clay to Mrs. Upton, 20 April 1908, ibid.

33. Laura Clay to Mrs. Biggers, 25 August 1909; to Jessie Ashley, 17 September 1910, ibid. The "Oklahoma" chapter in the final volume of the *History of Woman Suffrage* (6:525) is in error on Laura Clay's contribution; it gives it as $300. Mrs. Biggers to Laura Clay, 23 August 1910, Laura Clay Papers. Harper, ed., *History of Woman Suffrage*, 6:526. Clay's faith in the potential of Oklahoma was justified in 1918, when it became the first southern state to grant political equality to women. Although she took no part in that final victory, memories of her work there were still present. "Yesterday," a worker reported from Oklahoma, "I saw two mules named Anna Shaw and Laura Clay. That is a serious, honest to goodness story" (Marjorie Shuler to Carrie Chapman Catt, 1 September 1918, Sophia Smith Collection, Smith College Library, Northampton, Mass. Hereafter cited as Sophia Smith Collection).

34. Miss Shaw to Official Board, 27 January 1909, Laura Clay Papers.

35. Laura Clay to Miss Shaw, 28 January 1909; to Frances W. Munds, 20 January 1909, ibid.; Inez Haynes Irwin, *Angels and Amazons: A Hundred Years of*

American Women (Garden City, N.Y.: Doubleday, Doran and Company, 1935), p. 340; Laura Clay to Official Board, 29 March 1909, Laura Clay Papers; Frances W. Munds, "Arizona," *History of Woman Suffrage*, 6:12.

36. Mrs. Munds to Laura Clay, 22 February 1909; Laura Gregg to Laura Clay, 26 February 1909, Laura Clay Papers. Kraditor, *Ideas of the Woman Suffrage Movement*, pp. 123–46, uses the better part of one chapter in documenting the opposition of prominent northern and eastern suffragists to the enfranchisement of the new immigrants. Just as the southern women complained that ignorant Negroes had been enfranchised earlier than they, northern women railed against the new immigrants who were voting while natives were yet waiting for the ballot. Although Kraditor does not cite the material on the Arizona campaign, it supports her conclusion that there was a strong anti-immigrant feeling among suffragists. Alan P. Grimes, *The Puritan Ethic and Woman Suffrage* (New York: Oxford University Press, 1967), pp. 108–12. Grimes's thesis is that, contrary to popular opinion, woman suffrage first came to the West not as a result of its greater liberality and the traditional frontier love of freedom but as an attempt on the part of the Anglo-Saxon, nativist Americans to protect their power from the challenge of the newer polyglot American of the late nineteenth and early twentieth centuries. As a result, Grimes contends that the movement, particularly in the West, was as much a conservative as it was a progressive force.

37. Laura Clay to L. C. Hughes, 11 March 1909, Laura Clay Papers. Hughes, a Tucson newspaper editor, wrote Clay for her advice on handling this question.

38. To Col. William Herring [member of the Arizona House of Representatives], 10 March 1909, ibid.; Frances W. Munds, "Arizona," *History of Woman Suffrage*, 6:12; Laura Clay to Mrs. Munds, 18 March 1909, Laura Clay Papers.

39. Laura Clay to Mrs. Munds, 18 March 1909; to Miss Gregg, 30 March 1909; to Miss Gordon, 27 April 1909, ibid.; *Lexington Herald*, 1 March 1913.

40. Laura Clay to Official Board, 29 March 1909; Official Board to Laura Clay, 3 April 1909, Laura Clay Papers; Miss Gregg to Miss Shaw, 23, 16, 27 September 1910, Dillon Collection. Clay's confidence that Arizona was a promising field for suffrage activity was justified when the women of the state won the ballot in 1912 (see Laura Clay to Miss Shaw, 26 November 1909; to Mrs. Upton, 29 January 1910; Frances W. Munds to Laura Clay, 30 January 1910, Laura Clay Papers).

41. Martha G. Stapler, ed., *The Woman Suffrage Yearbook, 1917* (New York: National Woman Suffrage Publishing Company, 1917), pp. 176–77. These statistics were taken from the United States Census of 1910.

42. *Chicago Daily Tribune*, 15 February 1907; Kate Gordon to Laura Clay, 2 August 1907, Laura Clay Papers.

43. Laura Clay to Miss Gordon, 6 August 1907; Blackwell to Laura Clay, 11 September 1907, Laura Clay Papers. Beginning with Illinois in 1913, fourteen states had given women presidential suffrage by 1920. This gave women a voice in electing 339 of the 531 presidential electors, a powerful inducement to the submission and ratification of the Nineteenth Amendment (see unpublished manuscript, "A Brief History of Woman Suffrage," Sophia Smith Collection). Blackwell to Laura Clay, 28 September 1907, Laura Clay Papers.

44. Miss Shaw to Business Committee, 5 November 1907; Laura Clay to Miss Shaw, 30 October 1907, ibid.

45. Laura Clay to Blackwell, 14 October 1907, ibid.

46. Ibid.

47. Ibid.; Kraditor, *The Ideas of the Woman Suffrage Movement,* pp. 200–201.

48. Laura Clay to Blackwell, 5 December 1907; to Catherine Waugh McCulloch, 13 December 1907; Miss Gordon to Laura Clay, 5 December 1907; Laura Clay to Miss Shaw, 30 October 1907; to Mrs. McCulloch, 13 December 1907, Laura Clay Papers; Kraditor, *The Ideas of the Woman Suffrage Movement,* pp. 173–74.

49. Blackwell to Laura Clay, 20 November 1907; Laura Clay to Blackwell, 5 December 1907, Laura Clay Papers.

50. Ibid.

51. Laura Clay to Blackwell, 5 December 1907, ibid.

52. Laura Clay to Blackwell, 29 January 1908, ibid. There was a disagreement among the Mississippi suffragists as to why the campaign was discontinued. Kearney claimed that it was because she could not find a single legislator who would support the suffrage bill, but Somerville believed that Kearney's fear of antagonizing the prohibitionists and losing WCTU speaking engagements was the actual reason the campaign suddenly stopped. According to Somerville, Kearney ruined the chances of offering a bill at that session by announcing to the press that the suffragists would not seek any legislation (see Kate Gordon to Laura Clay, 15 January 1908; Nellie Somerville to Laura Clay, 10 February 1908, ibid.).

53. Claudius O. Johnson, *Borah of Idaho* (New York: Longmans, Green and Company, 1936), p. 413.

Chapter 7

1. Harper, ed., *History of Woman Suffrage,* 5:61.

2. Shaw to Anthony, 27 September 1906, Dillon Collection, Schlesinger Library, Radcliffe College, Cambridge, Mass. (hereafter cited as Dillon Collection); to Lucy Anthony, 4 October 1906, ibid.; Miss Shaw to Business Committee, n.d., 1908, Laura Clay Papers.

3. Miss Shaw to Miss Anthony, November n.d., 1908, Dillon Collection; Miss Gordon to Laura Clay, 7 May 1909, Laura Clay Papers.

4. Christopher Lasch, "Alva Erskin Smith Vanderbilt Belmont," in *Notable American Women, 1607–1950,* ed. Edward T. James, Janet Wilson James, and Paul S. Boyer (Cambridge: Harvard University Press, 1971), 1:126–28. Mrs. Belmont was divorced from William K. Vanderbilt in 1895, ending a twenty-year-old marriage. Soon after, she married Belmont. During this period, Shaw wrote the officers that she had secured Belmont as a life member. To Official Board, 20 March 1909, Laura Clay Papers. Ida Husted Harper, "What Do the Newport Suffrage Meetings Mean?" *Independent* 67 (9 September 1909): 575–79.

5. Alice Stone Blackwell to Rachel Foster Avery, 9 May 1909; Clipping, *Rochester (N. Y.) Union and Advertiser,* 17 July 1909; Clipping, *New York World,* 18 July 1909, Laura Clay Papers.

6. Minutes, NAWSA Executive Committee, 30 June 1909, ibid.; Harper, ed., *History of Woman Suffrage,* 5:248–50, 260–61.

7. Shaw to Anthony, 27 September 1906, Dillon Collection; Mrs. Upton to Laura Clay, 4 December 1909, Laura Clay Papers.

8. Clipping, *New York World,* 12 December 1909; Rachel Foster Avery to Laura Clay, 16 December 1909; Laura Clay to Mrs. Upton, 17 December 1909, ibid.

9. Minutes, NAWSA Official Board, 21–23 December 1909, ibid.

10. Laura Clay to Miss Gordon, 22 March 1910; Miss Shaw to Mrs. Upton, 12 March 1910, ibid. Immediately after the conference, Upton sent Clay the following piece of doggerel describing Lucy Anthony's appearance before the officers:

> There was a fat lady named Clay
> Who behaved most exceedingly gay
> When Lucy boo-hooed
> Miss Clay poo-poohed
> And said, "You will please go away."

(See night letter, n.d., ibid.)

11. To Mrs. Avery, April n.d., 1910, Dillon Collection.

12. To Laura Clay, Mrs. Avery, and Florence Kelley, 12 January 1910; Mrs. Upton to Laura Clay, March n.d., 1910, Laura Clay Papers. On one occasion she wrote three letters to Clay in a single Tuesday evening. Upton to Laura Clay, 7 March 1910, ibid.

13. Miss Shaw to State Presidents, 4 March 1910, ibid.

14. Washington Post, 15 April 1910.

15. Ibid., 18 April 1910; Harper, ed., History of Woman Suffrage, 5:275; Laura Clay to Mary L. C. Chisom, 21 January 1909, Laura Clay Papers. There are many letters to and from Clay in her papers relating to her work for the Great Petition. During her absence from Lexington in Arizona, she persuaded her sister Mary to take up the petition work and hired a secretary, Mary Reed, to help her with the correspondence. See Laura Clay to Mary B. Clay, 27 January 1909, ibid.; Minutes, NAWSA Official Board, 21–23 December 1909, ibid.; Votes for Woman (Seattle), May 1910, ibid.

16. National American Woman Suffrage Association, Proceedings of the Forty-Second Annual Convention . . . Held in Washington, D.C., April 14–19, 1910 (New York: NAWSA Headquarters, n.d.), pp. 85–87, 88–89, 93–94; Shaw, Story of a Pioneer, p. 336; Washington Post, 20, 21 April 1910.

17. Laura Clay to Catherine Waugh McCulloch, 20 May 1910, Dillon Collection; Harper, ed., History of Woman Suffrage, 5:282–83.

18. Miss Shaw to Lucy Anthony, 11 July 1910; Laura Clay to Mrs. Stewart, 23 December 1910, Dillon Collection.

19. Laura Clay to Anna Howard Shaw, 3 January 1911; to Mrs. McCulloch, 18 February 1911, Laura Clay Papers.

20. Laura Clay to Miss Shaw, 2 March 1911; Mrs. McCulloch to Clay, 11 March 1911, ibid.; NAWSA, Proceedings . . . 1910, p. 79; Miss Shaw to Official Board, 18 April 1911, Laura Clay Papers.

21. Ibid.

22. Laura Clay to Miss Shaw, 24 April 1911; Mrs. McCulloch to Laura Clay, 26 April 1911; Miss Gordon to Laura Clay, 4 May 1911; Miss Gordon to Mrs. Dennett, 6 June 1911; Laura Clay to Miss Ashley, 12 June 1911; Laura Clay to Miss Ashley, 30 June 1911, ibid.

23. Miss Ashley to Official Board, 29 June 1911; to Mrs. McCulloch, 18 July 1911; Miss Gordon to Miss Ashley, 23 July 1911; Laura Clay to Mrs. McCulloch, 27 July 1911, ibid.

24. Miss Ashley to Miss Gordon, 27 July 1911; Miss Shaw to Miss Gordon, 27 July 1911, ibid.

25. Laura Clay to Miss Shaw, 23 August 1911; Miss Shaw to Laura Clay, 30

July 1911; Miss Gordon to Official Board, 1 August 1911; Laura Clay to Miss Shaw, 12 August 1911; Miss Shaw to Official Board, 13 August 1911, ibid.; Miss Shaw to Lucy Anthony, August n.d., 1911, Dillon Collection.

26. Laura Clay to Mrs. McCulloch, 7 June 1911; Miss Gordon to Mrs. Dennett, 6 June 1911, Laura Clay Papers.

27. Laura Clay to Mrs. McCulloch, 14 June 1911; Emma M. Gillett to Laura Clay, 7 August 1911, ibid.

28. Ibid.

29. Laura Clay to Mrs. McCulloch, 7 June 1917; to Miss Gordon, 10 June 1911; to Mrs. McCulloch, 14 June 1911, ibid.

30. Alice Henry to Laura Clay, 2 October 1911, ibid.; Mrs. Dennett to Harriet Burton Laidlaw, 19 September 1911, Dillon Collection; Emma M. Gillett to Laura Clay, 21 August 1911; Laura Clay to Eugenia B. Farmer, 1 September 1911; Mrs. McCulloch to Laura Clay, 30 September 1911; Mary N. Chase to Laura Clay, 23 September 1911; Mrs. McCulloch to Laura Clay, 9 October 1911, Laura Clay Papers.

31. *Louisville Herald*, 24 October 1911.

32. *Louisville Times*, 20, 23 October 1911; *Chicago Daily Tribune*, 24, 20 October 1911.

33. *Louisville Courier-Journal*, 22 October 1911; National Woman Suffrage Association, *Proceedings of the Forty-Third Annual Convention . . . Held in Louisville, Kentucky, October 19–25, 1911* (New York: NAWSA, n.d.), pp. 184–86.

34. Ibid., pp. 204–5.

35. Mrs. Dennett to Harriet Burton Laidlaw, 19 September 1911, Dillon Collection. "If you could just be there [at the convention] through the election," implored Dennett, "that would be all that would be necessary." Mrs. McCulloch to Laura Clay, 30 September 1911, Laura Clay Papers; *Louisville Courier-Journal*, 20 October 1911.

36. Mrs. McCulloch to Laura Clay, 30 October 1911, Laura Clay Papers.

37. 6 November 1911, ibid.

38. *Louisville Herald*, 26 October 1911. Mrs. McCulloch to Sophonisba Breckinridge, 28 October 1911, Laura Clay Papers. LaFollette was the wife of United States Senator Robert M. LaFollette.

39. *Louisville Times*, 24 October 1911; Mrs. McCulloch to Laura Clay, 28 October 1911, Laura Clay Papers; *Louisville Herald*, 24 October 1911; Alice Stone Blackwell to Laura Clay, 1 January 1912, Laura Clay Papers.

40. Mrs. McCulloch to Miss Breckinridge, 28 October 1911, Laura Clay Papers. Laura Clay received many letters praising her past contributions to the NAWSA and her perseverance and strength in defeat. Among them were Mrs. Upton, 26 October 1911; Elizabeth J. Hauser, 1 November 1911; Frances Squire Potter and Elizabeth Gray Peck, 6 November 1911; Mrs. Stewart, 7 November 1911; Caroline I. Reilly, 20 November 1911, ibid.; Mrs. McCulloch to Laura Clay, 25 October 1911, ibid.

41. Laura Clay to Mrs. Upton, 1 November 1911; to Emma Maddox Funck, 2 November 1911; to Mrs. G. B. Longan, 3 November 1911; to Lida Calvert Obenchain, 3 November 1911; to Eugenia B. Farmer, 8 February 1912; to Mrs. Upton, 1 November 1911, ibid.; Telegram, Miss Breckinridge to Mrs. McCulloch, 24 October 1911, Dillon Collection; Laura Clay to "Dear Miss Sophonisba," 1 November 1911, Laura Clay Papers. The salutation is interesting since it is one

of the few times in her correspondence when Clay addressed a person by her given name. Correspondents of twenty years' standing, Upton or Gordon, for example, never became "Dear Harriet" or "Dear Kate."

42. Miss Shaw to Miss Anthony, September, n.d., 1911, Dillon Collection.

43. NAWSA, *Proceedings* . . . 1911, p. 227; Laura Clay to Mrs. Upton, 1 November 1911, Laura Clay Papers.

Chapter 8

1. "The harvest is ripe; it is time to put in the sickle" (Laura Clay to Mary Cherry, 25 January 1913, Laura Clay Papers). Laura Clay to Catherine Waugh McCulloch, 14 November 1911; Sophonisba Breckinridge to Laura Clay, 3, 15 November 1911, ibid.

2. Laura Clay to Alice Henry, 29 September 1911; to Mrs. N. S. McLaughlin, 25 September 1911, ibid.

3. Laura Clay to the Reverend Olympia Brown, 7 November 1911, 22 June 1915, ibid.

4. Madeline McDowell Breckinridge, "Kentucky," *History of Woman Suffrage*, ed. Ida Husted Harper (New York: NAWSA, 1922), 6:207–8.

5. Sophonisba P. Breckinridge, *Madeline McDowell Breckinridge* (Chicago: University of Chicago Press, 1912), pp. vii–xii. The author was the subject's sister-in-law.

6. Ibid., p. 196.

7. Mrs. Breckinridge to Kate Gordon, 1 October 1907; Laura Clay to Mrs. Breckinridge, 4 August 1913, Laura Clay Papers.

8. Laura Clay to Kate Gordon, 8 August 1918, ibid.

9. Madeline McDowell Breckinridge, "Kentucky," *History of Woman Suffrage*, 6:210.

10. Laura Clay to Mrs. Lafon Riker, 9 March 1910; Pamphlet, "What the Kentucky Equal Rights Association Has Done and What It Proposes to Do," Laura Clay Papers.

11. Laura Clay to Mrs. Upton, November n.d., 1912; Mrs. Hubbard to Laura Clay, 12 November 1912, ibid.

12. Laura Clay to Emma M. Roebuck, 3 February 1913, ibid.; National American Woman Suffrage Association, *Proceedings of the Forty-Sixth Annual Convention . . . Held in Nashville, Tennessee, November 12–17, 1914* (New York: National Woman Suffrage Publishing Company, n.d.), pp. 166–67; *Lexington Herald*, 1, 4 March 1913.

13. *Lexington Herald*, 26 May 1913; Walter Lord, *The Good Years: From 1900 to the First World War* (New York: Harper and Brothers, 1960), p. 278; Madeline McDowell Breckinridge, "Kentucky," *History of Woman Suffrage*, 6:210.

14. *Lexington Herald*, 26 May 1913.

15. Laura Clay to Mrs. Breckinridge, 10 September 1913; Kate Gordon to Laura Clay, 28 August 1912, Laura Clay Papers.

16. Laura Clay to Mary C. Roark, 17 February 1913; to Kate Gordon, 19 September 1914; Mrs. Breckinridge to Laura Clay, 19 August 1913; Laura Clay to Emma M. Roebuck, 19 September 1913; to Mrs. Breckinridge, 7, 23 October 1914, ibid.

17. Laura Clay to Lida Calvert Obenchain, 9 April 1913; Report of the Corresponding Secretary to the Kentucky ERA Convention, 22 November 1913; Clipping, *Hopkinsville* (Ky.) *New Era*, 25 April 1913; Laura Clay to Mrs. Upton, 3 September 1913, ibid.

18. Mrs. Breckinridge to Laura Clay, 26 July 1913, ibid.

19. C. P. White to Laura Clay, 6 June 1915; Laura Clay to C. P. White, 12 June 1915, ibid. Another man wrote that the women in Wickliffe had shown no interest in suffrage, and "if they do not want the ballot I am not inclined to insist." Clay answered that they expected him, as chairman, to ask for help, which she was certain the women would gladly give. G. O. Johnson to Laura Clay, 7 June 1915; Laura Clay to G. O. Johnson, 12 June 1915; Mrs. Margaret Van Winkler to Laura Clay, 7 June 1915; Laura Clay to Mrs. Van Winkler, 12 June 1915, ibid.

20. *Woman's Journal* (Boston), 4 April 1914, 9 October 1915; National American Woman Suffrage Association, *Proceedings of the Forty-Seventh Annual Convention . . . Held in Washington, D.C., December 14-19, 1915* (New York: National Woman Suffrage Publishing Company, n.d.), pp. 114-15.

21. Laura Clay to Hettie P. Adams, 12 June 1915; Leaflet, Kentucky ERA Press Committee, Laura Clay Papers. Internal evidence indicates that the leaflet was published after the Kentucky ERA convention of November 1915 and before the end of the legislative session of the Kentucky General Assembly in March 1916. Madeline McDowell Breckinridge to Ministers of Kentucky, 17 September 1915, ibid.; NAWSA, *Proceedings . . . 1915*, p. 114, 115; *Woman's Journal* (Boston), 13 November 1915, 9 February 1915.

22. *Lexington Herald*, 11 November 1915.

23. Laura Clay to Harriet Burton Laidlaw, 16 February 1912; Mary Ware Dennett to Laura Clay, 15 July 1912; Report of the Chairman of the Membership Committee, 1912, Laura Clay Papers.

24. Mary Ware Dennett to Laura Clay, 15 July 1912; Laura Clay to Mary Winsor, 8 November 1912, ibid.

25. *Lexington Leader*, 4 May 1913; Laura Clay Vita, 23 December 1923, Laura Clay Papers.

26. Officers of the Ohio Woman Suffrage Association [letter of appreciation] to Laura Clay, 29 May 1912; Laura Clay to Mrs. Upton, 11 June 1912, ibid.

27. Harper, ed., *History of Woman Suffrage*, 6:199-200; Lucy B. Johnston to Laura Clay, 4 October 1912, Laura Clay Papers; *Lexington Herald*, 4 May 1913; Harper, ed., *History of Woman Suffrage*, 6:199-200.

28. *Nashville Banner*, 10 January 1913; Newspaper clipping, 30 March 1913; Clipping, *Pontiac Press Gazette*, 10 March 1913, Laura Clay Papers.

29. Laura White to Laura Clay, 19 February 1915, ibid.; O'Neill, *Everyone Was Brave*, pp. 176-78; Laura White to Laura Clay, 13 May 1915; "Notes for Peace Address at Richmond" [Kentucky], May, n.d., 1915, Laura Clay Papers.

30. Laura Clay to Eugenia B. Farmer, 20 February 1917; to Laura White, 20 February 1917, ibid.

31. Laura Clay to Laura White, 20 February 1917; Clipping, Althea L. Hall to editor, Providence (R.I.) *Sunday Journal*, 1 April 1917, ibid.

32. O'Neill, *Everyone Was Brave*, pp. 183-84; Laura Clay to Eleanor Daggett Karsten [Office Secretary, Woman's Peace party], 15 June 1917, Laura Clay Papers.

33. Shaw, *Story of a Pioneer*, pp. 330-33. Shaw admitted that there were moves to unseat her from 1910 until she voluntarily stepped out of office in 1915. In a

paradoxical remark for inclusion in a complimentary letter, Catt wrote Shaw, "I have always thought it was a cruel mistake that you had to be National President." 2 January 1916, Dillon Collection, Schlesinger Library, Radcliffe College, Cambridge, Mass. In their efforts to replace Shaw, her fellow suffragists were partially restrained by two considerations: 1) because she was the best known and most popular lecturer among the rank-and-file suffragists, she would probably be impossible to defeat in the annual election; 2) replacing her without her consent would quite possibly split the movement and would certainly be used by the unfriendly press to tarnish it in the eyes of the public. *Woman's Journal* (Boston), 21 November 1914.

34. Harper, ed., *History of Woman Suffrage*, 5:675–78; *Woman's Journal* (Boston), 28 February 1914; Kraditor, *The Ideas of the Woman Suffrage Movement*, pp. 235–36, 267.

35. Judith Hyrms Douglas to Laura Clay, 13 February 1912; Kate Gordon to Laura Clay, 23 July 1913, Laura Clay Papers.

36. Clipping, *St. Louis Globe-Democrat*, April n.d., 1913; Laura Clay to Mrs. Breckinridge, 24 July 1914; to Catherine Waugh McCulloch, 14 November 1913, ibid.

37. Kate Gordon to Laura Clay, 21 November 1913; Mrs. B. B. Valentine to Kate Gordon, 14 November 1915, ibid. Belle Kearney to editor, *Woman's Journal* (Boston), 21 March 1914; Emma Maddox Funck to editor *Woman's Journal* (Boston), 30 May 1914. Gordon reported that Nellie N. Somerville had resigned from the SSWSC "on the score of my being too active against the National." She claimed that Somerville's real purpose in resigning was to curry favor with the leadership of the NAWSA. See Miss Gordon to Catherine Waugh McCulloch, 22 June 1915, Dillon Collection, Schlesinger Library, Radcliffe College, Cambridge, Mass. Kate Gordon to Members of Board [of SSWSC], 17 March 1917, Laura Clay Papers; *New Southern Citizen*, 9 December 1916, ibid.

38. Kate Gordon to Officers [of SSWSC], 7 July 1916; to Laura Clay, 28 March 1914; to Officers [of NAWSA], 13 April 1914; to Laura Clay, 8 April, 21 March, 19 August 1914, ibid.

39. 15 April 1914, ibid.

40. *Nashville Tennessean*, 11 November 1914; Kate Gordon to Laura Clay, 29 June 1915; Laura Clay to Kate Gordon, 3 July 1915, Laura Clay Papers; Kate Gordon to Anna Howard Shaw, 23 August 1915, Woman Suffrage Collection, Manuscript Division, Library of Congress, Washington, D.C.; Laura Clay to Kate Gordon, 3 July, 28 October 1915, Laura Clay Papers.

41. National American Woman Suffrage Association, *Proceedings of the Twenty-Ninth Annual Convention . . . Held in Des Moines, Iowa, January 26–29, 1897* (Philadelphia: Alfred J. Ferris, n.d.), p. 48; Harriet Taylor Upton to Catherine Waugh McCulloch, 2 February 1915, Dillon Collection.

42. Laura Clay to Catherine Waugh McCulloch, 14 June 1911, Laura Clay Papers. Clay and her sister offered McCulloch, a Chicago lawyer, $75.00 for expenses, if she would go to Washington to arrange a hearing on the bill. Clay was probably expressing her own concern when she added that her sister wanted to "take scrupulous care not in any way to seem to Congress to prescribe their own qualifications for voting *for state officers*, as our old Sixteenth Amendment [Anthony Amendment] proposed to do" [italics mine]. Laura Clay to Mrs. Antoinette Funk, 9 December 1914, ibid. It is interesting to speculate on Clay's bill in light

of the 1970 Supreme Court ruling that Congress could extend the franchise to eighteen year olds, but only in federal elections. See *On Bills of Complaint*, 401 U.S. 1–19 (1970). A logical argument for her bill would seem to be in Article I, section 4, which gives Congress the power to make or alter the regulations governing congressional elections. Clay seems to have feared that if Congress were acknowledged to have the power to exclude sex as a qualification for voting, it might open the door to other congressional regulations on literacy and property requirements and federal policing of the polls. Laura Clay to Catherine Waugh McCulloch, 21 May 1916, Dillon Collection.

43. Laura Clay to A. C. Price, 28 November 1914; to Kate Gordon, 28 October 1915, Laura Clay Papers.

44. Laura Clay to Mrs. Upton, 28 December 1914, 14 August 1916, ibid.; *Woman's Journal* (Boston), 21 March 1914.

45. Mrs. Harper to Laura Clay, 8 March 1914; see also Clay's scribbled notes on her interviews with a number of senators and congressmen in January 1916, Laura Clay Papers; Harper, ed., *History of Woman Suffrage*, 5:504.

46. Stapler, ed., *The Woman Suffrage Yearbook*, 1917, p. 91. The Shafroth amendment, which was drawn up by the Congressional Committee of the NAWSA, sought to amend the Constitution so that 8 percent of the voters of any state could require a referendum on woman suffrage. It was an attempt to ease the difficulties of amending the varied state constitutions, some of which were nearly impossible to change. The committee believed it would avoid the states' rights objections encountered by the Anthony amendment. See Harper, ed., *History of Woman Suffrage*, 5:411–18. Laura Clay to Catherine Waugh McCulloch, 2 October 1915, Dillon Collection; Harper, ed., *History of Woman Suffrage*, 5:501, 504. It is characteristic of the Clay family independence that Bennett did not give up her bill when Laura Clay drafted a similar one (see Laura Clay to "My dear Sallie" [Bennett], 27 January 1917, Laura Clay Papers). In addition to the sisters' two proposals, a Federal Elections bill, which had the same purpose as Miss Clay's measure but was based on a different part of the Constitution, had attracted some attention in Washington. Its sponsors were Clara Bewick Colby and the Reverend Olympia Brown of the Federal Suffrage Association. The result, as one might conclude, was a considerable amount of confusion among both suffragists and congressmen over the relative merits and differences in the three bills (see Harriet Taylor Upton to Laura Clay, 12 December 1915; Laura Clay to Antoinette Funk, 9 December 1914; Laura Clay to Grace Wilbur Trout, 9 July 1915, ibid.).

Chapter 9

1. *New York Times*, 9 September 1916; Arthur S. Link, "The South and the New Freedom: An Interpretation," *American Scholar* 20 (1951): 314–24; Richard M. Abrams, "Woodrow Wilson and the Southern Congressmen, 1913–1916," *Journal of Southern History* 22 (1956): 417–37; Arthur S. Link, *Wilson*, vol. 5, *Campaigns for Progressivism and Peace, 1916–1917* (Princeton, N.J.: Princeton University Press, 1965), pp. 38–42.

2. *New York Times*, 8 September 1916.

3. *Woman's Journal* (Boston), 3 October 1914, 9 September 1916.

4. David Mitchell, *Monstrous Regiment: The Story of the Women of the First World War* (New York: Macmillan Company, 1965), pp. 123–220, xvi; Catt to

Presidents of the State [Woman Suffrage] Associations, 9 April 1917, Laura Clay Papers.

5. Madeline McDowell Breckinridge, "Kentucky," *History of Woman Suffrage*, 6:210–11.

6. *Lexington Herald*, 7 May 1916; National American Woman Suffrage Association, *Proceedings of the Forty-Eighth Annual Convention . . . Held in Atlantic City, New Jersey, September 4–10, 1916* (New York: National Woman Suffrage Publishing Co., n.d.), p. 175; Minutes of the Executive Board of the Kentucky ERA, 14 November 1916, Laura Clay Papers; NAWSA, *Proceedings . . . 1903*, p. 66; Breckinridge, "Kentucky," *History of Woman Suffrage*, 6:208.

7. Laura Clay to Mrs. Catt, 2 December 1916, Laura Clay Papers.

8. Mrs. Catt to Laura Clay, 27 November 1916, ibid.

9. Laura Clay to Mrs. Sara M. Algeo, 23 April 1917, ibid.

10. *Lexington Herald*, 1–2 December 1917; Madeline McDowell Breckinridge, "Kentucky," *History of Woman Suffrage*, 6:211.

11. *Louisville Herald*, 2 December 1917; Mrs. Breckinridge to Christine Bradley South, 3 January 1918, Laura Clay Papers; *Louisville Times*, 11 March 1919.

12. To Laura Clay, 27 November 1916, Laura Clay Papers.

13. Mrs. Catt to Laura Clay, 12 January 1918; Laura Clay to "My dear Sallie" [Bennett], 14 January 1918, ibid.

14. Laura Clay to Mrs. South, 11 January 1918, ibid.

15. Laura Clay to "My dear Sallie" [Bennett], 14 January 1918; Mrs. Bennett to Laura Clay, 3 February 1918; Laura Clay to Kate Gordon, 8 February 1918, ibid. Maud Wood Park, *Front Door Lobby* (Boston: Beacon Press, 1960), p. 180. Park, who was chairman of the NAWSA's Congressional Committee, relates how many former antis, states' rights Democrats as well as Republicans, began to discover the justice of woman suffrage in 1918. Under pressure from Wilson, Theodore Roosevelt, and other leaders of both parties, the number continued to increase. The title of Park's book is interesting in light of some of the machinations she and Catt undertook to get the federal amendment through Congress. When the bill had passed the House and needed only three votes for success in the Senate, Catt wrote Park: "I have taken the liberty to write to Sen. [Key] Pitman [sic] about Bennett [unable to identify] and have told him we heard he wished an appointment and that I thought he [Pittman] was the one to engineer the appointment and the vote." 4 September 1918, Sophia Smith Collection, Smith College Library, Northampton, Mass.

16. Laura Clay to Kate Gordon, 7 February 1918, Laura Clay Papers. Stanley was one of the Democrats whose opposition to the federal amendment wilted under presidential pressure applied in the interest of the party. Under Wilson's prodding, Stanley appointed George B. Martin, who voted for the suffrage bill, to fill the unexpired term of Senator Ollie James, who died on 28 August 1918. A. O. Stanley Papers, University of Kentucky, Lexington; Mrs. South to Laura Clay, 2 February 1918, Laura Clay Papers.

17. Laura Clay to Kate Gordon, 18 March 1918; to Mrs. Catt, 16 January 1918; to Mrs. Breckinridge, 31 January 1918; to Kate Gordon, 4 June 1918, Laura Clay Papers.

18. Laura Clay to Kate Gordon, 4 June 1918; Desha Breckinridge to Laura Clay, 7 June 1918, ibid.

19. Laura Clay to Kate Gordon, 30 November 1918; to Anna Howard Shaw,

13 April 1918; to Ida Porter Boyer, 28 March 1918, ibid.; interview with Mrs. Cecil Cantrill, Lexington, Ky., 26 January 1969.

20. Laura Clay to Mrs. South, 6 October; to Mrs. Breckinridge, 9 October; Mrs. South to Laura Clay, 13, 18 October 1918, ibid.

21. Kate Gordon to Laura Clay, 6 September 1918, ibid.; *Louisville Times*, 11–12 March 1919; Laura Clay to Kate Gordon, 17 March 1919, Laura Clay Papers.

22. Laura Clay to Harriet Taylor Upton, 12 February 1919; to Kate Gordon, 21 February 1919; to Mrs. Upton, 17 February 1919, ibid.

23. *Lexington Herald*, 26 March 1919; Laura Clay to editor, *Lexington Herald*, 16 April 1919.

24. 26 March 1919.

25. *Lexington Leader*, 5 April 1919; *Lexington Herald*, 16 April 1919.

26. Laura Clay to Catherine Waugh McCulloch, 5 April 1919; Mrs. Breckinridge to Board [of ERA officers], 1 May 1919; Laura Clay to Kate Gordon, 26 April 1919, Laura Clay Papers.

27. *Lexington Leader*, 6 June 1919; Laura Clay to Kate Gordon, 30 March 1918, to Governor James D. Black [of Kentucky], 21 June 1919, Laura Clay Papers.

28. *Lexington Leader*, 12 June 1919.

29. "Open Letter to the Public," 2 June 1919, Laura Clay Papers; *Lexington Herald*, 3 September 1919; *Louisville Courier-Journal*, 5 September 1919.

30. Laura Clay to Kate Gordon, 23 May 1919, Laura Clay Papers.

31. Kate Gordon to Laura Clay, 6 September 1918, ibid.; *Louisville Times*, 11–12

32. Laura Clay to Senator James D. Phelan, n.d.; to Senator Hiram W. Johnson [California], 16 June; to Senator Miles Poindexter [Washington], 24 May; to Governor Oliver L. Shoup [Colorado], 17 July; to Governor Joseph M. Carey [Wyoming], 12 August, 1919, Laura Clay Papers. Joseph M. Carey to Laura Clay, 7 August 1919, ibid., "You are not willing in the South," he wrote, "to give the black man and woman the rights that they are entitled to in this country . . . . I am not in sympathy with you."

33. Ida Husted Harper to Laura Clay, 28 June 1919, ibid. Harper implied that Laura Clay was, in effect, in the camp of the antis. She, too, misunderstood the nature of Clay's objections to the federal amendment and sought to convince her that it would not be applicable to the Negro women of the South. Alice Lloyd to Laura Clay, 22 October 1919; Mrs. Joseph Alderson to Laura Clay, 14 June 1919; Eugenia B. Farmer to Laura Clay, 11 July 1919, ibid.

34. *Lexington Herald*, 3 August, 3 September 1919.

35. Mrs. Catt to Marjorie Shuler, 1 July 1919, Sophia Smith Collection; Ida Husted Harper to Laura Clay, 29 October 1919, Laura Clay Papers; *Lexington Herald*, 14 October 1919.

36. Laura Clay to Bessie E. Somerville, 3 January 1920, Laura Clay Papers.

37. Ibid.

38. Kate Gordon to Laura Clay, 23 July 1919; Judge J. B. Evans to Laura Clay, 13 September 1919, ibid. On another occasion, she told Kate Gordon that "We [Kentucky] have no negro problem." She then went on to warn her that "like the Western States, Kentucky is more or less tired of being hampered by the wishes of the colored belt to the neglect of their own or the Democratic party's interests. It is up to the colored belt to make some move to conform to the general interests of the Democratic party; or expect to find itself in a hopeless minority." Laura Clay to Kate Gordon, 8 February 1918, ibid.

39. *Lexington Leader*, 4 January 1920.

40. *Louisville Courier-Journal*, 7 January 1920; *Lexington Herald*, 8–9 January 1920.

41. Mrs. Breckinridge to Laura Clay, 1, 15 March 1920; Lida Calvert Obenchain to Laura Clay, 11 April 1920; Alice Stone Blackwell to Laura Clay, 15 March 1920; P. H. Callahan to Laura Clay, 10, 15 May 1920, 11 February 1939, Laura Clay Papers; *Lexington Leader*, 4 August 1920.

42. Laura Clay to Kate Gordon, 31 July 1920, Laura Clay Papers; *Lexington Leader*, 22, 11–21 August 1920; *Louisville Courier-Journal*, 2–26 August 1920; *Nashville Tennessean*, 19 July–21 August 1920; *Chattanooga Times*, 3–26 August 1920; *Chattanooga News*, 11–20 August 1920. Of these newspapers, all of which gave extensive coverage to the events in Nashville, only the *Lexington Leader*, 11 August, and the *Chattanooga Times*, 9 August, even mention her presence in Nashville.

43. Flexner, *Century of Struggle*, p. 322; Sinclair, *The Emancipation of the American Woman*, p. 335; Kraditor, *The Ideas of the Woman Suffrage Movement*, pp. 194–95, 214–15; Ida Husted Harper to Kate Gordon, 18 November 1918; John H. Wallace [Alabama Game Commissioner], "What a Southerner Thinks" (New York: NAWSA, 13 June 1919), Laura Clay Papers. This handbill, which was used by the NAWSA's Press Department at the height of the ratification struggle, assured southerners that the Republicans "will never seek to revive sectionalism at this late date by the enfranchisement of negro women along with white women of the country." The Reverend E. L. Baskerville [Archdeacon for Colored Work, Diocese of South Carolina] to Laura Clay, 23 December 1916; the Reverend E. E. Hall [St. Andrew's Church (Negro)] to Laura Clay, 30 January 1919; Anna Kelton Wiley to Laura Clay, 23 October 1911; Laura Clay to Corresponding Secretary, NAWSA, 17 February 1919, Laura Clay Papers. Clay, who is often accused of Negrophobia, voted for the Northeastern Federation of Women's Clubs without hesitation or comment at the very time Catt, acting through Harper, was trying to get the organization to postpone its application. See Kraditor, *The Ideas of the Woman Suffrage Movement*, pp. 213–15. Laura Clay to Kate Gordon, 8 February 1918; to Judge J. B. Evans, 17 September 1919; to Bessie E. Somerville, 3 January 1920, Laura Clay Papers.

44. "The Ideology of White Supremacy, 1876–1910," in *Essays in Southern History*, ed. Fletcher M. Green (Chapel Hill: University of North Carolina Press, 1949), pp. 124–56.

45. On one occasion, for example, she was offended by an article in *Woman's Journal*, which claimed that the southern states, especially Louisiana and Mississippi, first disfranchised their Negroes and then cut down on their school appropriations. Laura Clay to Alice Stone Blackwell, 23 May 1911. To satisfy her own mind on the matter, she wrote the superintendents of public education in Mississippi and Louisiana to inquire about the accuracy of the charge. Both officials denied it and claimed that appropriations for Negro schools had been increased. T. H. Harris [Superintendent of Public Education, Louisiana] to Laura Clay, 12 June 1911; J. N. Powers [Superintendent of Public Education, Mississippi] to Laura Clay, 16 June 1911. As a climax to this characteristically southern defensiveness, Clay demanded that the *Woman's Journal* refute the article. Laura Clay to Alice Stone Blackwell, 19 June 1911. As if to satisfy her conscience further about the South's treatment of the Negroes, she asked Gordon if Louisiana's property and educational requirements

applied only to Negroes. She made it clear that she thought they should apply to both races equally. Gordon answered that the law did not "discriminate in the letter; it of course leaves ample room for fraud, which the politicians have made ample use of to their advantage and the people's loss." Laura Clay to Kate Gordon, 12 July 1911; Kate Gordon to Laura Clay, 27 July 1911, all letters in the Laura Clay Papers. Taking time from her farm supervision and suffrage correspondence at the height of the discussion with headquarters in 1911, Clay's inquiries are some measure of her concern and disapproval of discriminations in the franchise requirements. Gordon, on the other hand, while complaining of the article's appearance in the organ of the NAWSA on the grounds that it was irrelevant to woman suffrage, did not question its accuracy. "Those of us who know the situation relative to the negroes' virtual disfranchisement," she added, "are not regretting it, for it remains a large vote against us whenever the question of votes for women is before the people." Kate Gordon to Official Board [NAWSA], n.d. [July–August 1911], Dillon Collection, Schlesinger Library, Radcliffe College, Cambridge, Mass.

46. *The End of American Innocence: A Study of the First Years of Our Own Time, 1912–1917* (New York: Alfred A. Knopf, 1969), p. 82.

Chapter 10

1. "I found another Cause awaiting all my zeal and devotion and so it will ever be." Laura Clay to Alice Stone Blackwell, 9 June 1931, Woman's Suffrage Collection, Library of Congress, Washington, D.C.; *Lexington Leader*, 22 August 1920; Goodman, *Bitter Harvest*, p. 64. The title of this brief biography of Clay is a more serious historical inaccuracy than the small errors of fact and interpretation which one might expect in a popular biography. *Lexington Leader*, 22 August 1920; Laura Clay to Mary Scrugham, 8 December 1920; Clipping, Richmond (Ky.) *Daily Register*, 15 August 1923, Laura Clay Papers.

2. Manuscript of speech to Democratic Women's Club of Kentucky, n.d., 1928, ibid.; interview with Mrs. Cecil Cantrill, Lexington, Ky., 29 January 1969; *Lexington Herald*, 1, 4 August 1920; Mrs. Arch Pool to Laura Clay, 28 May 1920; Laura Clay to Harriet Taylor Upton, 18 November 1921; Laura Clay to H. V. McChesney, 3 September 1920, Laura Clay Papers. Clay was in favor of the League, but she desired more "Americanizing reservations" than President Wilson or Governor Cox had accepted. Because of her doubts on these two issues, she refused McChesney's request that she make speeches for the Democratic party. McChesney to Laura Clay, 1 September 1920, ibid.

3. Laura Clay to Harriet Taylor Upton, 18 November 1921; Miss Blackwell to Laura Clay, 13 April 1922; Laura Clay to Alice Lloyd, 26 November 1921; Eugenia B. Farmer to Laura Clay, 21 February 1921; Miss Blackwell and Ida Porter Boyer to Laura Clay, 16 December 1933, Laura Clay Papers; Laura Clay to Miss Blackwell, 9 June 1931, Woman's Suffrage Collection, Library of Congress, Washington, D.C.

4. Clipping, *Lexington Kentucky Gazette*, 14 May 1892, Laura Clay Scrapbook; Henrietta Joy to Laura Clay, 12 May 1897; Laura Clay to Caroline Leib, 25 November 1905, Laura Clay Papers.

5. Address to Called Meeting of Woman's Auxiliary [Christ Episcopal Church], 16 January 1911; Laura Clay to Mrs. Upton, 5 April 1911, ibid.

6. *Woman's Journal* (Boston), 17 June 1911; Bishop Lewis W. Burton to

Laura Clay, 23 June 1911, Laura Clay Papers; Report on the Commission on the Memorial to the Sixteenth Annual Council, Petitioning for the Eligibility of Women to the Diocesan Council, 12 May 1912, ibid.; *Woman's Journal* (Boston), 13 June, 21 November 1914; *Lexington Herald*, 13 February 1920; Clipping, *Richmond* (Va.) *Times-Dispatch*, 22 November 1925, Laura Clay Papers.

7. Laura Clay to the Rt. Reverend Albion Knight, 12 September 1919, ibid.

8. Laura Clay to George S. Weeks [treasurer of Christ Church], 9 January 1920; Dean Robert K. Massie to Laura Clay, 17 January 1920; Clipping, *The Churchman*, 20 March 1920, ibid. The goal Clay sought was finally achieved forty-nine years later when women were admitted to the regular session of the university in September 1969. Catalog, University of the South, 1968–1969.

9. Clay once told an interviewer that "our work for suffrage is not over. We must teach the women that it is now their duty as well as their privilege to vote." Clipping, *Richmond* (Va.) *Times-Dispatch*, 22 November 1924, Laura Clay Papers; Laura Clay to Miss Blackwell, 9 June 1931, Woman's Suffrage Collection; *Lexington Leader*, 7 November 1923; the Reverend A. W. Denlinger to Laura Clay, 20 July 1923, Laura Clay Papers. On behalf of a mass meeting in Berea, Ky., Denlinger telegraphed Clay for her views on the pari-mutuel law. Her reply supported the law and claimed that the community had more to fear from fanaticism than from gambling, although she must have realized that it was not the answer which would find favor in Berea. Laura Clay to the Reverend Denlinger, 20 July 1923; Hugh Riddell to Laura Clay, 8 November 1923; Laura Clay to Mary Scrugham, 27 July 1923, ibid.

10. Laura Clay to Mrs. E. L. Hutchinson [President, Kentucky League of Women Voters], 4 October 1923; Mrs. Hutchinson to Laura Clay, 23 October 1923; Fred Vaughn [Secretary of State, Kentucky], to Mrs. E. L. Hutchinson, 5 December 1923, ibid. Nine of Kentucky's 120 counties had not reported their results when the above totals were reported.

11. *Lexington Leader*, 8 November 1923. The League of Women Voters probably took up the measure as a special courtesy to Clay; its president, Mrs. E. L. Hutchinson, was a friend of hers and one of the few suffragists in the Kentucky ERA who had voted with her for a state campaign in 1919. She wrote Clay that it was difficult for her not to refer to the bill as "your amendment," 23 October 1923, Laura Clay Papers. On the other hand, it was a rather strange alliance since as late as 1921, Clay did not approve of the League's "mode of action." Refusing to make a contribution to its legislative work, she wrote: "Now that we have the same voting power to effect legislation as men I believe that women should join with men for improved legislation, and not erect any division between the interest of the sexes." Laura Clay to Alice Lloyd, 26 November 1921, ibid.; Mrs. Upton to Catherine Waugh McCulloch, 5 March 1915, Dillon Collection, Schlesinger Library, Radcliffe College, Cambridge, Mass.

12. *Lexington Leader*, 30 June 1941; *Louisville Courier-Journal*, 4 February 1940; Laura Clay, manuscript speech for Governor Smith, n.d., Laura Clay Papers.

13. *Louisville Courier-Journal*, 28 November 1933.

14. *Lexington Herald*, 21 April 1935.

15. *Lexington Herald*, 1 July 1941.

Bibliographical Essay

Manuscripts

The majority of the material used in the preparation of this volume came from the Laura Clay Papers in the University of Kentucky Library. This is a particularly valuable collection because Clay, unlike many other prominent feminists who destroyed all or large parts of their personal letters, preserved her correspondence, personal and business, sometimes even failing to follow her correspondents' admonitions to burn certain letters. The collection is good for the entire period of her suffrage activities, 1888–1920, and particularly complete after she acquired a typewriter in 1904 and faithfully kept carbon copies of her letters. As a consequence of her industry and ordered mind, the Laura Clay Papers provide a unique insight into the life and activities of an individual suffragist and are especially helpful in understanding the internal dissensions which the feminists and their early chroniclers tried to keep from public view. Although used earlier by Aileen Kraditor and a few other historians, this collection has not received the recognition or attention it deserves.

Other manuscript collections were helpful on particular periods or special events in Laura Clay's life. The Clay Family Papers in the Filson Club at Louisville, Kentucky, are excellent on her early years, familial relationships, and the Clay women's early suffrage activities. Anyone doing research in woman's history will profit from the excellent archives at the Schlesinger Library in Radcliffe College, where the papers of a number of Laura Clay's contemporaries are housed. The Woman Suffrage Collection and the Breckinridge Family Papers, which include the letters of Madeline McDowell Breckinridge, in the Manuscript Division of the Library of Congress were helpful, although the latter papers are not well arranged. The Sophia Smith Collection in Smith College, which contains part of Carrie Chapman Catt's correspondence, was informative on the final fight for the Nineteenth Amendment.

Official Histories, Proceedings, and Reference Works

The History of Woman Suffrage, edited by Elizabeth Cady Stanton, Susan B. Anthony, Mathilda Gage, and Ida Husted Harper, 6 vols. (Rochester, N.Y., 1881–1922), is an indispensable reference work. While uncritical and somewhat encyclopedic, it contains valuable information unavailable elsewhere. The *Proceedings* of the national conventions, particularly those of the NAWSA, mirror the growth of the suffrage movement and describe the annual activities of the state associations, though, like the *History of Woman Suffrage*, they give little hint of the acrimony which sometimes accompanied the deliberations.

Notable American Women, 1607–1950, edited by Edward T. James, Janet Wilson James, and Paul S. Boyer, 3 vols. (Cambridge, Mass., 1971), is a highly significant and scholarly contribution to historical studies. This work is of immense value to those in woman's history and should encourage others to research in the field.

Newspapers and Periodicals

Newspapers are an invaluable, yet neglected, source for study of the woman's movement. Even in the early years, when much of the press wrote of the feminists with thinly disguised amusement or ridicule, they were apparently considered good copy and received prominent coverage. The press took particular delight in reporting any differences among the suffragists and is therefore enlightening where official proceedings and histories are silent and personal letters unavailable.

The *Kentucky Gazette* is important for the early history of the woman's movement in Kentucky, since Annie and then Laura Clay regularly wrote a "Woman's Column" for it. While a complete file of the papers is not available, many of the Clays' columns and related clippings were preserved in the scrapbooks faithfully maintained by Laura during the early years of her work. Other

Lexington newspapers worthy of special mention include the *Lexington Herald* and the *Kentucky Leader* (1888–1895), later titled the *Daily Leader* (1895–1901), and presently the *Lexington Leader* (1901–   ). Editor Desha Breckinridge of the *Lexington Herald* supported woman suffrage and his wife, the former Madeline McDowell, began contributing a weekly woman's page to the *Herald* in 1905. Because of the Breckinridges' wide interests in social reforms, the *Herald* is a storehouse of information on the Progressive era as well as the feminist movement.

The *Louisville Courier-Journal*, despite the editorial opposition of Henry Watterson to woman suffrage, was true to its present reputation as a great newspaper and faithfully reported the activities of the suffragists. The *Louisville Herald* and the *Louisville Times* were also very helpful, particularly on events in Louisville.

The large dailies of the major cities gave the suffragists good coverage, especially after the NAWSA headquarters was moved to New York in 1909. The *Washington Post* and the *New York Times* were good sources. Frequently the NAWSA conventions would be front-page news in the press of the convention city for as much as a week before the meeting began, carrying stories on the prominent suffragists and giving full coverage to the sessions of the convention.

The *Woman's Journal* of Boston was one of the few feminist periodicals which encompassed the full period of this study. Edited for the greater part of its lifetime by Alice Stone Blackwell, it was a quality publication which is full of information on the activities of the state equal rights associations and the suffrage campaigns of the NAWSA. *Progress*, the monthly organ of the NAWSA from 1907 to 1910, when the *Woman's Journal* assumed that role, is of minimal value. The *New Southern Citizen*, the monthly paper of the SSWSC, covers the activities and viewpoint of Kate Gordon and the strict states' rights suffragists.

Secondary Literature

Scholarly attention has begun to focus on woman's history only in the last few years. At the turn of the century feminists were complaining that historians had ignored women and even today the situation has been only partially rectified. Furthermore, as David M. Potter, "American Women and American Character," in *American Character and Culture*, ed. John A. Hague (DeLand, Fla., 1964) indicates, many of the great historical hypotheses and social generalizations are posited without any attempt to learn if they are as true for women as for men. Many facets of woman's history remain unexplored, although the spate of anthologies by or about women recently has at least drawn more attention to the subject.

Among the general histories of women in America, Eleanor Flexner, *Century of Struggle* (Cambridge, Mass., 1959), and William L. O'Neill, *Everyone Was Brave: The Rise and Fall of Feminism in America* (New York, 1969), are best. Andrew Sinclair, *The Better Half: The Emancipation of the American Woman* (New York, 1965), is well written but carelessly researched at times and, like Flexner, he misinterprets suffragists' positions on the issues of race and suffrage. Lois Banner, *Women in Modern America* (New York, 1974), is narrower in scope but highly readable and keenly interpretative.

Everyone in the field of southern suffrage history owes a debt of gratitude to A. Elizabeth Taylor for her seminal work. Well before the current interest in woman's studies developed, Taylor authored *The Woman Suffrage Movement in Tennessee* (New York, 1957) and has since written numerous scholarly articles which cover the origin and development of suffrage sentiment in virtually every southern state.

Several good biographies are available on women leaders, but much, both in reevaluation and original studies, remains to be done. Alma Lutz has contributed sound studies in *Susan B. Anthony: Rebel, Crusader, Humanitarian* (Boston, 1957) and *Created Equal: A Biography of Elizabeth Cady Stanton* (New York, 1940). I profited from Mary Earhart, *Frances Willard: From Prayers to Politics* (Chicago, 1944), which, contrary to contemporary detractors, shows the WCTU under its great leader to be an important social force in areas outside the realm of prohibition. Sophonisba Breckinridge, *Madeline McDowell Breckinridge: A Leader in the New South* (Chicago, 1921), is laudatory and workmanlike, but there can be no doubt that this great Kentuckian deserves a new and critical study. Clavia Goodman, *Bitter Harvest: Laura Clay's Suffrage Work* (Lexington, Ky., 1946), written before the bulk of the subject's papers were accessible, is a popular and uncritical biographical sketch.

Several volumes deserve special mention for their value in understanding the general historical context in which the woman's movement developed and grew. I have relied heavily upon the following: C. Vann Woodward, *Origins of the New South, 1877–1913* (Baton Rouge, 1951); George B. Tindall, *The Emergence of the New South, 1913–1945* (Baton Rouge, 1967) and *South Carolina Negroes, 1877–1900* (Baton Rouge, 1966); Albert D. Kirwan, *Revolt of the Rednecks: Mississippi Politics, 1876–1925* (Lexington, Ky., 1951); Francis B. Simkins, *Pitchfork Ben Tillman: South Carolinian* (Baton Rouge, 1944), and *The Tillman Movement in South Carolina* (Durham, N.C., 1926); Arthur J. Link, *Wilson*, vol. 5: *Campaigns for Progressivism and Peace, 1916–1917* (Princeton, N.J., 1965); George E. Mowry, *The Era of Theodore Roosevelt and the Birth of Modern America, 1900–1912* (New York, 1958); and Henry F. May, *The End of American Innocence: A Study of the First Years of Our Own Times, 1912–1917* (New York, 1969), a particularly insightful volume; Clement Eaton, *Freedom of Thought in the Old South* (New York, 1940), and *The Waning of the Old South Civilization* (Athens, Ga., 1968).

I am indebted to several authors for their works on the Clay family and its Kentucky environment. Worthy of special mention here is David L. Smiley, *Lion of White Hall: The Life of Cassius M. Clay* (Madison, Wis., 1962), an able and critical treatment of Laura Clay's father. My task would have been immeasurably greater without the excellent work in state and local history of Thomas D. Clark, *A History of Kentucky* (New York, 1937), and *The Kentucky* (New York, 1942); James F. Hopkins, *The University of Kentucky: Origins and Early Years* (Lexington, Ky., 1957); and J. Winston Coleman, *Lexington during the Civil War* (Lexington, Ky., 1938), and *A Centennial History of Sayre School, 1854–1954* (Lexington, Ky., 1954).

The scope and depth of writings in woman's history have been increased considerably since this study was begun. Anne Firor

Scott, *The Southern Lady: From Pedestal to Politics, 1830–1930*
(Chicago, 1970), has established her as the preeminent historian
of the southern woman. Broad in scope and keenly analytical,
Scott's work is noteworthy for the understanding of the southerners' sectional dilemmas which she brings to her writing. Aileen
S. Kraditor, *The Ideas of the Woman Suffrage Movement, 1890–
1920* (New York, 1965), is an excellent interpretative volume
which views the suffrage drive as an essentially conservative movement. She draws a meaningful distinction on the race issue between Deep South and border state suffragists and avoids Flexner's
and Sinclair's mistake of attributing racism solely to the southern
suffragists. Alan P. Grimes, *The Puritan Ethic and Woman Suffrage* (New York, 1967), challenges the old belief that state woman suffrage was enacted first in the West because of the democratic
spirit of the frontier. In a closely reasoned argument, he holds,
like Kraditor, that woman suffrage was a conservative movement
and demonstrates that the desire of the older, "native" stock,
American to retain political supremacy over the immigrant groups
strongly influenced its passage. One must legitimately ask, however, as Scott does, if this desire was anything more than one of
several motives behind the demand for equal suffrage. William
L. O'Neill, *Divorce in the Progressive Era* (New Haven, 1967),
is a scholarly investigation of a phenomenon which has strengthened women's rights.

A beginning has been made in the effort to study feminism in
a broader psychological and sociological context. I am indebted
to Christopher Lasch, *The New Radicalism in America, 1889–
1963* (New York, 1965), for his perceptive treatment of Jane
Addams, who, like Laura Clay, rebelled at the thought of a life of
"ceremonial futility." James R. McGovern, "Anna Howard Shaw:
New Approaches to Feminism," *Journal of Social History* 3
(1969): 135–53, is an excellent psychoanalytical study. Important
questions about the role and history of women are raised by Carl
N. Deglar, "Revolution without Ideology: The Changing Place
of Women in America," in *The Woman in America*, ed. Robert
J. Lifton (Boston, 1965), and in Gerda Lerner, "New Approaches
to the Study of Women in American History," *Journal of Social
History* 3 (1970): 53–62.

Index

LaVergne, TN USA
27 September 2009
159082LV00003B/8/A